D0204912

The Battle for Britain
THATCHER AND THE NEW LIBERALS

Stephen Haseler

The Battle for Britain
THATCHER AND THE NEW LIBERALS

I.B.TAURIS & Co Ltd
Publishers
London

For Bay

Published by
I.B.Tauris & Co Ltd
110 Gloucester Avenue
London NW1 8JA

British Library Cataloguing in Publication Data

Hasler, Stephen *1942-*
  The battle for Britain : Thatcher and the New Liberals.
  1. Great Britain politics sociological perspectives
  I. Title
  306'.2'0941

  ISBN 1-85043-148-5

Typeset by Selectmove Ltd, London
Printed and bound in Great Britain by
Biddles Ltd, Guildford and King's Lynn

91-3135

CONTENTS

Preface

A generation of Britons now reaching middle age have witnessed (certainly during the 1970s and 1980s) unprecedented turmoil in the formal politics of their country. At the beginning of this turbulent perriod – in the early 1970s – Britain not only witnessed the downfall of an elected government following a bitter struggle between the state and a powerful trade union, but also the first 'minority' government in a generation. At the end of the 1970s, it saw the election of its first ever woman Prime Minister, as well as in 1975 its first ever national referendum (in which the public ratified the ceding of the formal sovereignty many assumed it had possessed since ancient times). In 1981, it witnessed the birth of a new political party, which in alliance with an old one, was to secure more 'third-party votes' than at any time since 1929. In 1982, it went to war with a nation half a globe away. In 1985 the people watched as the country descended into what amounted to civil war between Margaret Thatcher's government and Arthur Scargill's Miners' Union. The 1980s were also to see the unprecedented spectacle (for modern times) of a single party, and a single Prime Minister, winning three elections in a row.

These unusual and dramatic developments were not, however, a series of random, unconnected events. They represented, instead, something more thematic and fundamental – a national transition (amounting to a national rite of passage) through which the country was passing, one as important as any in its history.

The idea for this book developed slowly during the early 1980s, born out of my increasingly strongly held belief that the economic restructuring of Britain (popularly known as 'Thatcherism') was being misunderstood. This book is an attempt to place the economic and social changes of the 1980s within the context of a broader (and, in my view, inevitable) historical transition through which the country was passing, and within which such changes should properly be viewed.

The argument in these pages is that, sooner or later, Britain would have to come to terms with its loss of Empire; that, sooner or later, it would have to modernize both its economy and its society in order to compete in an increasingly competitive world; that, sooner or later, its peculiarly antique paternalist structures and values would have to give way to a more enterprising, less deferential and more meritocratic society. Sooner or later, what I describe below as 'the century of paternalism' (the period of our national history starting around the last third of the nineteenth century, and lasting until the 1980s) had to be put to rest.

'Thatcherism' can therefore be viewed as the effect, not the cause, of an inevitable and profound change in the history of the nation. Thus, 'Thatcherism' is a misnomer for a broader and deeper radical phenomenon which, no matter the party complexion of the elected government, would have developed anyway. The fact was that the postwar decades had witnessed the emergence of new social groups possessed of new attitudes: automatic deference to authority was being replaced by a more instrumental and individualist social ethos; traditional *noblesse oblige* was giving way to competition as the preferred mechanism for measuring success; merit and talent were slowly replacing inherited social position as a valued social attribute. Of course, it has taken some time for the more democratic outlook and egalitarian attitudes of these new groups to take hold. After all, this postwar generation had grown up and matured within the carapace of a still very traditional and complacent society.

Britain had put off change for far too long. Well into the twentieth century it was a nation unlike any other in the advanced Western world; and its *unique* character was not particularly flattering.

As late as the end of the 1970s, Britain was a country still seemingly caught in a time-warp. To many foreign visitors (and to many of its inhabitants) it appeared somehow out of joint with the times, profoundly un-modern. It seemed in thrall to the lazy and complacent habits of a lost Empire; still exhibiting backward (indeed, quasi-medieval) political and social forms; still governed by a paternalist establishment (and a paternalist economic consensus) which treated its people like subjects on an estate, rather than free citizens.

To return to Britain from a visit to virtually any Western nation is still a jolting experience – something akin to entering a country in a time-warp, an island still largely untouched by the liberal bourgeois culture which has modernized the rest of the advanced world. Neal Ascherson's cruel depiction of his compatriots as resembling 'Ancient Britons', pre-modern people with pre-modern values, is hardly grotesquely overdrawn.[1] This national backwardness exhibits itself at both – hopefully now diminishing – ends of the social scale.

Social critics tend to focus upon the 'primitive' nature of some of the heirs of Britain's nineteenth-century proletariat: the punks, the football hooligans, those who read *The Sun* or demand fish and chips in Greece. These, though, are not 'Thatcher's children', the products of a mere ten years of free-market economics. This responsibility lies further back – in the deeper realms of the nation's culture.

Britain's 'backwardness' started at the top. In the name of paternalism the governing elites kept the 'propertyless mass' propertyless for far too long, thereby excluding too many of them from a stake in the nation and the self-confidence and maturity which comes with ownership and choice.

Contemporary historians are beginning to reveal the reasons for what Tom Nairn has described as a 'glamour of backwardness' which continues to grip the imagination of Britain's twentieth-century elites. Correlli Barnett locates the problem in the antiquated classicism which dominated the educational system, particularly the public schools of the mid to late nineteenth century. Martin Weiner's classic work, *English Culture and the Decline of the Industrial Spirit, 1850–1980*, reveals an English twentieth-century establishment unlike any other: reacting against the 'vulgarity' of industry and commerce, it lapsed back into a nostalgia for the arcadian values of a rural, indeed feudal, past.[2]

So, although Britain pioneered industrialism it nevertheless emerged from the remorseless modernization of the twentieth century as Europe's one remaining *ancien régime*, a country seemingly unable to throw off the shackles of the remnants of feudal sensibility. What – certainly when set side by side with most other Western countries – could be more 'backward' than a society in which a small family-based landed aristocracy still found itself comfortably ensconced within a feudal social pyramid (with Europe's only remaining lavish monarchical dynasty perched on top)? And what, too, could have been more 'backward' than the continuing dominance of the ideology of paternalism which has governed the thinking and statecraft of British politics even into the late twentieth century?

The traumas of the 1970s (which the first third of this book chronicles from the vantage-point of a participant observer) witnessed the welcome collapse of this increasingly embarrassing, and malfunctioning, paternalist consensus. And its displacement in the 1980s by a new radicalism (the subject matter of the last two-thirds of the book) now appears, certainly by comparison, as a profoundly progressive release and development.

At its core, the new radicalism is allowing (finally) the building of a vibrant and self-confident new middle class. For Britain, this is a potentially epoch-making social change, from which much else will ultimately flow. In a sense, it is the great irony of Thatcherism, that 'Thatcher's era' (and its 'enterprise culture') may well have done more to erode Britain's stubborn class system (and more to threaten the country's traditional Establishment) than all the previous, avowedly progressive, governments put together. This is the measure of the true radical import of the 1980s.

The economic and social changes ushered in by this new radicalism are, though, only the first stage of the long-overdue modernization of Britain. A truly liberal society – more open, mobile and enterprising than anyone now living has ever experienced, or thought possible – will ultimately *demand* a modernization of our deeply unmodern constitution.

A less dependent, and more self-reliant and self-confident, population will create new values, and new pressures. They will, over time, insist upon a modernization of Britain's peculiarly out-dated *ancien régime*. Modern Britons cannot live forever as *subjects* – without citizenship, without the basic, formulated rights which are enjoyed by every other advanced country in the world.

Yet, this outstanding, almost scandalous, national problem will only be dealt with when there is a popular demand for it.

Also, only a more self-reliant, and more 'bourgeois', society will be able to get to grips with the still largely taboo subject of Britain's pre-modern constitutional structure of Monarchy, Lords and Established Church. (In this sense, the central argument of this book proceeds from the proposition that although Britain deserves a written constitution (and a Bill of Rights) on the lines of the American or French examples, such constitutional change will only follow a change of public attitudes induced by economic change.)

The book not only attempts an analysis, but is also a chronicle of the times. The sketches presented here of some of the leading politicians of the 'old consensus' (as they grappled with the dilemmas presented by severe, often jolting, change) may at times seem harsh. Anthony Crosland, Harold Wilson, Ian Gilmour, Roy Jenkins, Shirley Williams, Bill Rodgers, Edward Heath, Jim Callaghan (and many others in the political establishment of the 1970s) were articulate and persuasive politicians (perhaps more so than the generation which has followed them). Yet, at least in the mind of this author, it became increasingly apparent that virtually all of these old-consensus politicians of the 1960s and 1970s – notwithstanding their rhetoric to the contrary – were essentially conservative in temperament, content with Britain's class structures and ancient 'upstairs-downstairs' habits of mind, secure only with managing decline. Indeed, they progressively assumed a composite political character, exhibiting the complacency, the insularity and, ultimately, the inadequacy of a failing political class.

Even so, I hope the final assessment which appears in these pages is one which places these unattractive qualities in a broader context of understanding. By comparison, the emerging 'successor generation' of politicians – those who rose to prominence in the 1980s – seem to be more in touch with the real problems of the life of the average Briton (perhaps the product of their less privileged backgrounds).

It is a measure of the national transition through which the country has passed, that our present party political leaders – Margaret Thatcher, Neil Kinnock, David Owen and Paddy Ashdown – appear to possess more in common with each other than with their respective party predecessors. Apart from all their differences of policy, even of ideology, they all share a refreshingly new political attribute: they are all 'post-imperial' in their outlook; they harbour few illusions and pretentions about Britain or its role, and thereby (unlike their predecessor generation) they are more grounded in reality.

In reconstructing many of the events I relate I have drawn upon my own correspondence and memory. Also, I am particularly indebted to my friend, Sir Reg Prentice, for making available to me his unpublished memoirs, many entries of which cover a remarkable period in Cabinet and government.

Stephen Haseler
London, 1989

1

A Nation in Transition

A cultural revolution?

> 'You know there are times, perhaps once every thirty years, when there is a sea-change in politics. It then does not matter what you say or what you do.' (James Callaghan, 1979)[1]

There appears to be a view, held as strongly abroad as at home, that the Premiership of Margaret Thatcher deserves the rare accolade of an 'ism': that 'Thatcherism' amounts not just to a change of course for Britain, but to a totally new political settlement – one even more important than that ushered in by the Attlee Labour government after the end of the Second World War.

Britain's 'Thatcher phenomenon' is no longer a remote blueprint. Well into its third government, the 'great experiment' now touches so many lives that public reactions to it are unusually emotional and polarized. They tend to be both personal and extreme, varying from devotion to hatred. Margaret Thatcher is, alternatively, either 'the saviour of our country' or 'the worst thing since the Luftwaffe'. Some even speculate, only half in jest, that 'Margaret Thatcher wants to be Queen'.

Such emotionalism about the personality and policies of a British Prime Minister is unusual; and it often serves to obscure or distort a cooler perspective upon the longer-term role being played by the Thatcher era in the life of Britain.

For instance, Margaret Thatcher's enterprise revolution (or 'great experiment') is often portrayed as an act of extraordinary personal political will, as a resolute (and dogmatic) decision taken – from amongst many others on offer – in favour of a new course for the country. This explanation of Britain's story in the 1980s, however, may rest too heavily upon Thatcher's personality; for the fact of the matter is that Britain – its institutions, its political parties, its peoples – had little choice in the matter.

By 1979 the country had run its earlier course. Britain's postwar love affair with the overblown corporate state, and with the increasingly out-moded and ineffectual 'brahmin' elite which directed and controlled it, was fading fast. The fact was that the whole postwar social construct (the interlinked and mutually reinforcing phenomena of a state commitment to full employment, an over-funded public sector regime, a universalist welfare state, and an entrenched role for trade unions) was simply no longer working. Its laudable social goals were coming into conflict with Britain's need to be competitive internationally.

Earlier predictions of a national reckoning to come (because of Britain's uncompetitive position in the world) had emanated from a host of politicians. In the early 1960s, Harold Wilson had regaled many an audience with the country's uncompetitive plight, and had illustrated the point by repeated references to its lowly place in the international economic league tables. Edward Heath later took up this refrain of uncompetitiveness in the lead up to the general election of 1970, although from a different vantage-point. Jim Callaghan returned to the theme during the International Monetary Fund crisis of 1976. Yet, these warnings lost much of their pith and moment as they fell foul of the country's seemingly miraculous ability (in both the 1960s and 1970s) to 'muddle through' within the existing postwar structures.

Margaret Thatcher was, in this sense, in a position no different from that of her predecessors in Downing Street. Like anyone aspiring to the leadership of the country during the 1970s she was bound, sooner or later, to confront the contradictions at the very heart of British life. The main contradiction, 'the British problem', was simple: the ambitious social goals established by the welfare society developed during the twentieth century could simply not be secured by Britain's resources – unless, that is, those resources could be improved by the creation of a more competitive economy and society.

Upon coming to office in 1979, Margaret Thatcher may have thought it best to confront 'the British problem' later rather than sooner. The new Prime Minister was not by nature reckless (certainly not more so than any of her predecessors), nor given to 'the gambler's throw' or the grand gesture; on the contrary, she was a careful woman whose career in the hidebound Conservative party had taught her to keep many of her passionately held beliefs in check. Thus, her natural judiciousness might, in normal times, have led her, as it did her predecessors, into working within the existing economic and social structures which she inherited.

However, by the late 1970s Britain's room for manoeuvre had, in fact – and as widely predicted – run out. The circle could no longer be squared, and something had to 'give'. The choice facing the country had already become clear during the International Monetary Fund crisis in the mid 1970s – between a welfare society which would slide ever lower down the economic league, or a nation which brought itself within the international economic disciplines in order to stay within range of its Western competitors. By 1979, after the collapse of the 'Social Contract' during the 'winter of discontent', the choice was even more apparent, and even more unavoidable.

In this sense, Thatcher's famous acronym, 'TINA' ('There Is No Alternative'), coined to justify her new economic strategy, possessed a fundamental validity. If, indeed, Britain was to remain in the Western system as a competitive nation, then it had indeed arrived at a point of decision. There was indeed 'no alternative' to a bold change of direction: to a radical re-fashioning of the economy in accordance with the realities of life in a competitive world.

The essential, and novel, ingredient in the 'radical re-fashioning' of the economy which proceeded after 1979, was the abandonment of the government's commitment to full employment. Although unemployment had risen dramatically under the administrations of the 1970s, a 'commitment' to its reduction remained declaratory policy, and whatever economic levers could be used to keep it relatively low were indeed pulled. Thatcher's 'radical' change essentially amounted to a strategy which allowed unemployment 'to take the strain' of the fight against inflation. Also, higher levels of unemployment secured twin objectives for the new administration: it both lowered the public expenditure needed for subsidizing employment, and it weakened the trade unions.

These higher levels of unemployment which emerged in the 1980s represented, in human terms, the severe (and, to some, the brutal) cost of the new economic strategy. Yet, there was another, more subtle, and more psychological, cost too. The obvious *need* for a radically new economic strategy, together with the lack of any clear alternative to it, served to expose some widely held illusions about the nature of Britain and its place in the world.

Britain had entered the postwar era not only severely wounded, but worse: riddled by a false view of its true position. Although no longer the protected heartland of a world wide Empire, Britain's peoples were still fed the illusion that they existed at the centre of the world, inhabiting a rich superpower run by an establishment whose writ still ran worldwide. The 1940s and 1950s Pathé newsreels, which now seem so innocent, nevertheless took their toll on reality. The silver screen presented an overblown picture of Britain's place in a changing world – projected to the British people through the distorted lens of the imperial sensibilities (and authoritative clipped accents) of a class, and nation, which in reality was in worldwide retreat.

Although national affluence had to be earned, it often appeared as though Britain's postwar leaders assumed that abundance was a divinely ordained British right. Although its competitors were creating modern socially mobile commercial societies, established opinion in Britain continued to believe that the country could survive and prosper in a post-feudal world without changing what was still its essentially rigid 'upstairs-downstairs' Dickensian social character.

British films for the mass market accurately depicted the sorry tale. Film after film (normally the second feature) displayed a social scene which amounted to a Ruritania rather than a modern nation. In the dramatis personae of the war movies military rank fitted the realities of civilian social class almost perfectly. The officer was invariably an 'upper-class twit' of a public schoolboy – not too bright, but very decent – who was usually never wholly in control of events; there was the bluff but efficient sergeant-major, a rough diamond smoothed down to Non-Commissioned Officer status, who ran the whole enterprise; and there was the cheerful and cheeky 'cockney sparrer' (or the statutory Welshman – 'Taffy' – or Scot) who lent a grateful hand, happy in his lowly lot. The Ealing Comedy films which depicted life in postwar Britain replicated these stereotypes in civilian life ('civvi street'), introducing the occasional entrepreneur, who was usually an unsympathetic working-class 'spiv'. The able classless person who could move easily between these hierarchies – in other words a rounded and confident individual – was notably absent.

This complacent dream-world – in which such an archaic social scene was widely considered as befitting a modern nation – took several decades before it was rudely shattered. Some commentators believed that Britain's humiliation during the Suez operation in 1956 would serve as the needed jolt. But it was not to be. The country was carried forward on the false dawn of the American-induced postwar consumer boom. Only during the traumatic decade of the 1970s did the chickens finally come home to roost; and only under the multiple pressures of inflationary oil price rises, continuing economic decline, industrial upheaval and a visit from the International Monetary Fund in 1976, did Britain's elites slowly begin to understand the need for a radical change of course.

It became increasingly apparent that Britain could no longer compete effectively whilst its inherited and antique anti-commercial culture – the attributes of 'England' which High Tory romantics often evoked as the very core of the country's character – continued to hold sway over its people. A marked disdain for trade, profits and commerce suffused, often unconsciously and inarticulately, many of the major institutions of British life. Anti-commercial sentiment was at its most pronounced amongst the leadership groups of some of the most powerful trade unions, and also amongst many of the socialist intellectuals who tended to support them. This coalition was beginning to question the very basis of the Western capitalist system; and, strangely, some of the bastions of Britain's archaic establishment – the surreal (yet very real) country of lords, castles, bishops and grand estates – were offering little resistance, their deep-seated cultural distaste for the commercial ethos of capitalism getting the better (and not for the first time) of their private enjoyment of its fruits.

By the late 1970s Britain itself had become rather like one of its old landed estates. A feckless but paternalist lord of the manor, dreaming of past glories whilst the money was running out, presided over a servile, but often grudging and rebellious, industrial serfdom. Such a rickety structure could not possibly survive. The old estate would simply have to be broken up, the family silver would need to be sold (much of it to foreigners), the family retainers would need to be let go, and the serfs set free into a life which was uncertain and insecure. The estate would have to reorder itself into one of those bourgeois modern nations like the United States or France, a more productive but less attractive arrangement of individuals, of financiers, engineers, designers, the upwardly mobile.

Such a metaphor for national decline is not overly fanciful. Britain had, in fact, been managed for most of the twentieth century by a cross-party paternalist establishment whose attachment to landed values and the past glory of Empire had obscured commercial and strategic realities. Viewing Britain's working people as adversaries rather than compatriots, they had treated them not as individual equals but as a collective entity to be 'bought off' by appeasing trade union power and creating a universal welfare state. In return for such appeasement working people would remain deferential, hardly ever challenging the uniquely class-based hierarchies of British life, even content to remain subjects rather than citizens with formal rights.

But, as in the metaphor of the estate, by the 1970s the money ran out. Britain's traditional, organic, hierarchical and deferential society (with everyone knowing, though not necessarily liking, their station in life) was no longer productive enough to survive, and could not be funded.

The sheer severity of the economic crisis facing Britain in the 1970s led, during the 1980s, to what amounted to a national reassessment of the postwar social democratic and corporate certainties which had governed the 'estate'. As, one by one, these verities were questioned, so too were some of the underlying historical biases upon which these certainties were based. The principal bias – one which sustained the moral ascendancy of postwar collectivism – was an image of Victorian Britain which portrayed nineteenth-century economic development as essentially socially malign, with few redeeming characteristics. The enterprise and productivity of the Victorian entrepreneur came to be overshadowed in this image by the undoubted deprivations (even horrors) of the life of the nineteenth-century urban proletariat; and the positive features of the provincial Victorian nonconformist work ethic became occluded by the distasteful aspects of Victorian hypocrisy.

This predisposition against the total Victorian industrial experience led ineluctably to a twentieth-century distaste for the economic liberalism of the nineteenth century. Productivity lost its appeal – and, in consequence, even the world of Isambard Kingdom Brunel began to appear as of less value than the effortless life of the rural idyll of Bladesover. So too did the validity of markets, free trade and competition. Economic liberalism not only lost its allure, but also its meaning. Liberal economics ceased to be thought of as having liberal consequences. Indeed, quite the contrary. By the 1960s (the high-water mark of the postwar consensus) nineteenth-century liberal economics had come to be seen as socially conservative, indeed as 'reactionary' – its liberal (indeed, in British terms, its radical) potential going unnoticed.

The sheer radicalizing effect of liberal economics – its ability to 'remake the world all over again' – is still only dimly perceived by many British opinion-formers. This is somewhat odd, particularly in view of its role in destroying the old feudal order during both the American and French revolutions. Both 1776 in North America and 1789 in France were essentially liberal revolutions, and, unlike the 1917 socialist revolution in Russia, ultimately beneficent. Of course, Britain's own unique pattern of development (in which the feudal forms and habits of mind were never fully expunged, either by the English civil war of the seventeenth century or by Victorian industrialism) ensured that liberal economics, and its associated social and political values, was neither fully developed in practice, nor adequately appreciated.

So in Britain, liberal economics is still regularly assumed to represent the economic face of the social status quo – a 'right-wing' economic dogma which serves to entrench, rather than dissolve, social rigidities and hierarchies. The case for liberal economics as a force for cultural and social democracy (as, that is, the economic mechanism for allowing an open, mobile and classless society, indeed, for social levelling), although understood throughout much of the Western world, is still not widely appreciated in Britain. During the twentieth century, socialism, not capitalism, came to be thought of as the progressive force in human development.

This was not always the case. During the eighteenth and nineteenth centuries the inherent relationship between liberal economics and social change was a given feature of political life. Indeed, some of the early apostles of the free market (such men as Tom Paine, Herbert Spencer and Auberon Herbert) were, in political terms, populists and radicals. Before the twentieth-century age of collectivism, a nonconformist 'laissez-faire' mentality would often go hand in hand with such radical dispositions as contempt for unearned social privilege, a dislike of aristocracy and opposition to the established church. For Tom Paine – perhaps the most exemplary exponent of free market political radicalism – 'the stratified society of privilege and rank would be levelled in a bourgeois world of competitive individualism'.[2] In the nineteenth century, the Liberal Member of Parliament, Auberon Herbert, continued to develop many of Paine's themes, albeit in an increasingly hostile environment. Herbert combined a visceral opposition to the collectivist state with a denunciation of the House of Lords and a personal declaration – in the House of Commons, amid scenes of considerable disorder – of republicanism.[3] Also, Herbert's mentor, the individualist political philosopher, Herbert Spencer, could wax indignant about 'the swindling and tyranny of the aristocracy' whilst at the same time, and quite thematically, proclaiming extreme free market views.[4]

The burst of economic liberalism which Britain has witnessed in the 1980s had revived interest in these pre-twentieth century free market radicals – and also in an understanding of how liberal economics may pose a greater challenge to traditional social hierarchy and rigidity than the economic corporatism of the twentieth century was ever capable of mounting. Indeed, the radical potential inherent in liberal economics – and the more specific notion that the liberal experiment of the 1980s may represent real change, and not necessarily simply a consolidation of the status quo – is increasingly being both accepted and conceded by a wide cross-section of opinion. Former Liberal party leader, Jo Grimond, has predicted that the party which adopts a combination of 'co-operation, community development and the free market . . . could become the radical element in our politics'.[5] Professor David Marquand, a leading social democratic political theorist, has argued that 'when the crisis came in the 1970s, Mrs Thatcher found it easier to strike the chords of the old, popular radicalism

than did the heirs of the radicals themselves'.[6] Both John Dunn
and marxist writer, Tom Nairn, have suggested that although
contemporary market liberalism may approach the problems of
modern Britain from a wholly different perspective from that of
the socialist left, it nonetheless exhibits a similar contempt for the
archaic and obscolescent features of British society.[7]

In many respects the kind of changes under way in the life of
Britain in the 1980s are as pregnant with possibility as were
those of the early Victorian era. Then, as now, Britain was not
encumbered by Empire; then, as now, the country was in a state
of economic change and social flux. Paul Webb has suggested that
then, as now, there was 'a great deal of money about, mostly in
"new" hands' and that 'the breakdown of traditional patterns of
work and behaviour, and the erosion of old class barriers, con-
trasted with continuing social (if not economic) pre-eminence of
the aristocracy and "old money"'.[8]

There is a vital difference, however between the early Victorian
prosperity and the 'new wealth' of the modern British. Whereas
early Victorian Britain was about to embark upon an imperial jour-
ney, modern Britain is not. Whereas the 'new money' and new
classes of early Victorian Britain were to become incorporated
into an aristocratic class which was to run a global show, today's
'old money' can offer today's 'new money' no such glory.

Consequently, today's 'new money' will have little time, and
less awe, for the habits, manners and customs of the 'old'. Its
confidence, and its place in the sun, will develop free from the
co-option and domestication into an aristocratic lifestyle which
was the lot of the early Victorians. As more and more 'new
money' comes on stream – through council house sales, wider
share ownership and lower tax rates for the average wage-earners
– a whole new generation of inheritors will emerge. They will have
a control over their lives – and a choice in the market – undreamt
of by the present inhabitants of Britain's rows and rows of council
houses and back-to-back terraces. But these sons and daughters
of new wealth will not, as was the lot of their early Victorian forebears, be disciplined, educated and carted off to serve an Empire.
Rather, they will become part of the new middle class of a modern
continent-wide European civilization.

Today's 'new money' is also more widely diffused than that of
the early Victorians. Whereas the 'new money' of Victorian times

was restricted to a small number – and this not very sizeable Victorian middle class lived side by side with the shame of a helpless propertyless mass, a huge proletariat whose soulless environment was to overwhelm all but the most hard-hearted – today's emerging middle class is the majority. The super-rich above them and the under-class below them will amount to only a fraction of the nation. Britain will then finally join the ranks of countries like the USA, France and West Germany – a largely middle-class society with a confident bourgeois outlook on life. Such a momentous social and psychological transformation will do more to open up a tired old country than all the words of radical poets. England's experience in the twentieth century may have taught the English to believe that revolutions are un-English; that *total* change, even when things are *totally* wrong, is somehow unhealthy. Consequently, we may no longer be able to recognize a revolution even when it is occurring. Of course, Britain's liberal 'revolution of the 1980s was *economic*, not *political*' — there was no storming of a Winter Palace or a Parliament House, no change in (let alone overthrow of) the political institutions of the country. However, the replacement of one economic consensus (particularly one which has been entrenched for so long) by a radically different one is no small matter. Thus, the economic transformation of Britain in the 1980s may indeed represent a more profound (than purely economic) change in the life of the nation – one amounting to a radical break with an underlying national style of thinking and action, so clean a breach with the past that it can accurately be depicted as a 'cultural revolution'.

It is the theme (and thesis) of this book that the liberal economic revolution of the 1980s did indeed both represent, and will continue to effect, a broader 'cultural revolution' against a previous national style of thinking and acting which throughout these pages I describe as paternalism. By the late twentieth century, the paternalist instinct (both as a general social attitude and, more specifically, as a method of domestic statecraft employed by a governing class) had become peculiar to Britain, every other major Western country having either overthrown or outgrown this essentially feudal mentality.

The paternalist inheritance

As recently as 1984 (almost eight decades into the twentieth century, and over a decade into the space age), Philip Norton, one of Britain's most widely published textbook writers, could describe his country to a worldwide student audience thus:

> A stress on responsibility as well as rights has been a significant and long standing feature of the British culture and has been well imbued by a large part of the nation's political elite. A paternalistic concern for the well-being of the nation has been a feature of most if not all monarchs and has been associated with a particular and often predominant tradition within the Conservative party.
>
> As long as the political system has been able to maintain the capacity to meet the demands and expectations of citizens, an allegiant orientation has been demonstrated by citizens. The longer the system has been able to do this and the longer people have been socialised into accepting the efficacy of the system the stronger and more enduring the allegiance has been.[9]

Norton here depicts Britain not as a *democratic* culture, or an *egalitarian* culture, or a *republican* culture, or a *money* culture, or an *individualistic* culture, or a *bourgeois* culture, or, even, as a *socialist* or *collectivist* culture. Somehow, modern Britain (at least to the sophisticated political mind) is unable to be classified by normal advanced world standards. The term which Norton selects, 'allegiant', could probably be applied to tribal societies, though hardly to modern nations.

Of course, 'allegiant culture' is only a polite way of describing an embarrassingly high and unusual public acceptance of authority. Yet, the sceptic might ask: to whom (or to what) is it that the British people are so allegiant? Whose (or what's) writ of authority runs so wide? The nearest a contemporary observer can come to answering this question is to point to the widespread public deference exhibited to 'those in charge' or the 'powers that be' – particularly when they are being benign, paternal, and obliging. Even so, the real answer, may lie in much deeper waters.

It can possibly be glimpsed in the mystical ideology of A. J. Balfour, who could write (in the early aftermath of the defeat of nineteenth-century liberalism) as if the Enlightenment and the Age of Reason (and Britain's contribution to it) had not existed:

It is Authority rather than Reason to which, in the main, we owe not religion only, but ethics and politics . . . it is Authority which supplies us with the essential elements in the premises of science . . . it is Authority rather than Reason which lays the deep foundations of social life [and] which cements its superstructure . . . if we would find the quality in which we most notably excel . . . we should look for it, not so much in our faculty for convincing and being convinced by the exercise of reasoning, as in our capacity for influencing and being influenced through the action of Authority.[10]

Such a startlingly undescribed (because indescribable) and undefined (because indefinable) notion of the power of 'authority' may seem, to modern man, like a philosophic confidence-trick. Yet, here was no eccentric professor! Balfour was a pragmatic leader of men, and was obviously giving voice to some deep authoritarian need in the British elite of his time. There was something bigger here than the 'nanny state', or even the 'nanny culture'. It amounted to a veritable 'nanny teleology', a mental and cultural framework umbilically linked back to feudal times. At the heart of the social thought of feudalism – which Balfour's late nineteenth-century proclamation, together with the paternalism of contemporary times, echoes – was the same notion that those in authority were automatically just (not, therefore, in need of being tested by reason or democracy), and that such authority would dispense its justice in return for loyalty.

Just how this feudal instinct of paternalism survived in Britain well into the twentieth century is a remarkable story which, of course, cannot be separated from the more general history of Britain's unbroken, evolutionary development – one which has allowed a relatively small landed social order to survive into the modern age, and, more importantly, ensured that its associated values suffused the culture of its broader society. The basic plot is also a subtle tale of swift, pragmatic, footwork on the part of this landed aristocracy, of the rapid adaptation of old interests, old money and older values to a new and threatening era.

Having compromised with, and thus stunted, the growth of a modern bourgeois society in the nineteenth century, Britain's landed social order – with its hierarchical and paternalist social sensibility intact – was even able to survive the arrival of the age of mass democracy in the twentieth. The full extension of the franchise, including votes for women, may have altered the party political landscape, but it made little impression upon the underlying popular sense of social hierarchy. Twentieth-century Britain became the only Western country of which it could be said of its people that they 'loved a lord', a metaphor for a wider belief in the efficacy of a society run from above, by 'those who know best'.

Paternalism was, thus, to be reinforced by popular demand, as the social forces 'below stairs' often encouraged rather than resisted the claims to authority emanating from 'above stairs'. To use the characters from the popular soap opera of the 1970s, *Upstairs, Downstairs*, the butler Hudson, the cook Mrs Bridges, and the maid Ruby, all, in their different ways, possessed something of a vainglorious attachment to the world which the British aristocracy was thought to have created (including the industrial might of the country, the Empire and the supposed special position of the British people, often then referred to as 'the British race'). This stable civilization – perceived by all classes 'below stairs' to be the remarkable achievement of the likes of Sir Richard and Lady Bellamy 'above stairs' – gave 'below stairs' what little place they could secure in the sun. The later traumas and exigencies of two world wars (and possible invasion) only served to further the notion 'below stairs' of a community of interest between the classes. 'We were', after all, 'all together in this thing.' In such an environment Hudson, Mrs Bridges and Ruby were hardly like to become rebels.

During the advancing democratic age, 'popular demand from below' increasingly counted. It was here that the genius of 'Tory democracy' (whether promulgated by Disraeli in the nineteenth, or Macmillan in the twentieth century) also counted. 'Tory democrats' would yield to, not confront, the people, and thus popular sentiment and power would be subtly co-opted within the traditional constrictions of paternalism.

In 1907, 'the democracy' (as the people were often somewhat quaintly referred to) was informed, in one of the most concise renderings of paternalism's new order, that:

> The principle of Tory democracy is that all government exists for the good of the governed; that Church and King, Lords and Commons, and all other public institutions are to be maintained so far, and only so far, as they promote the happiness and welfare of the common people . . . and that the mass of the people may

be entrusted so to use electoral power, which should be freely
conceded to them, as to support those who are promoting their
interests. It is democratic because the welfare of the people is the
supreme end; it is Tory because the institutions of the country are
the means by which the end is to be attained.[11]

'Democracy', then – at least for the British – was not to develop by
allowing popular sovereignty but, rather, by securing the 'welfare
of the common people' (or the commoners' welfare). The older
ideal of the 'Freeborn Englishman' as a critical, independent citizen
(who would measure institutions, and elites, against needs) was
overlain by a spurious collective entity known as 'the common people' – to whom, under 'Tory democracy', electoral power would be
'conceded'.

Having limited the democratic potential inherent in the extension of the franchise, the later development of state collectivism
in the twentieth century may have, on the face of it, posed an
even more serious threat to the paternalism of the landed order.
Under the impact of collectivist parties and ideologies, the state
could have become the mechanism for expropriating land (either
in order to nationalize it or to break up the large landholdings
and redistribute them). As it turned out, however, the landed
interest, and the landed ideology, remained intact; and through
its continuing cultural power it governed the way in which the
state would develop. In this sense, it appropriated collectivism to
itself, and moulded it to suit its own interests.

This uniquely English fusion between an old landed interest
and a developing collectivism produced in Britain in the twentieth
century a peculiarly paternalist flavour to the role of the state
and the growing public sector. Under the continuing impact of
paternalist values within Britain's elites, this enlarged collectivist
state became an obstacle to social modernization, to the creation
of a more open, mobile and classless society. On the face of
it this argument may seem peculiar. Was not the state (and
the enlarged public sector) the great instrument of social reform, the engine driving Britain away from the inequities built
up during the Victorian era and into a more socially egalitarian
society?

Well, not exactly. Although the enlarged welfare state provided
a safety-net for those who could not compete within the capitalist
system, this amounted to its only reforming social function. For,

under the patronage of its paternalist derivation, the twentieth-century welfare state did not become the means (a kind of state-sponsored launching pad) for securing the emergence of a more mobile middle-class society. Rather, the welfare state (at least as it developed in twentieth-century Britain) became – insidiously – a mechanism for limiting social mobility and individual aspirations and development. It did so by instilling in the *majority* of the British a sense of allegiance to a fixed place in an ordained social firmament.

A paternalistic social regime was skilfully maintained by a form of democratic feudalism in which, in return for welfare, 'the common people' would continue to owe 'allegiance'. Thus, not only was 'allegiance' secured, but a perverted view of 'welfare' emerged. As the twentieth century progressed, 'welfare' came to be almost universally viewed through the mental lens of a 'top-down' *noblesse oblige* and (its more contemporary partner) 'compassion'. The more egalitarian sense of welfare – whereby the strong and privileged do not look *down* 'compassionately' upon the weak and poor but rather look *across* to them with 'empathy' for equals who are down on their luck – never took hold.

The most impressive trick of all in paternalism's survival-kit, however, was the fact that Britain's socialist class also decided to play this 'welfare' game. Of course, these socialists (amongst them, John Ruskin, William Morris, and most of the Fabians) knew exactly what they were doing. The growth of a culture of 'welfare' would, *ipso facto,* result in a larger state apparatus, and that, in turn, would improve the future chances of establishing socialism in Britain.

These socialists added a scientific and rational gloss to the coat of mystical Tory paternalism, but they were nature's paternalists nonetheless. Their rage against the Tories of their day was rather like that of Caliban, as he saw his image in the glass. Many of the improving socialists of the early twentieth century saw civil society in virtually the same way as did the Tory paternalists: as, that is,

> a kind of estate to be managed in the most rational and benefi-
> cent way, its workers or retainers being kept busy producing
> the wealth necessary for their own maintenance as well as for
> . . . the functionaries and for the pursuit of public purposes.

> This was lordship of an effective and extensive kind involving the
> constant improvement, and so the enlargement of official interfer-
> ence. [12]

Even the politicians of popular radicalism – Randolph Churchill,
Joseph and Neville Chamberlain, and David Lloyd George –
ultimately succumbed to the paternalist embrace. Their populist
instincts would have normally led them to reject the 'top-bottom'
'upstairs-downstairs' High Tory view of society. Yet, ironically,
this same populism would lead all of them to see the paternal state
as the only mechanism for the remedy of grievances and injustices.
Consequently, they fell in, like sturdy and loyal sergeant-majors,
behind the Tory paternalist officer corps.

As the twentieth century progressed the essentially paternalist
character of the welfare state became increasingly apparent. After
all, who was to administer this enlarged welfare state? And, by
virtue of running it, who would gather more power both to themselves and to their values? As it turned out it was certainly not
to be the industrial workers (with their community-based values),
nor the merchants (with their commercial values), nor even the
professional middle classes (with their meritocratic values) who
manned the higher reaches of its bureaucracy.

All was revealed as the post-Second World War Labour government announced its list of those who, on behalf of the people,
would run its new nationalized industries and boards. It was soon
apparent that these new commanders of the enlarged British
state were to be drawn predominantly from the usual limited
social circle of the public school, and/or Oxbridge and Military
Academy-educated English upper class – all possessing the manners and ethos of the paternal culture. British European Airways
was to be run by Gerald d'Erlanger, CBE; British Overseas Airways by Sir Harold Hartley, KVCO, CBE, MC. FRS; the Road
Transport Executive by Major General G. N. Russell, CB, CBE;
the Central Land Board by Sir Malcolm Trustram Eve, Bt, MC,
TD, KC; The Forestry Commission by the Lord Robinson, OBE;
and the National Coal Board by the Viscount Hyndley, GBE.
It was also to become clear that the Civil Service mandarins
who were to run Labour's new state, were also to be cut from
the same cloth. Thus, under the guidance of Ernest Bevin and
Herbert Morrison, what were somewhat pathetically described
amongst the working classes as 'toffs' or 'gents' had reasserted

themselves. The values of the Raj had come home to run the home front.

If the growth of collectivism and the welfare state helped to breathe life into a paternalist culture which otherwise might have died, so, too, did the strange interruption of Empire.

Sometime in the late 1950s, a friend described his two uncles. One had served in the imperial civil service in India, and had returned to Britain on a relatively meagre retirement pension. The other had taken himself to America in his thirties and re-turned home late in life with lots of money but little to do. Both spent their declining years bemoaning the fate of their country, but seeing wholly different solutions. Their nephew, who himself had travelled somewhat, concluded that these two disaffected Englishmen symbolized two historic visions of Britain itself: 'One can think eastwards or westwards', the nephew suggested. 'To the east there was British India, to the west America. The In-dian vision was imperial, a vision of the noble cultivated Englishman civilizing a backward people as an act of paternalist *noblesse oblige*. The American vision was democratic, a vision of the boundless possibilities for ordinary people once they were released from guidance and control.'

In a sense, the Indian imagination was that of the English Tory, the American that of the English Radical. In the 'Indian imagination' the British people were also colonial subjects, who needed paternalist rule in order to be civilized; to the 'American imagination' all the British needed was to be set free on the path to self-reliance and self-development. And in Britain during the twentieth century it was the Indian imperial vision which won out over the American dream.

Paternalism's Indian summer

By the late 1950s, the reality (if not the lingering sensibility) of Empire was, though, largely a thing of the past. Nevertheless, as Harold Macmillan gave an elegant and languid wave to the crowds in Downing Street on the morrow of his victory over Hugh Gaitskell in the 1959 general election, Britain's postwar paternalist governing class still had much to congratulate itself about. A nation which had lost an Empire, and been devastated in a world war had, all in the space of a few years, seemingly re-created its former self. Macmillan was at the 'top table' of international summitry; the country was awash with consumer durables (particularly televisions!); above all, Britain was a seemingly stable partner, a key ally, in the expanding and confident Western economic and defence system. The country, which some in 1940 had counted out, was back.

The key element in the domestic success of this postwar establishment had been the 'mixed economy'. It became the accepted wisdom that this welfare society was a magic formula, representing the proper mix between private profit and public spending, the right balance between fairness and political freedom. That most cherished of paternalist goals, 'social stability', seemed with us forever. The tentative festivities of Labour's Festival of Britain had turned two years later into a full-blown celebration during the coronation of a new monarch. Britain's social democratic experiment (embraced by both political parties) was becoming 'the envy of the world'. And, perhaps, to an extent, it was. In foreign policy the British establishment had taken the lead in getting the Americans back into Western Europe, and had also succeeded in creating its own 'independent nuclear deterrent'. Britain was not only defended by the might of the United States, but also (unlike its European allies) could defend itself – alone if need be. (In Julian Amery's memorable and defiant phrase: 'The V-bomber pilots are determined to get through [to Moscow]'.)

By the late 1950s this Indian summer was cooling off, however. That something was seriously wrong with the British economy was becoming apparent. Yet, even though the inefficiencies inherent in Britain's postwar economic life were increasingly recognized, it was nonetheless assumed that judicious tinkering within the existing economic structures was all that was needed to deal with the problem. The old-codger postwar leadership retained, to the end, a woefully complacent assumption that Britain's rigid economy and fossilized society could somehow, some way, continue to compete in the modern world: it could 'muddle through' without need of economic surgery, certainly without the overhaul of cultural change.

'Muddling through' became a national fashion, and with it a whole new set of complacent public virtues were translated into a national style by a succession of Prime Ministers. The business-like qualities of Neville Chamberlain and Stanley Baldwin, the radical gusto of Lloyd George, and the heroic defiance of the wartime Winston Churchill had become decidedly outmoded. More languid and laid-back attitudes were promulgated from above. Clement Attlee set the postwar tone by making understatement and modesty look somehow awe-inspiring. 'Dear Laski', he wrote to his party opponent who had just threatened to topple him. 'Thank you for your letter, contents of which have been noted.'[13] Alec Home's pretended idiocy – when he proclaimed that he knew nothing about economics, and could only understand them by playing with match-sticks – won him as many friends as enemies. Harold Macmillan set a generation giggling by his studied aristocratic *hauteur* in the face of adversity. He got clean away (for a while at least) with his public reaction to his middle-aged War Minister sharing a mistress with a Soviet agent: 'I do not understand what young people are getting up to these days.'

There was a certain charm in this essentially aristocratic style which came back into vogue amongst the postwar political leaders. Its detached and articulate manner may seem preferable to the more engaged and earnest style which was ultimately to supplant it in the 1980s. Yet, there was a price to pay. For this 'detachment' of style truly represented an increasing detachment, on the part of its exponents, from reality.

So, only a decade after Macmillan's victory of 1959 this same paternalist class was presiding over a country on the skids. By the late 1960s the obvious failure of Wilson's Labour government had become apparent. Her Majesty's Government had publicly and humiliatingly capitulated to the trade union leaders by abandoning its mild reform proposals, and there was even talk of an attempt by Lord Louis Mountbatten (in league with newspaper tycoon, Cecil King) to topple the government in a military coup. Continuing comparative economic decline seemed irreversible.

Yet, even worse was to come. The 1970s were to make the late 1960s seem positively tranquil.

The contradictions of paternalism

What still surprises many – often foreign – observers is not how the essentially feudal political mentality of paternalism managed to last well into the first half of the twentieth century, but how it survived in Britain well into the 1970s, and even the 1980s! After all, today's British political spectrum (ranging from Tory 'wets', through to many Liberals and many socialists) is still straddled by those who stand in a lineal descent from this paternalist tradition – and their political influence (as well as their potential for translating that influence into government) is, even today, by no means minimal.

Part of the answer lies in the downward spiral in which Britain became caught up during the decade of the 1970s. The problem was essentially one of a seemingly unstoppable negative dynamic in which the various attempts at modernization all met resistance from obstacles thrown up by institutional obsolescence. The country's troglodite trade unions, its 'old-boy network' management, its traditionalist and restrictive professional groups (all reflecting a rigid class system and sensibility), its cultural conservatism, and its antique constitution – all reinforced each other in resisting change.

Of course, not all these problems were self-induced. The 1970s were to witness some severe jolts to Britain's stability from dramatic and unforeseen changes in the international system. The oil price rises following the Yom Kippur war injected an inflationary virus into the economic system which frayed the social fabric of a good many other countries as well as Britain. The geo-strategic instability caused by America's readjustment following Vietnam was also an unforeseen problem. Yet, Britain's postwar establishment had constructed both an elaborate welfare system and an over-extended global defence posture in the full knowledge of the country's weakened position in the world, and its vulnerability to the international winds of change.

Yet, by the early 1970s Britain had fallen so far behind its international competitors that some people even began asking whether participating in the 'international game' was worth the candle. Britain, they argued, should opt out. These 'opters-out' were led by an ever more protectionist, if not autarkic, faction within the Labour and trade union movement, and a sizeable Labour grouping was challenging the very rationale for Britain's membership of the Western economic system. By 1976 this 'alternative economic strategy' was accepted as official policy by the Labour party.

This 'alternative strategy', although specifically rejected by Downing Street, immediately found itself on the national agenda when the British government was forced to make a formal application to the International Monetary Fund for what later turned out to be the largest loan in the Fund's history. The serious dimensions of this crisis have tended to be underplayed by the politicians of the time, and hence by many journalists and commentators too; and it is still not in the interests of any of the major actors (the British government, or the allied governments involved in Washington and Bonn) to highlight the gravity of these events.

Britain's Prime Minister at the time has more than hinted, however, that the situation was unusual. He described how his Chancellor of the Exchequer, Denis Healey, 'sat for some time in my bedroom talking over the various drastic policy changes that would be needed if a loan was not forthcoming. They would have meant a bumpy ride not just for the British people but for the international community, with serious implications for our relations with GATT, the European Community and NATO, as well as the United States. On that night anything seemed possible.'[14]

How 'serious' these 'implications' might have become has rarely been revealed. William Rodgers of the US State Department was reported as saying about the British condition in 1976:

> We all had the feeling that it could come apart in quite a serious way. As I saw it it was a choice between Britain remaining in the liberal financial system of the West as opposed to a radical change of course, because we were concerned about Tony Benn precipitating a policy decision by Britain to turn its back on the IMF. I think if that had happened the whole system would have come apart.[15]

At the height of the crisis George Meaney, the leader of America's trade unions, wrote a letter to President Ford arguing that

> the United States must move forcefully now, as it did when the United Kingdom stood alone in the face of military disaster in World War Two . . . and place our strength and resources in the balance on the side of Britain. I urge you to declare, as strongly as possible, that the full faith and credit of the United States stands behind the British people in this crisis.[16]

Thus, almost three decades after the Marshall Aid package, Britain asked for, and secured, what amounted to another one. And, far from ensuring social peace and political harmony (one of the primary boasts of the postwar paternalist consensus) the country had, instead, ended the 1970s with a bitterly divided polity such as had not been seen since the labour unrest before the First World War.

Yet, even after the humiliating IMF experience, the paternalist consensus still held, at least for a time. The public expenditure cuts which were needed following the acceptance of the conditions for the loan would, obviously, meet resistance, and possibly even further polarize an already divided society. Labour's 'alternative strategy' was still on the national agenda, and its proponents were gaining an ascendancy in the Labour party. Such an uncertain environment served somewhat to reinforce paternalist sentiment within the political establishment. Although the new Conservative leadership in opposition was developing its own 'alternative strategy' (which would represent as decided a break with the consensus as would Labour's), the Tory paternalists were still able to weaken its appeal in the party by pointing to its dangers. Now was hardly the time, it was argued, for any breach in the postwar economic consensus. Too bold a free market experiment would only cause a vast increase in unemployment, and hence a public backlash which would be to Labour's advantage.

Only as it became apparent during the 1980s that Labour was in no position to take advantage of public anxieties about a change in economic direction, did the road become open for the economic liberals to develop their new strategy without hindrance.

The paternalist distortion

The remarkable survival of paternalism well into the late twentieth century has served to skew (and thus distort) not only an understanding of politics, but also the very meaning of political ideas and labels themselves. Consequently we shall continue, for some time to come, to get political words all mixed up. One example is the confusion over the widely used terms 'progressive' and 'reactionary'. Under the influence of paternalism, the political culture has impressed a bias upon the British, one which too readily associates a patrician mentality with positive values and a more democratic mentality with negative ones. Hence, paternalism itself, which derives from a feudal conception, and thus in the contemporary world can *properly* be described as 'reactionary', is nonetheless too often considered as 'progressive'.

For instance, a privately educated peer of the realm with bags of inherited family wealth (and maybe also bags of inherited social and racial prejudices) can expect, in modern Britain, to be described as 'progressive' simply because he *proclaims* a paternalistic 'compassion' for the poor (whom he may never meet) and wants the average tax-payer to foot the bill for welfare. Alternatively, a young entrepreneur from humble origins who, by merit and enterprise, has made some money (remitting much of it to his working-class parents) will too often be considered 'reactionary' simply because he believes that too large a state sector cramps initiative and enterprise.

The persistence of paternalism will also continue to distort a clear picture of the party political scene. British politics in the twentieth century has tended to be viewed and described as a contest between Labour and Conservatives, with the Liberals, (and latterly, the Social Democrats) somewhere in the middle. This, though, is only how the purely formal electoral debate is organized. The real political divisions (both those of ideology and interest) run, as they always have done, *through* the political parties and not *between* them. A less clouded lens might see the real political battleground in Britain rather differently: and, as far as paternalism is concerned, as a contest in which both its supporters and its opponents are to be found in all parties.

Of course, so powerfully entrenched was the paternalist ideology throughout most of the century that all the major parties (Liberals, Conservatives and Labour), and indeed both the major ideological traditions (socialism and conservatism) have, in their different ways, acted almost as though they were agents of a single paternalist governance. Whereas the nineteenth century saw a sharp division between, on the one hand, paternalists (reflected by the landed-interest-dominated Tories) and, on the other hand, classical liberals (reflected by the Liberal party), the twentieth century, in contrast, has witnessed hardly any clash of ideology at all. Instead, it witnessed an agreement, not a dispute: a paternalist-led collectivist consensus amongst the parties in which,

no matter the progressive and democratic rhetoric variously employed, the paternalist structures and ethos remained firmly in
place.

In a non-paternalist political culture the Labour and Conservative
parties would represent opposite poles in the universal ideological
tension between the principles of equality and freedom. Labour
(as the left-wing party) would place an emphasis upon equality.
Its programme and measures would aim at reducing economic
and social inequities even if such a reduction might impinge
upon traditionally understood freedoms. The Conservatives (as
the right-wing party) would take their stand on freedom and
liberty, even though the consequences of such a stand might
mean accepting, or even extending, inequalities of income and
wealth. Yet, this is not the way it has worked out: for both parties
have found their natural radicalism refocused, and their ideological
inclinations submerged, by a sovereign political establishment and
culture which has, in effect, used them as mere agencies for
reordering and rearranging the status quo. And in the process,
at least until recently, neither has Labour been able to make
Britain more equal, nor the Conservatives to make it more
free.

Labour's postwar domestic programmes are a case in point. Not
one of the Labour governments since 1945 (many of whose leaders
and supporters continued to see Labour as a 'party of the people'
in the tradition of radical reform, the Tolpuddle Martyrs, and the
Chartists) gave more than a passing thought to the question of
democratizing Britain, to opening up society and its institutions to
its peoples. Labour viewed constitutional change as a luxury. The
1945 government fed its energy into a programme of nationaliza-
tion and welfarism; and although it engineered a timid reform of
the powers of the House of Lords, the *ancien régime*, including
the hereditary element in the legislature, remained safely intact.
The 1964–70 Labour government, with the exception of Richard
Crossman's meagre proposals for reforming the House of Lords,
was just as constitutionally conservative as its predecessor. And
Labour's innate cultural conservatism also exhibited itself in its
attitude towards the education system, arguably the single most
potent arena for sustaining Britain's class system and sense.
Three decades and more of educational debate and 'reform' ended
up with the public schools intact, and the only ladder available for

bright and talented working-class children – the grammar schools – kicked away from under them.

In fact, Labour's more general failure to change the face of Britain should, on reflection, have surprised no one. Labour's more powerful state and public sector would ultimately serve only to enhance, rather than diminish, the power and influence accruing to the paternalist establishment. After all, Labour's expansion of the public sector was but a further extension of a structure which had originally been erected *not* by socialists, but rather by the paternalist aristocrats of earlier Liberal and Tory governments. Both Samuel Beer and W. H. Greenleaf have more than amply displayed how the 'New Liberalism' of the turn of the century (which gave the state its first, late-Victorian, boost), the later inflation of the state by the interwar Tory governments, and Labour's 1945 programme, can be viewed as a continuum, a thematic development of the paternalism inherent in aristocratic rule.[17]

Indeed, the Labour party and movement has historically been a god-send to paternalist governance. Labour's role in organizing workers both collectively and centrally (in trade unions) has allowed the established political order not only to organize (and thus govern) the society more effectively, but also to buy off its leaders. Labour's *penchant* for aggregating economic power was also counter-productive. Had Labour diffused economic power in Britain (even by using the state as an agency to 'break up' and redistribute the tightly controlled landed sector), rather than concentrating it further in the hands of the state, then the more plural centres of power (both private and public) which would have been created would have made the country less easily 'governed' in the traditional sense.

Also, Labour fulfilled a function which the Conservatives were congenitally incapable of performing. As Labour progressively during the twentieth century took over the mantle of the 'people's party' (from the Liberals) it thereby became the custodian of populist instincts and popular aspirations. Yet, it succeeded in squandering this inheritance by deflecting anti-establishment populist sentiment amongst its supporters away from democratization and into the safer shores of economic statism. Of course, the truth was that most of Labour's leaders were no more interested than most of their Tory opponents in creating a society free of deference, inhabited by self-reliant citizens.

Richard Crossman describes a pointed image of the life of politics as late as 1951, six years after the beginning of Labour's postwar 'social revolution':

> After dinner on Sunday Ben Nicholson . . . told an interesting story about ten days he spent at Windsor Castle as Deputy Keeper of the King's Pictures. On four of those days parlour games were played after dinner and the Queen chose her favourite game. The master of ceremonies took all the male guests outside and provided them with brass pokers, shovels, etc. After ten minutes practice they were then made to parade as a squad, with the shovels and pokers on their shoulders, in slow goose step down the long drawing room past the King, the Queen and the Princesses, who found it exquisite fun seeing Sir Stafford Cripps, Lord Ismay and Anthony Eden doing 'Eyes Right'. Nicholson said he hadn't seen anything like Stafford Cripps, who had been forced at two hours notice to spend a weekend at Windsor and who humbly obeyed the Royal command but suffered the full humiliation which Royalty seemed determined to extract from its Commoner guests. [18]

Thus they paraded like children. These great men of the democratic state (the radical socialist, Stafford Cripps, and the progressive Tory, Anthony Eden, then Foreign Secretary) were reduced to performing a scene redolent with feudal imagery, one unimaginable in any other advanced nation. 'Eyes Right' depicts not only the posture, but also the true political position of these children of reactionary paternalist collectivism.

Following the return to government of the Conservatives, it was obvious that the postwar Tories were as stunted by the overlain carapace of paternalism as was Labour. The welfare state was further entrenched by the Conservatives, indeed it was set in concrete, reaching the proportions of national symbolism, Britain's face to the world. It was hardly surprising that the Conservatives took to Labour's welfare state like a duck to water. After all, the postwar Conservative party was still a home for nature's paternalists, for aristocrats (and aristocrats *manqués*) uncomfortable with 'trade', 'commerce' and individual endeavour. Indeed, so suffused with the pathology of landed ideology were these postwar Tories that some even wanted to kick the businessmen out of the party. Lord Hinchingbrooke gave vent to much paternalist spleen when he rounded on the business class which had entered the Conservative party in the interwar years:

> True Conservative opinion is horrified at the damage done to
> this country . . . by 'individualist' businessmen, financiers and
> speculators ranging freely in a laissez-faire economy and creeping
> unnoticed into the fold of Conservatism to insult the party with their
> votes at elections . . . and to injure the character of our people. It
> would wish nothing better than that these men should collect their
> baggage and depart.[19]

Here was the authentic, untamed voice of Tory paternalism (or
what, later, came to be popularly known as High Toryism). Of
course, and unfortunately for Viscount Hinchingbrooke (and fortu-
nately for the young aspiring Margaret Thatcher), 'new money'
continued to 'creep unnoticed' into the Conservative party, to
'insult the party' with its votes and to 'injure the character of
the people'. Yet, the full extent of this subterranean process
of bourgeois change was only to become apparent much later.
Paternalism's grip upon the Tory party was to succeed in holding
back the merchants' advance, and the bourgeois modern world,
for a good few decades yet.

Following the end of the Second World War the political right in
most Western countries had accepted the imperatives and values
of the democratic age. This was not quite the case in Britain, where
influential opinion on the right remained largely unreconstructed,
still echoing attitudes, nostrums and values drawn from feudal
times. For instance, Britain entered the postwar era with the
West's only avowedly 'conservative' party, one which celebrated,
in its name apart from anything else, the accumulated tradition
of centuries. Also, the continuing influence of paternalist High
Toryism helped ensure that – again in the metaphor of the landed
estate – the Conservative party continued to view Britain and its
peoples not as a democratic polity to be governed, but as a feudal
organization to be ruled. High Tories told themselves that only
they (unlike the dangerous philosophers of liberalism) could both
ensure social stability and *dispense* 'justice'.

The stability of this 'feudal nation' would be guaranteed, so the
High Tory line of thinking ran, by a society where slow, organic
social development was fertilized by tradition (no matter how contrived), by the promotion of communal myths and ceremonies, and
also by the secular religion of nationalism (with which the priests
of High Toryism would attempt skilfully to associate themselves).
And the justice of 'the feudal nation' would amount to the 'justice'

of the manor – a humanitarian concern for the less well off, the weaker, based upon ancient notions of 'fair play'. This modernized conception of feudal lordship would ensure that 'justice' (through the welfare state) was administered to the 'serfs', that 'genuine' grievances were put right – but only, that is, as long as the 'serfs' did not flirt with ideas of possessing inalienable rights and were also prepared to render fealty.

Of course, this residual feudal mentality was rarely expressed systematically by Conservatives of a High Tory leaning. Indeed, part of the reason for the survival of such an anachronistic sensibility is the covert manner in which many of these old-fashioned prejudices – against the nouveaux riches and the bourgeois, against the modern notion of the individual, against commerce and industry – have been pursued. (In a sense, Hinchingbrooke, although he spoke for many a High Tory paternalist, let the cat out of the bag). Also, however, this High Tory attachment to feudalism has not only been covert, it has also been limited. After all, the High Tories of the contemporary era are descendants of the historic Tory party, the party of the court – and this party had, long before the modern age, abandoned its belief in arbitrary power and the divine right of Kings. For High Tories, the art of political survival has demanded an attempt to fuse their feudal instincts with the imperatives of democracy and industrialism.

This High Tory approach to government did not survive well into the last quarter of the twentieth century simply by accident. Nor was it imposed upon an unwilling people. Rather, its innate paternalism reflected a need amongst large swathes of the population for the security of an ordered and highly regulated society. This need for a relatively risk-free environment was the natural response of a population which had gone through two world wars and a depression, and whose lives during the twentieth century (and certainly amongst 'the propertyless masses') had been racked by financial insecurity if not poverty. In this less-than-confident environment, life had indeed been fearful, often lacking in even the basis for independence and personal growth.

It would thus need a sustained period both of affluence and of political stability for the British people, finally, to put the feudal embrace (and its paternalist distortion of politics) firmly behind them.

2

The Revolt
Against Paternalism

Early signs

Although the patrician edifice of British paternalism finally
cracked under the weight of the events of the 1970s, early
signs of erosion had appeared during the previous two decades.
The consumer boom, the spread of postwar affluence, and full
employment, all conspired to modernize British society, to give
it some of the flavour of the more rapid middle-class development
proceeding in North America and on the European continent.
A more 'classless' and socially mobile British way of life was
revealing itself. The 1950s were to see the emergence of the
mass consumer market, suburban development, and increased
foreign travel. Perhaps the most impressive of all the early signs
of bourgeois modernity was the mass popularity of the Beatles
popular music group with its vibrant, classless, provincial (and
indeed international) appeal.

The early 1960s witnessed the first 'irreverent' anti-establishment entertainment, called 'That Was the Week That Was'. Week
after week a mass audience was presented with the spectacle of
traditional authority being ridiculed. David Frost, a classless and
cosmopolitan Englishman if ever there was one, became (through
the power of the television medium) the nation's grand inquisitor,

wielding a cultural influence potentially even more powerful than
that of the scions of paternalism in the upper reaches of the British media. The new meritocratic militancy was also to mock the
backward restrictive practices of traditional 'working-class life', as
in the film 'I'm All Right Jack'.

Politically, it was the Conservative party which presided over
the consumer boom; and, as the Tories were still drawn from
a very narrow social stratum, this ensured that the country's
first-ever taste of mass affluence would run its course under the
political tutelage of paternalists. The postwar Tory leadership –
Churchill, Eden, Macmillan, Home – tended to view the onset
of mass prosperity in traditional paternalist terms, as though this
new consumer affluence was a kind of 'grace and favour' reward
to the workers for their war efforts and then for voting Conservative in 1951 and 1955. Harold Macmillan's throwaway remark that
'You've never had it so good' ('You', not 'We') was typical of this
paternalist mentality, as was Alec Home's later depiction of old-
age pensions as 'donations'.

Whereas the Tories (still largely landed, public school and Oxbridge in their recruitment system) remained untouched by notions of a more mobile society, ideas of social egalitarianism were
to express themselves politically amongst left-of-centre types. Labour revisionists, like Hugh Gaitskell, Anthony Crosland and John
Strachey, were becoming increasingly attracted by American-
style social and cultural openness.[1]

Anthony Crosland was one of the most impressive politician-
philosophers of this generation (an honour he shared with his
more left-wing counterpart Richard Crossman). Crosland's Plym-
outh Brethren background, and his intellectual arrogance, made
him something of a rebel. He delighted in being unconventional
in manners, and in pricking pomposity and complacency. (He
once rang me up to invite himself – at two hours notice –
to dinner, and walked round to my home in carpet slippers,
apparently believing that such informality was the prerogative
of the talented.) Crosland, like others in this Fabian coterie,
did not suffer fools gladly, particularly Tory fools. His rebellious
streak also allowed him to see through the shallow liberal elitism developing amongst many of his left-wing colleagues. As a
reaction he flirted with populism, and often invoked the virtues
of his 'working-class' Grimsby constituents. His pioneering book

The Future of Socialism was predicated upon the notion that the highest political value was equality. Yet, ultimately, he simply could not construct a workable public policy which would even erode inequalities. He wanted Britain to be culturally American-ized, but in the non-capitalist, risk-free, hierarchical structures of postwar Keynesian social democracy. Like so many of this leftist generation he was, at heart, an English paternalist.

More genuinely radical ideas were appearing on the intellectual front. Although the world of British letters was still largely in the hands of the establishment – in thrall either to the aristocratic and rural past or to the habits of mind of Empire (or both) – there were some remarkable exceptions. The most interesting appeared in a volume of essays, entitled *The Establishment*, published in 1959. In this volume a group of non-marxist, mainstream intellectuals set out the case for an open society via a devastating critical analysis of some of the central institutions of the paternalist state. Henry Fairlie (who is credited with discovering the term 'the Establish-ment') took on the BBC, Christopher Hollis, the Parliament, John Vaisey the public schools, Simon Raven the Army, and Victor Sandelson the City of London. In his introduction, the young Hugh Thomas (now Lord Thomas of Swynnerton) could write in terms which virtually called forth a liberal revolution:

> To those who desire to see the resources and talents of Britain fully developed and extended, there is no doubt that the fusty Establish-ment, with its Victorian views and standards of judgement, must be destroyed . . . the editor, however, cannot refrain from pointing out that it is in childhood that the men who make the present Establishment are trained; and that therefore we shall not be free of the Establishment frame of mind, permeating all aspects of life and society, and constantly reappearing even when apparently uprooted, until the public schools are completely swept away, at whatever cost to the temporary peace of the country.[2]

A year before *The Establishment* appeared, Michael Young's *The Rise of the Meritocracy* had caused an intellectual stir (and a temporary intellectual fashion). Young, also writing from a non-marxist, liberal perspective, ventured a prediction: that a new, modern 'classless' meritocracy was emerging in Britain which, al-though it would be resisted, represented the future. This startling anti-paternalist tract (although it was not called such) set about

Britain's worship of traditional authority in a manner not to emerge again until the age of Thatcher:

> Britain lived on ancestral capital, and the more it did so, the more it had to do so . . . A strange doctrine, I know, for a modern sociologist, but I am not alone in saying that too many people had too sharp a sense of history, along with too dull a sense of what the future might be persuaded to yield. It was not like this in the nineteenth century, but by the middle of the twentieth, tradition was over-valued, continuity too much revered . . . Britain, in other words, remained rural-minded long after eighty per cent of its population were collected in towns – altogether as strange an example of cultural lag on a mass scale as China before the Mao Dynasty . . . Ancestor worship took the form of reverence for old houses and churches, the most amazing coinage, the quaintest weights and measures, Guards regiments, public houses, old cars, cricket, above all the hereditary monarchy, namely the aristocracy, which could trace its descent from a more splendid past.[3]

These early outbursts of modernity in the cultural, political and intellectual realms of British life were not wholly isolated and random expressions of a country finally growing up. They were to some extent underpinned by what seemed to be important social changes.

By the early 1960s many believed Britain to be on the verge of 'embourgeoisement', a dry term for the creation of a middle class. Following the third Conservative election victory in a row (in 1959) a spate of studies set out to discover why the party which 'espoused' liberal capitalism could do so consistently well at the polls. The 'affluent worker' was discovered. This was a political animal who voted instrumentally (in his or her own material interests) as opposed to traditionally and deferentially.

The end of deference would indeed have been revolutionary. And for a while, it seemed as if the old patterns of class loyalty might be replaced by a more mature and discriminating individuality. A nation of individuals would replace the nation of predictable servitude to existing paternalist authority.

Yet, no sooner had this potential been raised than it was cruelly dashed. A whole school of scholars began to argue that this picture of Britain as an emergent modern society was cruelly overdrawn. A survey of Luton, north of London (picked because it was the archetypal 'affluent worker' town of the era) concluded that Britain's 'affluent workers' were not becoming like their 'blue-collar' American counterparts. Most of them, although better off, were retaining their 'working-class' cultural identity and their loyalty to Labour. It was a case of proletarians with wall-to-wall carpeting, but proletarians nonetheless. Deference to Labour (and amongst the 'working-class Tories', who voted 'for their betters', to the Conservatives) still held sway. They still knew their place.[4]

Harold Wilson, Labour's new leader, was not so sure. There was certainly something occurring in the life of Britain in the early 1960s: a certain radical sentiment in the air, an irritation with stuffy manners and ancient hierarchies. It was the age of 'Swinging London'. Consequently Wilson built his 1964 election campaign on the theme of social modernization. He attacked what he called the 'gentlemen and players' society, and savagely ridiculed the Tory Prime Minister, Alec Douglas-Home, as but a 'Fourteenth Earl'. His modernizing rhetoric, often evoking Lloyd George and Joseph Chamberlain, was used to devastating political effect. Wilson himself (a meritocratic lad from the North, in his classless Gannex raincoat) represented both in his media persona (1964 was a television election) and his political rhetoric the hope of creating a more classless, more modern nation that would finally put to rest Britain's ancient social forms and values.

Indeed, Wilson was an almost perfect British embodiment of the confident 'mid-Atlanticism' that Kennedy had established as a political genre on the other side of the Atlantic. It seemed to some that a 'New Britain' (Labour's slogan for the 1964 election campaign) was indeed about to dawn, and that it would bring with it the 'unleashing of talents' (much talked of at the time) through a social and economic system which would reward efficiency, merit and enterprise. Within two years, however (and after a further Labour election victory in 1966) it was obvious that Wilson's 'New Britain' was not to be taken seriously. The Labour government was reeling under serial economic crises (mainly derived from a worsening balance of payments), and Labour loyalists argued that Labour's programme had been 'hi-jacked' by 'events', mainly international; that the 'New Britain' had been 'blown off course'.

Yet, the incipient 'New Britain' – which was 'blown off course' – was hardly much different from the 'Old', which, implicitly at least, it wished to replace. What the 'New Britain' really amounted to was an attempt to achieve higher economic growth than its Tory predecessors. This growth was to be achieved by a greater measure of planning – induced by a Department of Economic Affairs, which would restrict the authority of the Treasury. Policies that would make a reality of the rhetoric of 'an open, mobile, classless society' were non-existent. The Labour government was certainly not to be in the business of securing modernization by 'bourgeoisification', by the mechanism of state disengagement, and the rule of markets, choice and enterprise. Labour's plans for redistribution of income and wealth would address the problem of 'poverty' only by weakening the middle income sector. Apart from Richard Crossman's failed attempt to 'reform' the House of Lords there were to be no plans for constitutional modernization. Harold Wilson, Britain's 1960s 'new man', was to end up with the Garter as Lord Wilson of Riveaulx.

Labour's upper-middle class 'Gaitskellites' were critical of Wilson's conservative leadership of their party, but were no more radical than Wilson himself. The last thing these revisionists seemed interested in was the creation of a vibrant and self-confident middle class. A striking characteristic of most of the members of this influential 1960s political grouping (as it appeared to this young biographer) was their social and cultural sameness. Virtually all of them were from financially privileged backgrounds, deeply imbued with upper strata values deriving from the late Victorian disdain for industrialism and 'capitalism'. After all, most of these 1960s Labour leaders were brought up in the feudal environment of the interwar public schools, and those who were not were later inducted into antiquity by the Oxbridge of the 1930s.

Although they proclaimed liberal values they could not bring themselves to embrace liberal economics. Like many in the Labour party of that time, Keynesian economics, and its big state, were to remain their instruments for change, even whilst the state was controlled by an establishment they claimed to despise.

The problem with this dominant social democracy of the 1960s was superbly described by the Canadian-born economist Harry Johnson. He suggested that, in Britain, there were

the social values underlying Keynes's approach to economic questions [which] were typical of the British academic milieu, particularly that of Oxford and Cambridge. Centered around the colleges, which remained in spirit 'feudal institutions', this way of life . . . encouraged a paternalistic and static attitude towards the working class. The main social obligation of the authorities (like the college fellows vis-à-vis the college servants) tended to be seen as that of guaranteeing employment. The 'social problem' was fundamentally that of providing security for the masses.[5]

These 'progressives' (like their counterparts today who are so hostile to free market economics) saw themselves as an intellectual elite whose duty was to guide 'the workers' over whom, in some indefinable way, they were 'set'. (Most of them were ill at ease in the company of their 'working-class' constituents.) A freer economy and society would threaten this ascendancy as much as it would the status of Britain's aristocratic establishment.

Labour's 1960s left wing were as tame as the Labour right. Drawing their Bevanite ideas from John Ruskin, Charles Dickens and William Morris, they were as much affected by the late Victorian revulsion against capitalism as any High Tory. Like their right-wing counterparts (and their Conservative opponents) they had little interest in setting 'the workers' free from their life-time ghettos in council estates or trade union clubs.

A young Labour MP, green around the gills and still enthusiastic for change, once suggested in a caucus meeting of London's Labour party that the party should sell off its council housing stock – to its existing tenants. 'At least they will be able to paint the front door whatever colour they want', he proclaimed, 'instead of having to get a bureaucrat's permission.' He was immediately upbraided by an elderly councillor who normally spent most of his time in such meetings half asleep. 'Young man', he shouted across the room 'those folk are our voters. We want to keep them that way.'

In the 1960s, the Labour hierarchy, like the Tories, would set their faces like flint against a more bourgeois society.

The trade unions of the 1960s were no more radical. They sought collective advancement, not individual development through embourgeoisement. Nor did they want to use their collective muscle in order to secure individual achievement. Their mental apparatus was a mirror image of that of the landed elites. A society of individuals, each gaining control over their lives, increasingly presented with greater choice (both of goods and services), free to develop their own tastes, and their own sense of self-esteem and physical and psychic space, was anathema! It would wreck the carefully contrived structures, built up over centuries, in which the establishment of land and the establishment of labour (and the establishment of letters) all had their assigned places.

So, Harold Wilson, even had he personally wanted to make a 'dash for freedom' during the 1960s (which was anyway unlikely), would have found the road blocked by his own party and movement.

As the 1960s progressed whatever small instinct for change existed was to dissolve amidst the economic crises and social instability which engulfed the country from the mid-1960s until the early 1980s. The British peoples' search for security was to lead them back into the embrace of paternalism for most of this troubled time.

Yet, strangely, the 1970s were to open with a determined burst of liberal optimism. The new man at the top (Edward Heath) proclaimed, of all things, the need in Britain for a 'Quiet Revolution'. And the 'revolution' he had in mind was a bourgeois one.

Heath's instincts were not those of the traditional Tory, since he was bereft of both rural sentimentality and a love of the archaic. He was the first Tory leader since the war who had nothing of the patrician in him; and, remarkable as it may now seem, the first-ever to be elected! He seemed to be that most unusual of twentieth-century Tories, a meritocrat. His reaction against Britain's decline took a visceral technocratic and modernizing form.

Whilst Prime Minister, he was to become irritated with the slothful and tradition-bound habits of much of reactionary British industry. He seemed to understand that the day of the quaint English rural idyll was over. He once proclaimed, much to the annoyance of arcadian Tories, that 'the alternative to expansion is not, as some occasionally seem to suppose, an England of quiet market towns linked only by trains puffing slowly and peacefully through green meadows. The alternative is slums, dangerous roads, old factories, cramped schools, stunted lives'.[6]

As Leader of the Opposition during the 1960s Heath had presided over a Conservative party policy review which had culminated in the Selsdon Park programme, the most radical neo-liberal prospectus ever developed by a modern British political party. During January and February of 1970 Heath's Shadow Cabinet, in order to prepare the ground for his 'Quiet Revolution', engaged in a a series of speeches, clearly signalling that a Heath government would make a clean break from the postwar social democratic consensus. In one such speech, Sir Keith Joseph spoke of the need for a new national economic strategy which would involve no automatic partnership between government and industry; each, he argued, had a distinctive role, and the government's was to create a background in which the free enterprise system could work more effectively through changes in company and taxation law. Another speech by David Howell (a former director of the Conservative Political Centre) reflected Heath's views on how the quality of government could be improved by defining areas and activities from which the government would distance itself. He promoted Heath's view that new administrative techniques developed in America, designed to test and evaluate government accountability, and to streamline its structure, were needed in Britain.

By the time of his first party conference as Prime Minister (held in Brighton in October, 1970) Heath had re-formulated the 'Quiet Revolution'. It amounted to nothing less than an assault upon the whole postwar Attlee consensus, as radical an appeal as any that Margaret Thatcher was later to deliver in the 1980s.

Heath's theme for the conference was the need to create a more self-reliant society, a pointed rejection of traditional Tory paternalism. He argued that his 'revolution' amounted to '. . . less government, and of a better quality'. And he outlined a daring programme of governmental disengagement whereby individuals were to be encouraged to be more responsible for themselves and their families, free to make their own decisions, if they wished to, rather than having them imposed by bureaucracies. Disengagement was to extend to private industry as well: 'lame ducks' would no longer be rescued. Heath's 1970 prospectus amounted to Thatcherism without privatization.

After a major review of public expenditure in October 1970, Heath's Chancellor of the Exchequer, Anthony Barber, outlined his budget proposals for 1971, anticipating a saving of public funds of £1,000 million by 1974/5. His proposals included cuts in the defence budget (whilst honouring commitments in the Far East and the Gulf states), a cut of 6d (2½p) in income tax for most wage-earners and a reduction in Corporation Tax of 2½ per cent. The new government was firmly opposed to an incomes policy.

The details of Heath's economic policies remained, for the moment, consistent with the theme and strategy of radical neo-liberal disengagement.

Yet, the course of Heath's 'quiet revolution' was to run for only a few more months. Over the next three years its central planks were dismantled, one by one. The 'dash for freedom' was therefore virtually over before it had began. The 'U-turn' (as it was dubbed) amounted to the sharpest reversal of declared domestic political strategy seen in a life-time. The patrician edifice, constructed on the building blocks handed down by John Maynard Keynes and William Beveridge, was to remain in place for another ten years.

A revolt aborted

Heath's fabled 'U-turn' was indeed spectacular. It was as if his 'dash for freedom' had touched the rawest of nerves, had affronted some historic English folk-memory which awoke to resist this alien onslaught on its very identity. Perhaps it had. Dismantling the patrician state – with so many intertwined vested interests and hierarchies – would be no easy matter. Heath had obviously not thought through the consequences of so rapid a burst of liberalization.

The Heath men were obviously shocked at the bitter resistance encountered from both organized labour and established capital. A Tory grandee of somewhat innocent liberal disposition had his fellow diners in the Carlton Club in gales of laughter when he asked, 'What on earth is all the fuss about? After all, we're going after stupid management sucking off the public teat as well as for the union fellas?'. That, of course, was the point, the very rub.

When Heath's 'lame-ducks' strategy was put to the test by the Upper Clyde Shipbuilders sit-in, and the Chief Constable of Glasgow told him that he could not guarantee public order, he backed off. Nor had he foreseen that the first phase of liberal economics would mean higher unemployment. When the unemployment figures topped the million mark he took fright. At the first whiff of grapeshot, he ran away.

First, there were the early economic policy reversals (in the first six months of 1971) which brought the monetarist and free market economic strategy to a shuddering halt. There followed a group of further statist measures (enacted in the first few months of 1972) which formed the sharp bottom curve of the 'U'. Then came the greatest reversal of all, the introduction of a compulsory incomes policy (announced in November, 1972) which pushed the line up, to complete the 'U'.

In good paternalist fashion the trade unions were 'told' what their wage levels should be. But it was this attempt to impose wage levels which caused the first signs of the inner contradictions of paternalism (what Samuel Beer has called the 'contradictions of collectivism') to appear. The same paternalist state, which over the previous century had encouraged trade unions, now found that these same unions (by the 1970s less deferential than their fore-bears) would simply no longer tolerate the word of government.

The trade unions, the most majestic source of inertia in Britain's traditional society, not only defeated the 'Quiet Revolution', but also placed a roadblock in the path of Heath's return to economic paternalism. Following his defeat at the hands of the National Union of Mineworkers, the battered Prime Minister left office in February 1974, and handed the administration of Britain's tottering paternalist consensus back to Harold Wilson.

Wilson had not expected to become Prime Minister again. It was no doubt a pleasing shock to find himself, yet again, standing on the steps of 10 Downing Street waving to the crowds. But this time, the thrill of office must have been tempered somewhat by a sinking realization of what had, once again, fallen to him: the management of a nation in severe crisis.

'Management' was indeed to become Wilson's watchword. This time he would not even seek to change the course of British history. Rather, he saw his role as serving the ramshackle established order. He would hold the ring. In favour of what, he was not clear. Against what: he was somewhat clearer. Labour, with its special relationship with the victorious trade unions, could save the country from social upheaval. His private boast was that if as Prime Minister he was able to 'get everybody in the Kingdom back to bed at night without too many heads being broken', then he would consider himself a success.

He regarded Heath's flirtation with bourgeois radicalism – during the 'Quiet Revolution' – as a grievous, destabilizing error. The old actor-manager (by this time more cynical and worldly-wise than the stunned, innocent Heath) would appease, not confront, the trade unions. So Wilson inaugurated a novel system of national management. It was called the 'social contract' – an arrangement whereby government and unions co-operated to determine the domestic policy of the nation. Even the composition of his Cabinet was to be determined by trade union leaders.[7]

By bringing the union leaders into the very heart of government Wilson was not (as some of his critics alleged) taking the country to the verge of 'red revolution'. He was rather marching to the beat of the ancient drum of paternalist statecraft, exhibiting the traditional instincts of England's ruling class when it meets a challenge to its vital interests. Domesticate, do not enrage, the insurgent; appease, do not confront, the opponent; maintain power by the appearance of sharing it.

And the union leaders played their part. As day after day they were to be seen on Britain's television screens emerging from 10 Downing Street, it was as if the ermine was already wrapped around their shoulders, draping them in the embrace of an ancestral acceptance, more worthy than any mere industrial reward. Their members had other ideas; but that particular rude awakening would await the next Prime Minister, the real architect of the 'social contract', Harold Wilson's successor, James Callaghan.

Britain's eighth postwar Prime Minister identified with the trade union movement. Jim Callaghan came from a southern English upper working-class background. He was a merchant seaman, and then an employee of the Inland Revenue, and as a young man made his way in Labour politics through the Inland Revenue Staff Association. Like others from a similar background (such as George Brown, Ray Gunter and Bob Mellish) he relied heavily upon right-wing trade union votes for political advancement. Callaghan could relax easily with trade union leaders, a social coterie with which he felt at home. For all his seemingly detached political style, and his cold self-assurance, Callaghan was socially insecure, like so many from his background during his generation. Consequently, he invested immense emotional capital in the Labour movement.

One of his Cabinet colleagues could suggest:

> An endearing feature was his genuine gratitude to the Labour party for all the opportunities it had given him. He was justly proud to be the only politician of the century to have held all

four of the senior offices of state: Chancellor of the Exchequer, Home Secretary, Foreign Secretary and, finally, Prime Minister. In turn he thought he owed the Labour party his total loyalty and this meant accepting the trade union link, bloc votes at conference and the arguments between right and left. These were, in his view, an inevitable part of the Labour party and they had to be endured.[8]

Nothing could shake Callaghan's determination to work with the trade union leaders; and, although the 'social contract' became increasingly shop-soiled during his tenure in office, he stood by it to the end. The Callaghan-led Labour government was even more collectivist in its underlying assumptions and ethos than that of Wilson. Wilson – an individualist, university-educated and meritocratic – had, after all, at least flirted with social modernization as an objective, believing that weakening trade union power was one way to create a more open and socially mobile society. Callaghan, on the other hand, was by background a trade union employee and a trade union-sponsored Member of Parliament, who assumed that the only possible method of improving the conditions of the poorer, weaker and less wealthy sections of society was by 'collective advancement' under the auspices of the Labour movement, working within a framework of established economic and social relations.

The 'working class' could achieve a place in the sun, as he had, only by collective action. In Callaghan's view, British labour should work through the existing paternalist system, veering neither to the 'left' (and attempting to overthrow the system) nor to the 'right' (with a free market economy which would lead down the slippery slope to individualism). For Callaghan, there was little that was morally repugnant in the paternalist national structure and ethos which he inherited as Prime Minister. After all, the paternalist state had allocated the 'workers' (and the Labour movement) an assigned place within its total structure, and the function of Labour governments was simply to improve, at the margin, the position (in terms of lifestyle and life-chances) of what was to Callaghan its most valuable component part. Thus, it was not Labour's role to create the conditions for the emergence of a modern class-less society, one in which 'the workers' would cease to be treated as a single social 'category' (a category to be advanced, appeased or resisted) and instead assume the aspect of individuality.

Callaghan's instinctive lack of radicalism (and distrust of modernity) was aptly displayed when, late in his political career, he followed the path of generations of successful Englishmen and retreated to the country, to the life of the land. Like Stanley Baldwin before him, rural values and farming became a subject upon which he could wax eloquent.[9] Callaghan became the patrician state's last Viceroy. Like Harold Wilson he ended up in the House of Lords.

When the public service unions finally destroyed the 'social contract', during the 'winter of discontent' in 1978-9, it was not only the end for Callaghan, but the end, too, of a paternalist era, indeed of a paternalist century.

Seeds of revolution

Britain's liberal revolution started, like all revolutions, in the world of ideas, in the minds of men and women who refused to accept automatically the imperatives of orthodoxy, tradition or fashion. Of course, the classical liberal ideas at the heart of the changes since 1979 have (as argued above) a long pedigree. But their postwar resurgence in Britain began when social democracy started fraying at the edges in the middle 1960s.

So total was the social democratic consensus during the postwar decades that few would veer from its embrace. Inevitably, as the crises gathered in the 1970s many intellectuals left for the pastures of extreme socialism. Few supported the free market solutions of economic liberalism. The great exception was to be found at the Institute for Economic Affairs in Lord North Street. Set up in the 1960s, the IEA was careful not to brand itself politically. Led by Ralph Harris (who is not a Conservative, and sits on the cross-benches in the House of Lords) and Arthur Seldon (who was a Liberal party officer in Orpington in the 1960s, and describes his position as 'Whiggish'), this tiny opinion-forming body was seen for many years as an essentially fringe stage-show.

The IEA school, as it affected British politics, concerned itself primarily with economics. Adam Smith, not Tom Paine, was its hero. Its members were convinced free marketeers, monetarists and supply-siders, but steered clear of such controversial (in Britain) questions as political culture, social class and constitutional reform.

Professional intellectuals can often afford to be more courageous and adventurous than politicians, whose livelihood depends upon the art of compromise demanded by interest groups and political parties. Yet the IEA had some early party political adherents, most of them in the business wing of the Conservative party. Its ideas had a short burst of life during Heath's 'quiet revolution', but following the 'U-turn' the pamphleteers of Lord North Street (although always stimulating company for those who turned up to their monthly lunches) remained lone figures, swimming hard against the dominant patrician collectivist tide.

The economic ideas of the IEA had some dedicated supporters in Fleet Street, mainly amongst some of the younger leader writers. Andrew Alexander of the *Daily Mail*, who describes himself as a radical not a conservative, John O'Sullivan and Michael Harrington of the *Daily Telegraph*, and later Derek Hill of the *Daily Express* were amongst the most forthright.

Margaret Thatcher's election to the Tory leadership in 1975 was the breakthrough which the neo-liberals needed. While still Leader of the Opposition, she brought into the centre of British politics much of the pent-up anger and betrayal felt by the radical Conservatives over the 'U-turn'. Although some believed it was another false dawn, and that she would ditch her radical instincts once she was in power and the going got tough, it soon became apparent that she might be a wholly new kind of Tory animal. Soon after becoming leader she, and Sir Keith Joseph, set up a Conservative party think-tank, the Centre for Policy Studies, which began propagandizing for what was later to become known as 'the enterprise culture'. The guiding hand behind the CPS was former communist Alfred Sherman, who was later to be succeeded by Hugh Thomas, who had left Labour for the 'dry' wing of the Tory Party in the mid-1970s.

Even the CPS found it difficult to make headway, however. An authentic commitment to the 'Free Market' and 'Monetarism', let alone to the 'the Enterprise Culture', only touched the outer fringes of the Tory party. Many of those Tory MPs who today proclaim neo-liberal views were loyal supporters of Heath, but, more importantly, instinctive Tory 'wets' and paternalists.

Support for the cluster of ideas behind popular capitalism had few friends in the Labour or Liberal parties in the mid-1970s. Isolated figures like PLP chairman Douglas Houghton, trade union leader Frank Chapple, or Liberal MP John Pardoe, would turn up at IEA and CPS lunches, as would some of the officers of the Social Democratic Alliance.

Whatever support liberal economics secured from within Labour had more to do with the necessities of life following the International Monetary Fund crisis of 1976, than with any systematic ideological liberal conversion. The IMF crisis did, however, serve to give the small group of radicals a boost. Following the loan, Callaghan became the first postwar Prime Minister prepared to give the country a lecture on the virtues of liberal economics. Consulting his son-in-law, Peter Jay, ahead of his 1976 Labour conference speech, Callaghan asked him to produce some paragraphs which would 'make the fur fly'.

In front of the serried ranks of staid trade unionists he proclaimed:

> For too long, perhaps ever since the war, we postponed facing up to fundamental changes in our society and in our economy. That is what I mean when I say we have been living on borrowed time. For too long this country – all of us, yes this conference too – has been ready to settle for borrowing money abroad to maintain our standards of life, instead of grappling with the fundamental problems of British industry . . . The cosy world we were told would go on forever, where full employment would be guaranteed . . . that cosy world is now gone . . . We used to think we could spend our way out of a recession and increase employment by cutting taxes and boosting government spending. I tell you in all candour that that option no longer exists, and that insofar as it ever did exist, it only worked on each occasion since the war by injecting a bigger dose of inflation into the economy followed by a higher level of unemployment as the next step.[10]

Callaghan did not stop there. Under the shadow of the IMF he also became the first postwar Prime Minister to talk the language of the IEA about the dominance of 'producer' over 'consumer' interests in collectivist Britain. He was later to suggest

> I also wanted to support the producer, but felt that the balance had shifted too far, to the extent that welfare services, and especially

local government, were increasingly run entirely for the conveni-
ence of those who worked in them without concern for the needs
of the ordinary citizens (and voters) who paid for them through
taxes and who tried to use them . . . In fact, in all my many
dealings with the National Union of Teachers at the time I never
once heard mention by it of education or children.[11]

Labour, though, (and, as it turned out, Callaghan too) was not
to be seriously moved by these unusual injunctions. For well over
a decade following his public flirtation with liberal economics, the
accumulated historical ideology of Labour continued to weigh in
the balance against accepting that Britain needed 'fundamental
changes' in society and economy, at least of the kind suggested
by Callaghan.

By the early 1980s, however, the nascent ideological stance of
the political centre was more promising for the new liberalism.
Two years into Thatcher's first government radical liberal ideas
were becoming fashionable amongst the higher socio-economic
groupings, and, for a time, it became a toss-up whether or not
the new Alliance (between the SDP and the Liberals) would run
with them, indeed would allow this emergent ideology to define
its electoral appeal. By the mid-1980s two distinct strands had
emerged within Britain's new political grouping of the centre.
David Steel and the Jenkinsite wing of the SDP – the grouping which guided the direction of the Alliance in its first few
years – retained their fundamental sympathy with the old Fabian
certainty.

Later, though, stark divisions began to emerge between Steel
and Jenkins on the one side and David Owen on the other. Owen
introduced into SDP policy-making the idea of the 'Social Market'
(a concept pioneered in West Germany by Ludwig Erhard, which
accepted the virtue of a market-oriented system, but placed it
within the context of social goals), and was supported by John
Pardoe and SDP MPs John Horam and Neville Sandelson. These
neo-radicals within the political centre were, however, soon to be
isolated by the political guile of Britain's most impressive liberal
paternalist, Roy Jenkins. Jenkins, particularly after he became
the SDP's first leader, was to be successful in steering the new
party away from the 'Social Market', and back to an economic
strategy which was hardly any different from that which governed
the thinking of the second Wilson government. John Pardoe was

subsequently to leave politics altogether; John Horam joined the
Conservatives; Neville Sandelson left the SDP and founded the
Radical Society; and David Owen went into the political wilder-
ness.

If, in the early 1980s, the political support for the new liberalism
was negligible, the social base upon which it could be constructed looked even less impressive. Socially, Britain could hardly
claim either a numerically large, or culturally vibrant and self-
confident, middle class – the essential pre-requisite for a bourgeois
revolution. Also, there was a general impression that the early
Thatcher years were producing a hardening of class solidarities –
particularly in the old industrial regions where unemployment was
rising dramatically and amongst trade union activists who were
witnessing the progressive repeal of the legal advances they had
secured under Labour.

A freer economy, let alone a neo-liberal cultural revolution,
could simply not proceed whilst the trade unions were so powerfully entrenched in the economic system. Yet, few at the time
apparently understood the role which trade union militancy was
playing in the unfolding British political drama. In one sense the
assertive trade unionism of the 1970s and early 1980s was a force
which reinforced the corporate state, in that with every trade union victory the instinctive reflexes of the politicians led them to
renew their efforts to bind the trade unions into an alliance with the
state. Yet, in another sense, trade union militancy was a symptom
of a more widespread assertiveness in British society, a sign that
'workers' at least were no longer content to accept their allotted
position within the paternalist state. An undeferential workforce
was, in theory at least, fertile ground in which the seeds of a liberal
revolution could grow.

When the public sector employees breached the guidelines of
the 'social contract' during the 'winter of discontent' it hardly
appeared possible that they had anything in common with the
radical liberal intellectuals who were beginning to influence the
thinking of the Conservative party in opposition. Yet, both groups,
although acting separately and with distinctly different objectives,
managed to erode the foundations of postwar paternalism. The
workers in the unions destroyed the collectivist consensus; the
liberal ideologues in and around the Conservative party came up
with the cluster of ideas which would serve to replace it.

For the ideas of the IEA and the CPS to take root, however, they would need to be turned into the concrete policies of government. Following the Conservative election victory of 1979 the Battle for Britain moved from the rarefied atmosphere of pamphlets, articles and position papers, to the realm of high and hard politics.

Thatcher's victory

In the summer of 1979, the radical liberals around the new Prime Minister had little real support in the country. The new economic philosophy being promulgated from Downing Street had, after all, been floated before, by Edward Heath during the 'Quiet Revolution'. The same interest groups which had forced Heath to back away from the strategy were still entrenched. Thus, Thatcher's new liberalism, although exciting considerable interest (particularly in the light of the failure of the previous consensus), was, nonetheless, viewed as a fancy – as coherent theoretically but, ultimately, unapplicable to Britain. It went against the grain.

Such an ambitious economic restructuring of the country could not be carried through in the lifetime of one Parliament. Thatcher's radicals needed at least a decade, if not longer, to implement their new economic strategy, to overcome the inevitable initial resistance, to acclimatize people to the benefits they were certain a freer economy would ultimately bring, and also to create an environment in which a new party political consensus (one including Labour as well as the political centre) could cohere.

Surprisingly, startlingly, they were to get the time they needed, for the Conservative government was to be returned to power in three successive general elections. Yet, what on the surface appears as a spectacular series of electoral triumphs for the Conservatives was, in reality, rather less impressive. The fact is that the whole Thatcher era – and its revolution – has been underpinned by a popular vote which has consistently fallen well short of a majority of the electorate. In the 1979 general election the Conservative share of the vote was 43.9 per cent, and this share fell by 0.2 per cent in 1983, and again by a further 1.4 per cent in 1987 – a so-called 'landslide victory' in which the Conservative party received a smaller percentage of votes cast than did

Hugh Gaitskell's Labour party in 1959 when it suffered a 'landslide defeat'. The Conservatives were able to translate this series of minority popular votes into a series of 'landslides' of Parliamentary seats because they benefitted from the vagaries of a multi-party electoral system which tends to deliver a disproportionate number of seats to the party which can secure over 40 per cent of the vote.

Even so, the fact that the Conservatives *did* succeed in achieving over 40 per cent of the vote in three successive elections was no mean achievement, given the considerable economic and social dislocations which the new economic strategy brought in its wake. The intriguing question is why this Conservative vote should have remained so firm for so long.

Part of the explanation obviously lies with the high level of antipathy towards Labour exhibited throughout much of the south and the midlands of England during the 1980s. Yet, from the Conservatives' point of view, there was also a positive side to the story. A careful reading of the detailed electoral statistics reveals that the new liberal economic strategy of the 1980s was able, over time, to create genuine support for itself amongst a growing 'middle-class' electorate. And 'middle-class' here is not meant to depict, solely, the traditional Conservative enclaves in the Home Counties and amongst the suburban salariat.

One of the most intriguing aspects of the politics of the 1980s has been the changing voting habits of one of Britain's most pivotal voting blocs, the skilled manual workers. Between the elections of 1983 and 1987, the percentage of these workers (and their families) who voted Conservative *rose* by 4 per cent.[12] This helps to explain the historically (and remarkably) high level of Conservative votes recorded in predominantly urban safe Labour constituencies throughout the southern half of England. Such erstwhile Labour strongholds as Thurrock, Walthamstow and Wolverhampton North-East were *gained* by the Conservatives in 1987; and in seats like Barking, Dagenham, Coventry South-West and Corby (as well as in a range of other predominantly urban and highly unionized constituencies) the Conservative vote reached levels that it had never seen before.

Previous decades had witnessed fluctuating 'working-class' support for the Conservative party, but what was new about the 1980s was the sheer size of the conversion in particular blue-collar areas in the southern half of England. The electoral map of southern England began to lose its class flavour, as the traditionally 'working-class' seats could no longer be so easily distinguished from the rest. This electoral consensus, however, represented something even more important. A process was obviously under way which was beginning to blur the lines between the old, stubborn, British social stereotypes of hourly paid workers living in council houses (who voted Labour) and the salaried middle class with mortages (who voted Conservative). 'These divides' it was suggested by *The Economist* of 16 May 1987 'are now crossed by millions who would be called upwardly mobile if the yuppies had not got to the term first.'

Yet, although the election results of the 1980s reflected what amounted almost to a dissolution of the traditional British class divide throughout much of the southern half of England, the same could not be said of the nation as a whole. The class inequalities which the 1980s had somewhat 'ironed out' in the southern half of England, had stiffened in the North (including Scotland). Large tracts of the urban North and of urban Scotland were untouched by the economic changes proceeding in the south (and the rising trend in unemployment north of the Trent had ensured that, far from eroding social barriers, ancient social divisions were, if anything, hardening).

The old image of 'the North' as one vast wasteland was never particularly apt, however, for such an image hardly took into account either the areas of northern prosperity or, indeed, southern poverty. This image somehow tended to omit from view the vast number of acres held in private ownership throughout the North and Scotland, the sizeable middle-class suburbs surrounding many Northern and Scottish cities, and, indeed, the quasi-bourgeois character and aspirations of some of the more prosperous families in the mining areas. Thus, 'the North's' reaction to the popular capitalist experiment of the 1980s was more complicated than the traditional image would normally have allowed. In fact, during the 1980s 'the North' was only marginally less well-disposed to the Conservatives than was the rest of the country. Between 1983 and 1987 the Conservative vote fell by only 2 per cent in the North–West and by 2.3 per cent in the North (Scotland was the genuine exception where it fell by 4.3 per cent and the Labour vote rose by 7.3 per cent).

The consistently solid level of public support (around the low 40 per cent mark) for the radical liberal economic strategy of the 1980s contrasts sharply with the notion that Britain had become utterly resistant to change, locked forever in the embrace of traditional behaviour and paternalist governance. By the time of the third Conservative election victory, the London correspondent of *The New York Times* could argue that:

> None of the opposition strategies seemed to admit the possibility that in an ossified society – where inheriting has long been deemed the only truly proper way to acquire wealth – Mrs Thatcher's strivers' code might exert an almost clandestine appeal. [13]

Of course, a series of election victories for the Conservative party during the 1980s is hardly the same thing as a popular national mandate for radical change. Nor does it tell the whole story about the underlying instincts and opinions even of those who voted Conservative. For amongst Conservative voters those who identified themselves with economic change (and wanted more of it) were probably outnumbered by those who sought the defence of the status quo, who voted Conservative as a means of keeping Labour out. If anything, 'old money' probably supported the Conservatives as fervently as did 'new money', landowners as determinedly as the new entrepreneurs, and the older traditional middle class in greater numbers than the upwardly mobile 'workers'. A marked shift in the underlying social attitudes of the Conservative voting constituency should not therefore be pushed too far. Although popular motives can never be properly adduced from polling results, it would seem likely that a large percentage of the Tory popular vote in both 1983 and 1987 was still grudgingly given.

The fact was that throughout the 1980s a sizeable section of the traditional Conservative vote was instinctively 'centrist'. These were the folks who were relatively comfortably off and economically secure. They were the 'old middle class' of the rural villages and richer suburbs who normally did well under an old-style Conservative government, and who had, initially, seen Thatcher as the traditional Tory lady come *only* to slay the socialist serpents in the Labour and trade union movement and in local government. 'Isn't She Marvellooos' some of the more 'county' types amongst them would almost coo to each other.

But their reservations about Thatcher grew with every passing month, as they began to realize that she was no Tory of the old school. Above all, they were fearful that her new radicalism might, by confronting the unions, also destabilize their own world. Labour's 'shadow' Foreign Secretary, Denis Healey, had attempted to exploit these fears during the 1987 campaign by exposing Thatcher's known anti-establishment instincts. 'Thatcher', he asserted, 'has declared war on the BBC and the Church of England.'[14]

A leader in the *Sunday Telegraph* of 7 June 1987, published on the eve of polling day, also struck a High Tory traditionalist note, one which spoke for many who in the end also voted Conservative. Entitled 'Bourgeois Triumphalist Threat to Mrs Thatcher', it issued a warning:

> Wealth-creating is a good thing . . . in their case [that of the new financial elite] the possession of wealth seems to carry with it absolutely no sense of obligation or service whatsoever . . . To some extent the resentment they provoke is due to envy, since they flaunt their wealth with a degree of brazen insensitivity the like of which has not been seen since the days of the Edwardian nouveaux riches. But the resentment is also due to genuine concern that the values yuppies espouse, or rather the lack of values, threaten this country's long record of civilised governance.

This concern to ensure 'civilized governance' echoed more widespread fears amongst many Conservative supporters about whether or not a more entrepreneurial society would endanger the kind of 'stability' with which traditionalist Tory voters had historically felt comfortable. A healthy economy fired by entrepreneurial spirit and values was not – so the argument went – *ipso facto* a stable society. Yet these same Conservative supporters were aware that the 1970s had not been a stable decade either. Economic decline had produced serious social instability and, what is more, an instability which expressed itself collectively (through trade union action) rather than individually. In an age in which deference was waning and aspirations were rising, a rich society was likely to be more stable than a poor one. Hence, traditionalist Conservatives, *in the absence of any 'acceptable alternative'* (or 'soft option' as it was dubbed by the Tory 'dries') continued to support, albeit reluctantly, Mrs Thatcher's radical agenda.

The first port of call for these Conservative voters in search of a 'soft option' was the newly created SDP-Liberal Alliance. Yet this 'acceptable alternative' fell progressively from favour as it became clear that voting for the Alliance entailed too great a risk. The new Alliance had simply not enlisted enough support in its first years of life to 'break the mould' and thereby 'hold the balance'. Thus, the fear was that voting Alliance would let Labour in by default. Large numbers of potential Alliance voters in the villages and more affluent suburbs of southern England therefore ended up by voting Conservative in both 1983 and 1987. By 1987 the Alliance popular vote had fallen by 4 per cent from its high point in 1983.

The second potential 'soft option' for this kind of voter appeared when Neil Kinnock took over from Michael Foot as Leader of the Labour party in 1983. But this 'alternative' disappeared within months as it became clear that Labour under Kinnock's leadership would not be moving to the safe centre. It would still be beholden to the trade unions, and was not going to repeal its policy of unilateral nuclear disarmament. In 1987 therefore, the option of voting Labour was not available.

In this respect the electoral contest of 1987 was like no other since, arguably, that of 1935. In twelve general elections since then (from 1945 to 1983) the voter could record a vote for either of the two main parties secure in the knowledge that the declaratory ideological direction of the chosen party (rarely very sharp) would be mitigated by a 'moderate' (or paternalist) faction within the winning party once the counting was over and Parliament assembled.

For almost forty years – since Churchill accepted the Beveridge plan during the Second World War – all major parties contending for government could, once in office, be expected to work solidly within the parameters of an agreed and imposed national strategy. The election of 1987 – with its stark counterpoising of 'peoples' capitalism' and neutralist socialism – finally marked the end of this era. Thus, 1987 became the year in which British politics was 'disestablished', in the sense that neither major political party offered to the electors *either* an 'establishment' programme *or* the likelihood of a reversion to such an 'establishment' programme once it was elected. Voting Conservative in the summer of 1987 entailed what it had never done before in the twentieth century: it amounted to a conscious decision (no matter how reluctantly) to support a party determined to make a radical break with the past. It was in this manner that much of establishment England was recruited to serve in effecting its own defeat.

The 'disestablishment' of the Conservative party – perhaps the most remarkable political development of the 1980s – was the end-product of a reordering of social power within the party which had been under way over the whole postwar period. This Pareto-style 'circulation of elites' – in which the upwardly mobile, commercial, and populist faction of the party (the 'dries') edged ever nearer to an ascendancy over the landed and 'liberal' wing (the 'wets') – became evident with the political demise of a generation of 'One Nation' Tory paternalists. During the 1980s such leading 'wets' as Norman St John Stevas, Jim Prior, Sir Ian Gilmour and Lord Carrington were progressively replaced at the Cabinet table by more radical and meritocratic figures like Geoffrey Howe, Keith Joseph, Nigel Lawson and Norman Tebbit.

Later still, this vanguard was supplemented by a whole new generation of younger Conservative politicians – like John Major, John Moore, Cecil Parkinson, Kenneth Clarke and Norman Fowler, who represented the more classless grass-roots base emerging through the Conservative party itself. The party leadership was no longer dominated either by the landed classes or the stereotypical products of public school and Oxbridge. People with very different formative experiences and values had taken over the helm.

These 'new Conservatives' were part of a mutually reinforcing internal party dynamic which ran through the politics of the party during the 1980s. The new breed of Conservatives helped Mrs Thatcher to establish her ascendancy over the party and she, in turn, used her influence to further widen the social base of the leadership. And, in turn (again), as the party became more classless Thatcherism's writ within the party ran ever more powerfully.

Margaret Thatcher's ascendancy over her own party is a remarkable achievement, by any recent historical standards. It is a story made all the more intriguing by being against the grain and the odds. It involves doses of political courage, no little guile, great luck, and considerable tenacity on the part of Britain's first woman Prime Minister. There are many twists and turns along the way in this tale of the in-house revolution within the party. Her achieving the leadership in the first place (in 1975) was something of a fluke. And, ever since, her Tory opponents have been waiting for a suitable excuse to weaken, and even oust, her.

Looking back on the 1980s there now appear to have been three vulnerable phases through which her premiership has passed. Had she lost the 1983 general election, she would almost certainly have been replaced as leader by a more 'soothing' figure. Yet, the Falklands war shored up her party (and consequently her premiership) at the very moment (in the spring of 1982) when the newly formed SDP-Liberal Alliance was looking extremely formidable in the polls, and on course for take-off. If the Alliance had succeeded in holding the balance in Parliament, Roy Jenkins would have worked with the Conservatives, but not with Mrs Thatcher.[15]

Having got through 1983, the next hurdle for the radical Conservatives emerged in the following year when the National Union of Mineworkers found itself in dispute with the Coal Board over projected pit closures. The prospect of a conflict between the NUM and the state aroused considerable anxieties within the Conservative party and government. Ever since 1971 – when the NUM unexpectedly won what was to become the first of a trilogy of industrial battles with the elected govern- ment – British politics had proceeded in what amounted to a twilight world of authority. The question raised in the first general election of 1974, 'Who governs Britain: government or unions?', remained a legitimate subject for speculation well into the 1980s. (Some months before the 1983 general election a European *chargé d'affaires* politely asked an embarrassed Tory MP whether the NUM President, 'Mr Scargill', had a 'veto' over the further development of the Thatcherite revolution. 'He surely', enquired the foreigner, 'will not allow privatization of energy?')

The natural instinct of many Tories was to appease the NUM. Indeed, Margaret Thatcher had done so herself when she yielded to the union in an earlier dispute a year after coming to power. By 1984, however, the government was prepared to see out the strike, but this decision to confront the union was another high stakes gamble. Of course, the challenge from the NUM would have to be met sooner or later if the process of economic restructuring – of winding down the paternalist state – was to be allowed to run its full course. Yet, had the strategy to confront the NUM failed – and the dispute gone Arthur Scargill's way – then not only would the NUM have established 'veto power' over at least some aspects of the liberal economic strategy, but also the re-emergence of an under-current of fear for the future of the social fabric would have strengthened the hand of the Tory 'wets'. Thatcher's revolution, and possibly Thatcher herself, would have been over. As it turned out, the conflict with the NUM (and indeed Britain's 'trade union question') was finally settled in the late spring of 1985 when thousands of defeated miners – the 'lions who had been led by donkeys' – returned to work, covering their humiliation at the hands of the Conservative government by marching in columns under their banners with bands playing. Thatcher had survived yet again.

By the spring of 1986, Margaret Thatcher was confronting yet another threat to her premiership when the 'Westland helicopter affair' came remarkably close to removing her from office, this time by an attempted 'palace coup' within the 1922 Committee of Conservative backbenchers. 'Westland' was essentially a contrivance, and an opportunity for Thatcher's remaining opponents to oust her in time to allow another Prime Minister to see *himself* into the job before the coming election. Thus, the merits of the issue became of less interest than what the affair revealed about the line-up of 'dry' and 'wet' forces within the Conservative party seven years into Thatcher's era. It was soon quite clear that the radicals had indeed won the battle for the Tory soul, for the 'wets' could simply not muster the parliamentary numbers needed to overcome a determined resistance from Number Ten.

Yet, even during the 1987 election campaign (when it seemed that Labour might be doing very well indeed in some of the marginal seats) there were leaked speculations that, in the event of a narrow Conservative victory, Mrs Thatcher would have to be replaced. On election night, as the BBC computer mistakenly forecast just such a result, the jubilation in the Corporation was barely concealed.[16]

Margaret Thatcher probably overcame most of the rebellions against her from within her own party because, when the question of whether to remove her or not finally concentrated the minds of Conservative MPs, any possible replacement would have been considered too electorally risky. The connecting theme in Thatcher's successful battle with her own party is that it has stuck by her because she is a winner, above all electorally. Thus, the triumph of radicalism *within* the Conservative party can hardly be divorced from the string of election victories accumulated by the party under her leadership.

These same election victories, however, need to be set in a broader context. It had been a truism of British politics during the twentieth century that divisions of the left help the Conservatives. Such was the case when Labour edged out the Liberals as the major opposition party during the 1920s; such, too, was the outcome after the Labour government broke up in 1931. It is also a truism that divisions on the left are endemic, a part of the furniture of British politics, a product of deep ideological tensions, indeed irreconcilabilities. These strains, however, were contained for a good three decades following the 1945 political settlement. They began to surface again during the 1970s as the uneasy coalition between the socialist and social democratic wings of the Labour movement began to fray at the edges. It was Margaret Thatcher's inordinately good fortune that they finally erupted in 1981 only two years into her first government; for the electoral fissure between Labour and the SDP which was produced by this political earthquake was to give her revolution a fair wind for another ten years.

Revolt on the left

No account of the surprising success of the new radicalism in establishing its ascendancy in British politics can be complete without understanding the pivotal role played by the SDP. The day after the 1987 election it was finally clear that the high hopes for the SDP of only a few years earlier were to come to nothing. The 'mould of British politics' was not to be 'broken', and a 'hung Parliament' remained as remote a prospect as ever. At a reception at the SDP conference later in the year, one of the Trustees of the new party offered the following conclusion as to what it had all meant: 'Well, we may not have broken the mould, but we have dished Labour, and for a generation'. He was not far off the mark.

The crude facts about Britain's odd electoral system prove his point. Fact One: the system gives the party which gets the most votes a disproportionate number of seats. Fact Two: when there is a three-way contest between three more or less equal parties, the party which gets over 40 per cent of the vote, whilst the other two hover between 25 and 30 per cent each, gets a wildly disproportionate number of seats.

The fanfare of publicity surrounding the launch of the SDP in 1981 succeeded in giving the Liberals their long-needed boost; but the upshot was that the new Alliance (of SDP-Liberals) could only raise the proportion of the popular vote for the centre parties to the mid-20s. This sorry outcome was the worst of both worlds for most of the SDP leadership. Their public support was not high enough for them to hold the balance in Parliament (which would have stopped Thatcherism dead in its tracks); but it was enough for them to have split the opposition vote, thereby securing three terms for Thatcherism.

When the dust had settled, the much trumpeted 'realignment of the left' had ended up with an ironic twist. The Keynesian liberal paternalists who had set up the new party had helped secure, by the very act of wounding Labour, the end of the paternalist era. Had Roy Jenkins, Shirley Williams, Bill Rodgers and David Owen known, in those early, heady days surrounding their launch of the new party, how they were playing into Thatcher's hands they might not have embarked on the endeavour at all.

The SDP affair cannot be seen only in this grim and ironic context, however. The declaration of the new party in 1981 was not a random event, rather it had its roots in the contradictions of Labour's history. Labour had nearly split apart several times during the 1960s and 1970s. But, somehow, its explosively combustible contradictions always seemed to be contained, yet another testimony to the sluggish hold of tradition on the mid-twentieth-century British. The great battles of principle and ideology – between marxism and social democracy – were always seemingly subsumed under the inertia of habit.

Hugh Gaitskell (Labour's leader from 1955 to 1963) came near to splitting the party in 1960 when he made his famous 'Fight, Fight and Fight Again' speech against Labour's left – in essence challenging them to accept his defence policy or throw him out. During this traumatic period for the party, personal loyalties and cohesive political groupings were forged on the Gaitskellite right which were to surface two decades later. Many of the actors in the later SDP drama were schooled and blooded in these years.

Gaitskell, however, was somewhat different from many of his friends in his political circle. He was an intriguing man, possessed of a personal confidence rare in British politics, and rare too amongst his friends. He was a man of open emotion, exactly the opposite of Aneurin Bevan's wickedly unfair quip about his being a 'desiccated calculating machine'. But this attribute allowed him to enjoy the cut and thrust of intellectual combat, and not be fearful of being contradicted, as long as he sensed that the battle was intellectual, not political. Some of his younger academic supporters used to meet at his home in Hampstead in the early 1960s and bat ideas back and forth. He would take part with relish, and without the contrived distance often employed by other, less personally (and politically) secure leading politicians.

Gaitskell was a peculiar hybrid, both a paternalist and a radical. His background – son of an Indian civil servant and with a public school education – meant that he could never fully break with the mental and emotional framework of upper-class English rulership and with its paternalist 'top-down' view of politics. Yet, within these limits, he was also a genuine radical who, as radicals must, always tried to go 'to the root of the matter'. The Wykehamist intellectual in him enhanced his radicalism, producing a temperamental aversion to ambiguity. Once he had made up his mind on an issue he would propound it ruthlessly, irrespective of the sensitivities obtaining at the time. Gaitskell was a 'conviction politician', as convinced in his day as Mrs Thatcher was to be in hers that political risks were an attendant feature of a political life with a purpose beyond mere party management.

This authentic English radicalism led him, unlike many others in his coterie, towards a belief that the class system was central to Britain's problems as a nation. On a personal level he was un-en-thralled by upper-class affectations, manners and pretentions. He saw through them. Towards the end of a rather dry speech in 1955 on the nationalized industries, he suddenly put aside his prepared text and declared: 'I would like to tell you, if I may, why I am a Socialist and have been for some thirty years. I became a Socialist quite candidly not so much because I was a passionate advocate of public ownership but because I disliked the class structure of our society.' He elaborated upon this theme in 1959, declaring that he sought 'a society without the snobbery, the privilege, the restrictive social barriers which are still far too prevalent in Britain today'.[17]

As with many genuine social egalitarians, Gaitskell was fond of the American way of life, which he saw as refreshing and enterprising. Roy Jenkins, a completely different political character with quite different ambitions and tastes, reported of Gaitskell that:

> He became strongly pro-American, not uncritically, nor to the exclusion of some tough bargaining with them, but deeply because multi-dimensionally so, liking the country, the life, the intellectual style. He always, *I am afraid*, much preferred Americans to continental Europeans.[18] (emphasis added)

Attitudes to America are, in a sense, one of the great unspoken dividing points in British political life. British politicians are rarely neutral on the issue; and Gaitskell (like Thatcher, but unlike Heath and Jenkins) was very decidedly on the American side.

A son of the establishment, Gaitskell was nevertheless an anti-establishment figure. Born into a family of the Raj, he rejected imperialism as his social vision for Britain turned westwards (to egalitarian America) not eastwards to the hierarchy of India. An atheist, a robust intellect, both nonconformist and confrontational: these attributes rebuked the honed-down and careful upper-class English habits of mind of his day. He was incapable of the flamboyant posturing of Welsh radicals like David Lloyd George or Aneurin Bevan, but that made him all the more serious, and potentially deadly (had he lived beyond 1963).

When, in the late 1960s, Roy Jenkins finally took over the leadership of the Labour right from Gaitskell, the establishment (albeit its liberal wing) was back in control. From then on the politics of the Labour right became all about how to save the paternalist state (from the threat from the left) rather than about how to change Britain.

The debate within the Labour right on how to handle the 'left-wing problem' was often heated, indeed acrimonious. It always came back to the same question: should the left be 'smothered' by our staying within the Labour party, or should we leave and either form a new party or try a coalition with the Conservatives.

Many discussions took place 'across the floor'. They normally came to nothing. Yet, in early December 1976, a realignment looked to be on the cards. Callaghan's majority in the House of Commons had disappeared and consequently a very small number of Labour MPs could effectively bring down the government. For some years past the arguments for a realignment had been taken seriously by a section of the Conservative party who had been close to Macmillan. Since 1973, Reg Prentice had taken a lone path, one which would eventually take him out of the Labour party and into the Conservative fold. In the meantime, in league with Roy Jenkins, he had sought ways of bringing down the Callaghan government.

His advocacy had struck a chord with some Conservatives, amongst them Robert Carr, Nicholas Scott and Patrick Cormack. These, and others, were beginning to meet, together with Labour MPs, on an increasingly regular, though informal, basis. A meeting finally took place in Julian Amery's house – Amery himself, Patrick Cormack, Maurice Macmillan, Reg Prentice, John Mackintosh and Brian Walden – to argue through the case for bringing down the Callaghan government. The consensus emerged that an attempt was worthwhile, and Prentice, who had come straight to the meeting from a Labour Cabinet meeting chaired by Callaghan, made arrangements to meet secretly with the Opposition leader, Margaret Thatcher.

> The key people would be Margaret Thatcher, Roy Jenkins and David Steel, in that order. Margaret would have to lead such a government, as the Conservatives would be the biggest party in it, although they lacked a majority in the House. Would she be interested? If she were, then Roy Jenkins would be the one person in the Labour Party with a wide enough personal following to bring in a substantial Labour contingent. Only if this happened would the Liberals be likely to join. Arrangements were made for me to see Margaret Thatcher. Nobody else was present and no notes were taken. I do not recall all the details of the discussion, but I remember her strong views on the economic crisis, so much more incisive that anything I had heard at the Cabinet table. She was angry and worried at the drift of events and was afraid that the government would 'fudge' the issue again. As to a political realignment, she did not commit herself, but I was left with the impression that she would feel bound to participate if there were evidence of wider support. The clear implication was that I should take further soundings.[19]

Everything therefore hinged on the attitude of Roy Jenkins. He was technically a backbencher, but he had an office in the Cabinet Secretariat building – as he would be taking up the Presidency of the European Commission on 1 January the following year. As an MP still, he was politically and constitutionally available to take part in the contemplated political moves. Jenkins, however, was to reject the overture, and the opportunity. He told Prentice that 'the proposed realignment would lead to a government nominally "national" but in fact "Conservative"'. He also argued that 'Although I would be a senior figure in the new government, supported by other right-wing Labour members, we should be supporting an essentially Conservative administration, rather like Ramsay MacDonald and his friends in 1931.'[20]

Jenkins was at that time haunted by the 'MacDonald analogy', with its image of 'betrayal'. At the same time, he obviously believed his refusal to 'break out' during the 1970s was another kind of betrayal. The formation of the SDP, in which he was the incomparable guiding hand, was, in a sense, an act of redemption on his part for these past missed opportunities.

Once he had made up his mind, Jenkins set about the task with some relish. His strategy for the new party, and its electoral alliance with the Liberals, had been clear from the start. The SDP-Liberal Alliance was to be in the business of holding the balance in Parliament. This it could do only by taking enough seats from the Conservatives in the south of England. Once it held the balance it would force a change in the electoral system, and thereby secure a permanent place for itself in a future of British coalition politics.

The whole SDP game-plan was therefore predicated upon a 'soft' Conservative vote, one which, as frustration with Thatcher grew in the south of England, would fall into the Alliance's hands like a ripe plum. This strategy only truly fell apart when the Falklands conflict erupted. The Policy Committee of the SDP met in their Cowley Street headquarters as the task-force was steaming south, slicing down the middle of the Atlantic Ocean. The 'Gang of Four' (Roy Jenkins, David Owen, Bill Rodgers and Shirley Williams) gathered round the table dejected and defeated, somehow overnight diminished in size and stature. All four of them knew what the Falklands meant for the future of their political careers. It would shore up the Tory vote in the south of England, and the great gamble would be lost.

Jenkins had become convinced, some time before the new

party was even launched, that if the Alliance could replace any party then it had to be the Conservatives. Labour's vote was considered too solid to erode more than just at the margins. In this assessment he was to be proved correct. Yet, it was also a confession of weakness: of the inadequacy of the new party (and the new Alliance) to attract the upwardly mobile 'working class' who were instead becoming increasingly attracted to Thatcher's radicalism. The truth was that the new party (and Alliance) was not populist enough, branded (accurately) as it was with the image of the kind of paternalist socialism which was out of kilter with the times. 'It's his posh accent, I tell you', said one frustrated SDP activist about his leader, when confronted with polling figures showing lack of SDP appeal among 'working-class' voters.

Jenkins was a multi-faceted political personality, never quite taking his contrived distant and fastidious manner over-seriously. The languid aristocratic carapace which covered his more complex personality was to hurt him politically, however. Although a superb parliamentary, and even better platform, performer, he was an appalling canvasser. The image remains of Jenkins meeting the ordinary folk of Warrington, during the by-election of 1982: of a huge, bloated grandee of a figure, obviously at a loss as to what to say, descending awkwardly upon an unfortunate local. 'How long have you lived heaaar?' he asked haughtily. 'All me life' came the startled reply.

The SDP was essentially a conservative and paternalist force. The leading Social Democrats had a peculiar attitude towards social change, and towards the rigidities and hierarchies of British society and culture. They proclaimed radical credentials. The Limehouse Declaration (the party's first salvo) talked of the need for 'classlessness' and for an end to 'the class-based parties'. Yet, for all the ringing declarations, the prescriptions for change (whether economic, social or constitutional) which emerged from the SDP Policy Committee were very slight.

David Marquand's major pamphlet, written specifically for the newly formed party, was appetisingly called 'Russet-Coated Captains', referring to the radical officers in Cromwell's New Model Army. However, all it amounted to was a call to arms on behalf of the standard Keynesian paternalism, and a recitation of the need for social conciliation rather than radical social and cultural change. The new party was also heavily influenced by

Keynesian Professors Meade and Layard whose economic strategies, rarely placed in the context of the need for modernizing social change, hardly differed from those of the Labour right or the Tory 'wets'. Apart from David Owen (whose propagation of a Social Market economy made him a lone voice on the Policy Committee of the new party), the leading practitioners and theorists of the SDP were all re-tread paternalists, uninterested in new ideas for creating a more open and bourgeois society.

The fact is that the Social Democrats of the early 1980s were not radicals in any serious sense of the term. The reason for this strange truth may lie partly in the social background and aspirations of the leading members of the party. None of the original 'Gang of Four' were from extravagantly privileged backgrounds, none born into real wealth or status. Roy Jenkins – although his demeanour and accent belied it – came from a middling Welsh family. His father, though by no means a typical workers' representative, had gone to prison for trade union activities, a fact which caused his mother some embarrassment. David Owen's ancestry was Celtic, a fact about which he could sometimes become emotional.[21] Bill Rodgers was a Mancunian, a grammar school boy with provincial roots. Shirley Williams hailed from a self-consciously intellectual family which seemingly rejected the conformist upper-middle class standards of the day.

As the playwright, John Mortimer, wrote:

> Mrs Williams it seems was born with a silver spoon in her mouth, perhaps one of those her mother, the writer Vera Brittain, who inherited wealth from a family business in the Potteries, used at her elegant tea parties attended by a maid . . . She had a father, who, as his son candidly admits, gave the appearance of being a frightful snob. The temptation to take such a spoon and stir a chipped mug of strong Typhoo in the nearest and greasiest working man's caff must have been irresistible.[22]

These backgrounds, however, did not unite the Social Democrats in a radical rejection of the values and attitudes of High Tory paternalist England. Rather, and peculiarly, they led many of them into a lifetime's desire to emulate them. Consequently, they tended (with some exceptions) both to accept, and to see themselves as leading participants in, the governance and the governing ideology of the British elite as it operated and controlled the postwar consensus. The Gang of Four were, thus, all paternalism's children; Jenkins being the most integrated, David Owen the most wayward. And, from amongst the original founders of the SDP, only Owen was to attempt to adapt his politics to the post-paternalist age.

3
The Radical Challenge

The former MP, Robert Kilroy Silk, paid a short visit to the United States in March 1988, and returned with some alarming news:

> They [the Americans] also know that America is their country. It belongs to them. All their history, their teaching, ideology, literature and laws tell them so. The rules and the laws are made for them . . . Britain, we know, doesn't belong to us. We don't know who it does belong to, but it's certainly not the people – that's why our laws treat us as nuisances and America treats its people as citizens; that's why its government is open with its people and ours keeps secrets.[1]

Presumably, Kilroy Silk is not suggesting that the problem with Britain is simply one of unjust ownership of land. His implication is of something far more intangible, yet also more all-embracing: of a country in which no one (no matter how much land they may hold) has a personal stake, and in which everyone owes allegiance not to themselves, but rather to something mystical outside themselves, something which they cannot quite discern or describe.

This sense of 'the people' being locked out of their own country (even out of its history) has, according to historian Norman Stone, been the major preoccupation of the intellectual life of A. J. P. Taylor.

> Taylor's English history 1914–1945 said that the rising well-being of the people mattered more than anything else – more than battles,

peers, archbishops, Oxford colleges, the Empire. These were all noises off; part of that Establishment which Cobbett, a hero of Taylor's, called 'The Thing'. Taylor himself, a northern radical by origin, believes in the people . . . He is certainly the historian with the greatest popular following . . . he writes in a style open to all.[2]

Railing against 'The Thing' has been a constant theme of British popular radicalism. It reached its most articulate form in the eighteenth century in the life of the free market capitalist, Tom Paine. His frustration with England's still-born seventeenth-century revolution eventually led him abroad. His compensation (or revenge?) was to help found the United States of America, that commercial republic which Paul Johnson has described as 'the posthumous child of the English revolution'.

Tom Paine is now being resurrected. A statue has been erected to him in his native Norfolk; he is the subject of a play (recently performed at the Arena theatre in Washington, DC); Margaret Thatcher includes his quotes in her speeches; learned works about the man are appearing, the most recent by the philosopher A. J. Ayer; and his name and works are used in support of calls for constitutional reform and a Bill of Rights. David Marquand has captured Tom Paine well:

> It is not, however, as a thinker that he [Tom Paine] deserves to be remembered. It is as the embodiment, symbol and shaper of a tradition of British popular radicalism which has gone underground for most of the twentieth century but which may well hold the key to the politics of the next. For obvious reasons, this tradition has always been weaker than its American or French equivalents . . . Central to it are the notions that power should flow upwards from the sovereign people, not downwards from some sanctified authority.[3]

What, though, were these 'obvious reasons' why Paine's vision for his country has never been realized; why in Britain, now uniquely amongst major Western nations, does power still flow 'downwards'? Tom Nairn suggests that everything was set in concrete before Paine even came on the scene. He suggests that by the late seventeenth century the English establishment was so 'irreparably traumatised by its Ugandan experiences of 1640–60 – warfare, regicide, massacre and military dictatorship' that it 'erected a state with no house room for democracy. Democracy, that is, in the sense which was to be theorised in the Enlightenment and tested out by the American and French revolutions a century later'.[4]

This is only half the story, however. Tom Paine, it should never be forgotten, was an individualist, an entrepreneur and a man of commerce. One of his private obsessions was to build an iron bridge across the Schuykill River in Philadelphia, and his heroes were the English men of commerce, the Arkwrights and the Wedgewoods. He would have had little time for the big state collectivists who were to take over the radical mantle during the Victorian age, and even less for the 'top-down' Fabians and trade union collective bargainers who were to follow them. The bosses of these collectivist movements might rail against Cobbett's 'Thing', but they could never deal with it. The large institutions they created, particularly the state, were simply taken over by 'the mandarin culture of the English South East'[5], and 'The Thing' was reinforced.

Tom Paine's radical challenge to the England of his day was not only to reject the aristocratic world and the 'quixotic age of chivalric nonsense', but to do so by creating a bourgeois ethos of individualism as a condition for its overthrow. This challenge was never met. A century of British 'radicals' could simply not understand that you cannot have US-style popular sovereignty without a US-style economy and society. It has taken a long time (well into the 1980s) for the two strands in Paine's thinking – the free market individualism, together with the popular radical attack upon aristocratic values – to be reunited.

Like Tom Paine, today's Thatcherite revolutionaries have isolated the lack of a national sense of the 'individual' as the core British problem. During the paternalist century, the land which prided itself upon giving space to the creative eccentric ('the character', 'the mad scientist', 'the crazy professor', 'the explorer') yielded to the world of the bureaucrat and the mandarin. The English language even lost its purchase on enterprise, as its competitor global language gave the world the word 'entrepreneur'.

In the paternalist century, the 'individual' was overwhelmed by class on the left, a spurious national identity on the right, and, more generally, by a mythic notion of 'community'. The individual as an active and responsible citizen (a concept remarkably powerful during Victorian times) had been overlain, as the twentieth century progressed, by a syrupy and almost folk-lorish 'subjecthood'. The two war efforts repressed individual aims, rights and desires by constant evocations of national collective will; and the mass movements (particularly the trade unions) eroded nonconformity amongst the propertyless mass.

Britain's love affair with the collectivist nostrums of national unity and national community even led to such absurd notions as that states and groups could possess obviously personal attributes like consciences, characters and wills. Pompous grandees would talk of the 'conscience of the nation' being affronted by some event, Enoch Powell evoked national identity, Labour leaders the 'will of the movement', as though all the separate and distinct individuals involved were somehow magically one: forged into a single John Bull or Wat Tyler figure.

This reluctance to place the individual at the centre of existence has now been overcome. For present-day Britain, a heightened sense of individual worth is the dynamic and radicalizing agent for realizing some, at least, of the populist goals of the old radicals.

It was the essence of the old radical cry that the ordinary people had been 'dispossessed', robbed of their rights by scheming aristocrats or capitalist robber barons who rigged the market by their intrigues at court. Shelley's sonnet said all there was to say about the old radical image of a cheated common people:

> Rulers, who neither see, nor feel, nor know,
> But leech-like to their fainting country cling . . .
> A people starved and stabbed in the untilled field.

Yet, how to repossess the 'dispossessed'? How, in contemporary Britain, can the diminishing 'propertyless mass' begin to assume a stake in the country and attain at least some of the attributes of citizenship? Many of the old radicals saw the answer in the 'collective' marshalling of popular expression through large organizations such as the political parties of the left, the Labour movement or the state itself. These organizations may indeed have served the purpose of providing a mechanism for a limited amount of such social mobility. These are the ladders up which the young Jim Callaghan climbed in the 1940s and 1950s – the movements which 'gave him everything'.

But, too often, these same large organizations, rather than providing an escape from propertylessness and poverty, have tended to degenerate into hierarchical structures of rulers and ruled. Council tenants were no less propertyless simply because a Labour government was in office; back-to-back houses in Sheffield were no more inviting an environment in which to live because the local council was controlled by the party of the left; and the car worker in Dagenham hardly felt more of an active citizen because of his membership in a militant trade union. These large 'top-down' organizations solved neither the problem of powerlessness, nor the problem of hierarchy. The collectivist century simply created a new group of 'lads at the top'. And this new breed of leaders from more humble backgrounds, rather like the earlier Victorian businessmen, were easily absorbed into the older hierarchies.

Privilege was simply re-entrenched. By the 1970s – after a century of the advance of the 'working-class' mass movement and Fabian socialism – the populist and egalitarian aims of the old radicals were as far from being realized as ever. Because of this failure, questions about the moral validity of collectivism (when added to scepticism about its economic benefits) led ineluctably to a reappraisal of how market mechanisms might be as 'just' – maybe even more so – in allocating resources.

Matthew Parris is one of the few political observers who has glimpsed the potentially populist and egalitarian consequences of the contemporary market-led enterprise culture:

> The devastating free market argument against entrenched privilege – inherited wealth, private education, the whole apparatus of unmerited advantage so beloved of the British establishment – is deeply embarrassing to a party which believes in 'merit'. It is almost never put . . . It could be – and this would indeed be very serious – that Thatcherism does pose more of a threat to Monarchy than socialism does or did. For after all, Welfare Statism is very much a modern adaptation of the idea of the Monarch as father of his people (paternalism) . . . Just what the role of the Monarchy would be in the Thatcherite dream bourgeois society, made up of mostly self-sufficient individuals, is less easy to imagine. [6]

That individuals, working their will through markets, could act as bulldozers for change, would have seemed a bizarre proposition to many of the old radicals who placed their faith in state action. In particular, 'progressive' intellectuals in the universities had erected aa veritable ring of steel, linking the enlargement of the state to the advancement of 'the people'. Such a chain may now be broken. In Britain it finally became obvious that 'the state' was not the same thing as 'the people'. After all, The Man On The Clapham Omnibus did not 'own' the state (let alone London Regional Transport) in any serious sense. The definition of 'ownership' is the ability to sell what is owned. The only say in the running of London Regional Transport allowed to its so-called 'owners' was a vote on election day. And the sense that voting once every four years or so amounted to 'ownership' became laughable.

'The state' has today become the symbol of authority, not the proud 'possession' of a people. Rather than the centralized instrument of the will of the electorate, the state is often 'them' as opposed to 'us'. 'Them' decides and, in the welfare society created since 1945, 'dispenses'. 'Us' serves: off-stage, as extras, as an entity to be constantly evoked, appeased and catered to, but an entity essentially manipulable, not individuals worthy in themselves. The modern British state cannot possibly be seen as 'Us' whilst its subjects do not even possess inherent and formulated rights.

'Power to the people' was the incoherent but eloquent cry of the old radicals. Yet, as the state socialists of the twentieth century took over the radical mantle from the liberals, the left's hold on the populist image (of 'the people' against the establishment) was tragically forfeited. By default, populism is now becoming the prerogative of the Tory radicals.

By the late 1980s it was the 'new Tories' who were playing the populist, anti-establishment tunes. Tory radicals like Teddy Taylor and Norman Tebbit seemed to possess a more authentic understanding of the real needs of the 'common people' than did their left-wing opponents. More libertarian Tories were also taking up radical themes. One such was 'dry as dust' Tory libertarian MP, Richard Shepherd, who, in 1988, led the parliamentary attack upon Britain's secrecy laws. In a strange inverted twist, Shepherd echoed the cry of the old radicals when he argued that his Conservative party was 'the populist party, fighting on the side of working people and not the grandees'.[7] Margaret Thatcher's own brand of populism is essentially of this liberal kind: believing, as did Paine and Herbert Spencer before her, that 'government' is the enemy of 'the people', and that once freed from 'government' their innate virtue will display itself.

Populists believe people count; that a country is ultimately determined by its people, not its elites. Whereas twentieth-century socialists have tended to ignore 'the people' (in favour of ideology), Thatcherite radicalism wanted to change them, or, at least, their prevailing values. There was a decided aspect of liberal social engineering in this Thatcherite nostrum that 'If we can get the people right' then all else would fall into place. Margaret Thatcher's own stark views about her own compatriots was revealed when she was reported (obviously in a moment of despair) as admitting, in almost Gaullist terminology, that 'at times she had wondered whether the British people still retained the drive to seize the opportunities they had been given under Conservative rule'.[8]

This somewhat cold logic nevertheless echoes a nineteenth-century liberal sensibility that there can be no discontinuities between people and policy, not even foreign policy. Only a resilient and independent people can, in the long run, see the need for a strong defence and understand the need for their position in the Western international system. And, as Thatcher looked across the ocean at the United States, she obviously saw the link. In fact, on a private visit to Washington in July 1987 (to bolster her flagging friend Ronald Reagan during the height of the Iran-Contra Hearings) she argued that the United States was basically safe because it had millions of 'self-reliant' people. That people *mattered* was, at bottom, the populist aspect of her new radicalism. To the new radicals, although the values of 'the people' certainly needed to be changed, they mattered! This is hardly the 'top-down' Toryism of the old leftist demonology.

The populist challenge posed by the new radicalism is, thus, relatively simple. Britain's future, it would argue, is not dependent upon the techniques of paternalist governance, but rather on its people who, once released from the embrace of the paternalist state, will be free to develop their individuality, ensuring not only their own futures, but the country's too. This 'ideal' enterprise culture 'individual' was once described by *The Times* journalist, the late T. E. Utley:

Someone who, by hard work, does his best to look after the needs of his family; who tries to purchase some measure of personal independence by buying his house or by taking shares in his firm; who pays his tax honestly, and with whatever is left over, does something for his less fortunate neighbour, is laying the foundations not only of his own, but of his country's prosperity.[9]

The revolution versus class

Britain's recent burst of popular capitalism may also deal a body blow to that other old radical demon: the class system. During the paternalist century, the British fixation with class (both loving it and hating it) was proportionate to the country's inability to do anything about it. By mid-century, England's most notable radical man of letters, George Orwell, could still complain that Britain was 'the most class-ridden country under the sun'. Orwell's dictum remains true even today. Whereas no Western country has achieved equality of wealth and income, most have at least either obliterated or flattened out hierarchies based open feudal sensibilities. The capitalist West (with Britain as the odd man out) is therefore largely 'classless', at least in the social sense.

This 'classless' potential of capitalism has been a recurring theme of the guru of Thatcherism, Sir Keith (now Lord) Joseph. A member of a leading Anglo–Jewish family who represented a northern constituency in the House of Commons, Joseph is, by background and temperament, a social egalitarian. Samuel Beer described his approach, linking it back to the Victorian liberals:

> He (Sir Keith Joseph) shared the Victorian liberals' vision of a classless society which could be achieved by a 'common value system' . . . He regretted that 'Britain never really internalised capitalist values'. On the contrary, the rich man sought to get away from his background in trade and industry, giving his son an education 'not in capitalist values but against them, in favour of the older values of army, church, upper civil service, professions, and land-owning'. With his praise for liberal individualism and his rejection of Tory paternalism went an equally bold rejection of the patrician mode of rule.[10]

Joseph was entering territory into which many a contemporary 'radical' analyst would not dare to tread. Like some of the old radicals, this modern free market radical was going to the root of the matter. By arguing that his country's uniquely contorted class system was based upon something far more profound than the mere arrangement of formal economic power, Joseph was raising the infinitely more tricky and fundamental question of the cultural power of paternalism. Britain's real 'class problem', he was suggesting, could be dealt with only at the highest levels, by operating on the exclusive, restrictive and hierarchical values emanating downwards from such bastions of privilege as the professions, the upper civil service, the army and the established church.

'Internalizing' capitalist values in these areas of English life is a revolutionary nostrum, threatening the whole structure and security of the paternalist nation and the ancient establishment which brought it into being.

'Truth to tell' noted a Sunday newspaper as though it was a revelation, 'Thatcherism is profoundly egalitarian, in the sense that its moral message is the same for everybody, for all walks of life, for rulers as much as ruled . . . old aristocratic values have been consigned quite expressly to the dustbin of history.'[11]

The levelling social effect of radical capitalism has also been a theme of another leading member of the neo-liberal nucleus around Margaret Thatcher, Sir Geoffrey Howe. Howe (like Joseph and Thatcher herself) is essentially a Tory outsider, a Welshman, and a self-improver. He came to prominence during the abortive modernizing phase of the 'Quiet Revolution', when he introduced the 1971 Industrial Relations Act. He has described himself, in very un-Tory terms, as a 'quiet revolutionary', and prefers to think of his economic liberal philosophy as descending from a somewhat egalitarian non-patrician nineteenth-century lineage.[12]

Margaret Thatcher later built upon Howe's political theme that by embracing the free market the Conservatives had become a socially egalitarian party. In March 1988, she asserted that 'It's not just the socialists who want a classless society. So do I – and, unlike them, I really mean it.'[13] Norman Tebbit went further. 'One by one', he argued in April 1988, 'the bastions of class privilege . . . have fallen to that most remarkable of animals: a Radical, Populist Conservative Party.'[14]

Howe, Joseph, Thatcher and Tebbit all saw Britain's archaic class system as an obstacle to the creation of a modern 'enterprise culture'. Tory leaders are still somewhat reluctant, however, to take the 'classless' issue beyond the small print of isolated public speeches, and into full-blown campaign rhetoric. Such an abrupt swivel of ideological appeal would still sound somewhat contrived, and, anyway, would not be appreciated by the more traditional Tory functionaries.

Nevertheless, Thatcher's era has witnessed a change in the social composition of the Conservative party which should reinforce its social egalitarian image for the future. The party in the country is less landed and more suburban than ever in its history; and it appears to be attracting into its ranks a new generation of 'classless' individuals. Young Conservative activist, Andrew Tinney, may be a case study in such change. From a manual working-class background, and LSE-educated, such a young aspirant would in previous decades have contemplated joining the Labour party; but he 'regards the Conservative party as a natural vehicle of expression, socially and politically, because it is the most classless political habitat for young people of enterprise'.[15]

The Conservative party in Parliament is moving in the same direction. The general elections of 1979, 1983 and 1987 brought in a new breed of upwardly mobile Tory MPs from working-class backgrounds. This contrasts sharply with the 1960s when the Conservative Parliamentary Party was so overwhelmingly dominated by the products of the public schools that it almost appeared as though it was one itself. This pre-Thatcherite Tory party in Parliament could boast only one trade unionist – Ray Mawby – who was virtually elevated by his Tory colleagues to the level of a social token.

These changes in the social composition of the party still rankle with its more patrician elements. The ageing Harold Macmillan once declared that he was shocked to hear on the wireless a senior Tory Cabinet Minister (Norman Tebbit) possessed of an East End accent. However, the more primitive forms of social narrowness tend increasingly to be concealed from public view. Backwoods opposition to social change within the party now tends to be expressed either privately, or in terms of impotent resentment – as when 'Knight of the Shires' MP, John Stokes (following a speech by Norman Tebbit to the Radical Society praising the modernization of the Tory party) wondered, somewhat facetiously, whether there was any room left in it for the landed interest.[16]

In many respects, it is the career of Tebbit (more so even than those of Howe, Joseph or Thatcher) which typifies the changing social composition of the historic party of Crown and land. An airline pilot from Edmonton, holding a seat in suburban north London,

Tebbit's demeanour and style are more akin to the politicians of Labour. His regional accent, untainted by Received Pronunciation, is an important clue to a future in which politicians of the right may no longer seek to be absorbed by the social ethos (and attitudes) of traditional Toryism. This time, the bourgeois revolution may not be co-opted or domesticated.

These social changes in the Tory party only reflect even deeper changes wrought upon Britain's antiquated class system by the enterprise revolution. Commentators are already noticing how in the 1980s the ancient hierarchies created by paternalism are in the process of flattening out, making Britain more like other, more classless, Western nations:

> Britain is not yet a classless society in the way that, say, America and Australia are. But its class system is less rigid, and its people less inclined than they were to do things in tribal groups. The most popular leisure activity is watching television. The most popular sport is fishing. Nothing collectivist about them. Since the next century's economic prizes will go to those countries where people work with their brains in small groups, a Britain of individualists will at least have a place at the starting line. [17]

This American or Australian model of social development which Britain began adopting in the 1980s was the first serious alteration of its class patterns for a century. Britain's 'social pyramid' was being chipped away at its foundations by the more individualistic emerging society and being replaced by a 'diamond-shaped' social structure. At the centre of the 'diamond' was a huge 'middle class' – at once the most numerous and the most dynamic grouping, which would set new manners, tone and style for the nation.

Such a 'flattening out' of the traditional 'social pyramid' would, on the face of it, be welcome news to those generations of radical critics who had seemingly so despaired of the country's antique class system. During the high-tide of postwar paternalism a whole bevy of social critics had discussed little else than the malign nature and character of 'class' in Britain. George Orwell, John Strachey, Richard Hoggart, Michael Young, Anthony Crosland (and others) had set a critical tone which was taken up by a generation of postwar consensus politicians: 'One Nation' Tories and the labour social democrats alike. The speeches and articles of people like Hugh Gaitskell, Ian Macleod, Harold Wilson, Edward Heath and Roy Jenkins were replete with calls for such egalitarian social goals as the creation of an 'open society', the 'opening of society to the talents', a 'classless society', and the need for 'social mobility'.

Their 'classless' words, however, were not matched by deeds. Class solidarities and 'tribal' sentiments hardened, rather than weakened, during the postwar consensus, finally leading to the bitter class confrontations of the 1970s. One (less than charitable) explanation may be that these essentially meritocratic politicians of the postwar consensus had already – before they had even uttered a socially egalitarian word – been co-opted by Britain's smoothly efficient patrician polity. Whatever residual egalitarian sentiments remained to be expressed were, therefore, in reality weakly held.

Another explanation lies with the realities they faced. They simply couldn't make silk out of a sow's ear. No matter how committed to egalitarian social change they may have remained, these reformers of the 1960s could not implement their ideas within the framework of the collectivist system in which they operated. How could a 'classless' society be encouraged in an age dominated by assertive and self-conscious trade unionism? Or through the mechanisms of a public sector dominated at its apex, in the higher reaches of the civil service, by what amounted to a narrowly drawn social caste?

Yet another explanation may lie in the fact that the postwar critics of 'class' were heavily influenced by the elitist Fabian way of looking at the world. The Fabians were certainly social reformers, but of a peculiar type. Sons and daughters of Empire, they were schooled in notions of hierarchy and order. The very last thing they wanted for Britain was to open it up by extending property rights and widening choice for ordinary people. When they were in the mood to challenge the total economic system, they went overboard, and (like Sidney and Beatrice Webb) embraced Soviet Communism. Otherwise, they were content simply to reorder the inequalities of income as between various sections of the masses within the 'social pyramid'. Schooled in social statistics, the Fabians were drawn to economic inequalities (who has what?) rather than to the more intangible inequalities of worth (who feels what?), which were the real and distinctive 'British disease'.

George Orwell and Richard Hoggart were amongst the few postwar critics who understood that the 'class problem' in Britain was as much cultural as economic. Both were literary figures more than social scientists, and they described in vivid detail the huge cultural chasms which existed between the people of their island home. Yet both of them tended to portray Britain in cosy, familial, terms. Orwell, in a famous aphorism, which said much about his native conservatism, saw Britain as a family. It was 'A family with the wrong members in control', but 'Still, it is a family'[18]. Hoggart seemed to find the regional and hierarchical distinctions of British life, which he analysed so incisively, a pleasing, rather than a disconcerting, patchwork.

The striking point about the postwar social critics is that, at bottom, they were ultimately satisfied with paternalist Britain, with its organic nature, and with the nation as 'family'. They assumed the aspect of rebellious children, seeking some reordering of resources within the family fortune, but ultimately loyal to the paterfamilias. Little headway could be made amongst this pre-Thatcherite generation by evoking the model and images of America, Australia or even postwar Germany. Bourgeois capitalism, with its images of the nation as a series of families (as opposed to 'one happy family' or indeed 'one unhappy family'), had little appeal. Indeed, it would often meet with a fierce reaction. Anthony Crosland once suggested that America's open and mobile society would create in Britain 'psychosomatic illnesses on a large scale'.[19] In other words, a more open and socially mobile society was 'dangerous'; Britain was fundamentally alright as it was!

The great test for the Fabian social reformers came with the issue of the grammar schools. These meritocratic public sector schools were the only true and trusted educational ladder by which the bright sons and daughters from families of average income and below could rise in society. Handed down by the Butler Education Act of 1944 (a product of the 'classless' imperative of war), their very existence threatened the static society of postwar paternalist Britain. Yet the upshot of all the reforming zeal of the 1960s was to be a 'progressive' coalition directed at removing this ladder of social mobility. The grammar school issue highlighted the lack of serious commitment amongst the 1960s social reformers to a more 'classless' society. They neither sought to break down class barriers by spreading private education more widely throughout society, nor, alternatively, to abolish the public schools.

The connecting thread running between the so-called social reformers of the pre-Thatcher era was an abiding fear – almost amounting to terror – at the prospect of opening up British society by allowing the development of a bourgeoisie, a new 'middle class'. Such a new class might challenge the values and structure of the paternalist nation. The existing 'middle class' of the postwar decades posed no such threat. It was relatively small by international standards, it did not incorporate 'the workers' (who still saw themselves as distinct). It was also divided – between its public sector, socialist wing (which led the Labour movement) and its private sector, 'commercial' wing which aspired to aristocratic values.

A vibrant and confident 'middle class' (of the kind which inhabited America and Australia) was, however, a wholly different proposition. Its pushy individuals and egregious entrepreneurs would upset the cosy, though ill-arranged, paternalist system, and with it the special place assigned in that system to the 'social reformers'.

A new middle class.

In a half homily to Thatcher's social revolution, Conor Cruise O'Brien draws an interesting parallel with England's first outburst of serious bourgeois sentiment:

> The political division of modern England in regional terms corresponds quite closely to the line of division at the time of the first English revolution. Then, as now, the line ran between the South and East on the one hand, and the North and West on the other. The old domain of the Puritan revolutionaries is now the domain of Mrs Thatcher. The old Royalist areas are now held by Mr Kinnock's socialists . . . I don't think this is a mere curiosity or fortuitous paradox . . . Mrs Thatcher likes to be compared with Queen Elizabeth 1 and Queen Victoria . . . I think the Iron Lady is closer in spirit to Old Ironsides. [20]

This analogy is, of course, somewhat overdrawn. In 1980s Britain, there is no political violence, no involvement of the military in governance, and no question of royal absolutism. Whereas Cromwell was pioneering a revolution which would reverberate round the world, Thatcher's new radicalism represents exactly the opposite dynamic: the overdue adjustment of an old evolutionary nation to the imperatives of life within a revolutionary modern world.

Yet, the forces behind the changes under way in Britain in the 1980s seem just as formidable, and just as potentially triumphant, as did Cromwell's New Model Army after Naseby; and the forces of opposition, restricted to a *laager* in North Britain (as in Conor Cruise O'Brien's intriguing geographic replay), look just as desultory. And, now as then, a militant 'middling' class is flexing its muscles, and drawing its political strength from the sense of influence – and power – accruing to new centres of money, trade, and commerce.

The ultimate test of the durability of Britain's 'classless revolution' of the 1980s will, however, rest upon the strength of the social base of small capital ownership and accumulation. Put crudely: the more personal power people possess – the greater the number of 'islands of freedom' – the more irreversible the middle-class revolution will become.

By the 1990s the growth in small businesses, though, will still be minimal. The West's more mature bourgeois competitors will still be producing far more 'new' entrepreneurs than will Thatcher's Britain. The much vaunted 'wider share ownership' campaign has, in reality, been a meagre affair. Twice as many people owned shares in 1987 as in 1980; and employee share ownership schemes had been enlarged from around 30 in 1979 to over 1,000 in 1987. But this only scratches the surface, incorporating into the enterprise culture only a very small section of the manual working population.

On the other hand, the new radicalism did take one decisive step to widen 'at a stroke' the ownership of private capital. It sold off council houses, allowing 'the working class' who were trapped in the serfdom of council ownership and control to take over at least one part of their lives, their homes. The addition, between 1980 and 1988, of one million more home owners can hardly be undervalued in terms either of reality or of symbolism. Joel Krieger has ascribed to this process a serious political dimension, coining the term 'the ideological suburbs' to describe the potential effect of council house sales upon the wider political contest:

> those attracted by the appeal [of home ownership] could feel good about themselves: they were not simply abandoning socialist community for individual interest but participating in a broad inter-class modernising movement. [21]

This 'inter-class' (or classless) modernizing dynamic has been further boosted by increased geographic mobility. Norman Tebbit's 'On Yer Bike' injunction was seen as an insensitive piece of political imagery (particularly in a still frozen society where such a freedom was virtually impossible). Yet, as a social goal for a modern society, the enabling of lower-income people to relocate more easily (and thereby take advantage of job opportunities) is unexceptionable. In 1986, more than two million families moved home, more than in any year since the war. The pattern of movement in that one year suggests substantial additions to medium-sized towns and their environs. Towns such as Milton Keynes (which added 60,995 people), Peterborough (37,752), Northampton (36,910), Telford (30,106), Colchester (26,749), Bournemouth, Chelmsford, Aberdeen, Widnes, Wigan and Redditch all gained at the expense of losses in the big cities – London (740,781), Glasgow (166,193), Manchester (145,375) and Liverpool (134,371).

This movement from cities to towns means that the nation is 'levelling out' horizontally as well as vertically. The south of England is slowly becoming one large classless suburb. As the older 'working-class' ghettos in the large cities dissolve, the new areas of population are located in what are essentially the suburban environs of the growing towns. These new suburbs bring in their wake a more classless, consumer environment (including American-style shopping malls).

As the British people spread out to inhabit their own country, one wonders why it all took so long. It seems remarkable that one of the most densely populated landmasses in the world could have sustained, well into the twentieth century, such proportionately vast tracts of uninhabited land. In the name of protecting the countryside, Britain's planners placed ring fences round both the medieval 'village' and the industrial nineteenth-century 'city'. This frozen 'village and city' pattern was ultimately dependent upon a freezing of social and geographic mobility, and was further secured by piling 'the propertyless masses' of the old inner-cities into tower-block developments, rather than allowing a freer and more lateral pattern of development.

The suburbanization of Britain poses the most serious threat yet to the old 'cities and villages' model (and mentality) which sustained the class structures (and images) of postwar paternalism.

As the more affluent working people and their families now finally move into suburbia, they will leave behind them severe problems for 'the city'. The inner areas of the big city of the future may become bereft of all but the super-rich and the underclass. We can expect, as Tony Travis has pointed out, 'a growing polarity in places like London between those established in the housing system, and those hoping to break into it'.

The inner-city future may not be as stark as this, however. 'Every year since 1980,' reports Professor Duncan Maclennan, 'middle income households' – particularly the younger ones – have been going back into these [inner-city] areas as part of a general urban regeneration policy . . . They diversify the population and add to local service demands'.[22]

The pressures of mobility upon an erstwhile relatively static society will also change the face of rural southern England. Government projections argue that between 460,000 and 610,000 new homes will be needed in London and the South East between 1991 and the year 2000, of which 210,000 will have to be located in the green-field sites of the peculiarly named 'Home Counties'. Thus, radical market imperatives come into conflict (as they must) with another bastion of traditional High Tory privilege – in this case, the 'rural interest' centred around the cherished 'English village'.

That the image of the 'English village' has its charm, entrancing locals and tourists alike, can hardly be in dispute. Its hold on the English imagination – as a refuge from the rigours of modern life – remains as strong as ever, particularly amongst those whose lives are essentially urban. But charm (particularly induced charm) has its costs. In evoking a positive image for 'the village' we also, implicitly at least, accept pre-capitalist and pre-individualist habits of mind. 'The village', by definition, is small and thus exclusive; too large a village becomes a 'town'. Also, in many of the villages of southern England the British class system is played out in miniature form. Modern-day 'lords of the manor' often preside over a social hierarchy not unlike that of medieval times. Below them, there is a local 'gentry', a local vicar, and, further down, a modern propertyless 'peasantry', usually hidden from view on the small council estates.

England's rural lobby – seeing itself challenged more effectively by market forces than it ever was by socialist planning – now

increasingly couches the defence of its privileges not in terms
of protecting 'village life', but rather in the more acceptable garb
of 'conservation', of 'conserving a national heritage'. Of course,
this 'heritage' was never truly 'national', because so much of
England's green and pleasant land was owned and controlled by
so few. There are only two ways properly to ensure that Britain's
rural heritage becomes 'national'. One is to nationalize the land, a
strategy which incurs all the disadvantages of socialism. The other
is to allow an increasing proportion of the British people to own
non-farming land in small parcels. Late twentieth-century Britain
is taking the second road. The rising expectations unleashed by
the enterprise revolution will inevitably mean that more and more
people with average incomes will seek to live (if not work) in England's countryside, and not simply pass through the green fields
during holiday times.

As the British spread out into their own country (and countryside), the defenders of the 'rural interest' are increasingly placed
at a moral disadvantage. The 'Not In My Back Yard' instinct has already become a famous acronym (NIMBY) depicting both selfishness and hypocrisy. Nicholas Ridley, the Thatcherite Secretary of
State for the Environment, will annoy many of his own traditional
Tory supporters by declaring that 'I cannot and will not say that
because I have a nice house and a good life I do not care about
anyone else', and that 'the city dweller's life should not be made
a misery in order to save others a picturesque view'. [23]

This social battle – between the southern 'ideological suburbs'
and static village England – may seem an exclusively South
Eastern concern, at least for the moment. But the resolution
of the conflict could have immense ramifications for the rest of
the nation.

Conor Cruise O'Brien's depiction of the South East as a 'power
base that can dominate the rest of the island'[24] can, of course, be
interpreted as moral obloquy, as a battle cry against a potential
southern-led bourgeois imperial conquest of the North. Yet it can
also be viewed through a different lens: as a positive 'spill-over' (or
'trickle down') from the most prosperous to the most depressed
parts of the country.

This 'trickle down' (or 'trickle up') can take various forms.
Cultural and political power is still located in the South, and if
the battle for the South is won by the forces of modernity, then

it will have its knock-on effect upon the whole country. Already, under the economic framework established in Westminster, the early signs of an indigenous new bourgeois order are present in many parts of North Britain. Also, the North/South divide has already been somewhat eroded – in a perverse kind of way – by market pressures in the South. The inflation of property prices in the South East of England has already led southerners to cash in on their property profits, and invest in cheaper personal and commercial property in the North. In these and other ways, the more classless and mobile bourgeois South East can indeed become a vast regional platform from which a market-driven modernity could, by stages, be launched upon the rest of backward and deprived Britain.

An international invasion

Just as liberal economics knows no regional boundaries, so, too, it knows no national boundaries. The very first act of the new neo-liberal regime in 1979 was to remove exchange controls; and this symbolic departure – perhaps even more than entry into the Common Market in the early 1970s – represented a fundamental act of adjustment on Britain's part to the modern world outside its borders.

British capital was finally fully free to expand overseas – to the point where, in the late 1980s, it had become the single most important foreign investor in the United States. In return, foreigners bought up more and more of Britain – encouraged not only by a welcoming government, but by weakened trade unions and a more competitive domestic environment. This increasing penetration of the domestic economy by foreign capital produced a 'culture shock'. One by one, some of the country's most 'English' of institutions fell into the hands of foreigners. Harrods went to the Arabs, Rowntrees to the Swiss, 'quality' Sunday newspapers and 'prestigious' publishing houses to Australians and Canadians. Also, and more crucially, a people only previously allowed to see the world through the lens of their elites, were to have available to them foreign-owned television channels.

This invasion put an end to any lingering sensibility of the country as an economically sovereign nation-state. Gone was the image of Britain as a corporate economic identity whose future could be shaped by the fine-tuning of its mandarin class. In its place appeared a new reality: the country as little more than an off-shore territorial 'entity' upon which a complex of financial, industrial and commercial players (some domestic, some foreign) could work their separate and multiple wills.

Of course, the more internationalized domestic economy ushered in since 1979 only accelerated a process already under way during the last decades of postwar paternalism. 'Splendid isolation' never seriously appeared on the postwar British national agenda. Clement Attlee's generation, as it looked hopelessly on at the end of Empire (and its protected markets), could hardly afford to insulate itself from the wider world. Nor could Harold Wilson's generation – even though some amongst them embarked, in the 1970s, upon a brief flirtation with the Cambridge school's alternative protectionist strategy.

During the 1970s the realities of the international economy impinged ever more sharply upon the British domestic scene. The country entered the European Community in 1973; was forced to accept the IMF's conditions for a loan in 1976; and witnessed the life-belt provided by foreign risk capital as it exploited the North Sea's oil reserves, and thereby helped stabilize the nation during the traumatic transition from the Attlee to the Thatcher consensus.

Long before the twentieth century Britain's economic culture had been anything but insular. From the works of Adam Smith through to, and beyond, the Manchester Liberals of the nineteenth century, Britain had pioneered the modern conception of Free Trade. The old adages still ring in modern ears: 'Britain is a trading nation or it is nothing'; 'If Britain has to choose between Europe and the Open Sea, it will always choose the Open Sea'; 'Trade follows the Flag'. These aphorisms of Empire displayed a keen sense of a world beyond the home base, and an outward-oriented patriotism. Indeed, the English imperial ruling class prided itself upon its global sensibilities, despatching the beneficent largesse of a European civilization abroad to less fortunate peoples. The Britain of Empire, it was suggested, positively basked in the glow of 'ostensibly a-national grandeur – in the anti-narrowness of those born . . . to give examples to others'.[25]

This 'anti-narrowness' was, though, never quite what it was cracked up to be. Britain, after all, 'Ruled The Waves' from an impregnable power base; and its imperial mentality was a world view of rulership, not a democratic global vision. The 'White Man's Burden' was certainly outward-looking, but to an ever widening horizon filled with English manners, language, religion and rule. One sadness of the British Empire was that it precluded the English elites who ran it (and through them the British people) from ever being able to measure their own national culture in honest competition with others.

This 'narrowness' made the country's later adjustment to the competitive postwar world environment all the more difficult – certainly more painful than that of America, of defeated and reconstructed West Germany and Japan, and even than that of France. The sores of a lost Empire (and a lost world role for Britain) are still open; and they continue to irritate those sections of British society (mostly found outside the new middle class) who still have much emotional capital invested in British 'grandeur'. An unreal sense of Britain's importance in the world exhibits itself in a tragic provincialism which believes that some of the most advanced and confident of modern nations (not only Canada and Australia, but the United States as well) are still somehow 'colonies' – if not politically, then at least culturally. The received and untested notion that British institutions (particularly the BBC) are the 'best in the world' is still prevalent. This time-warped provincialism can often degenerate into a defensive xenophobia, typified by proletarian football hooligans who parade and rampage through civilized European cities chanting 'We won the waooor'.

Britain's postwar socialist intellectuals are hardly any more outward-looking and cosmopolitan. There is a whiff of chauvinism in many of the routine attacks upon 'international finance' and the role of the City of London. One marxist writer seems to speak for a generation when he argues that the 'real Britain' is a 'far flung wasteland of garden gnomes and factory chimneys' which 'is in effect an image of nation-state prostration before the City's hegemony'.[26] Hence, the one sector of Britain which has adjusted most effectively to the modern world is portrayed as the dominating partner. The 'real Britain', on the other hand, is evoked as the downtrodden wife, not as the beneficiary of an enterprising husband's survival by adaptation.

What insular sentimentality remains in the bosom of the political right tends to focus less on 'the City' and its financial institutions, and more upon the obviously 'foreign' European Community. That most singular apostle of modern High Toryism, Enoch Powell, destroyed his political career on the issue of Britain's entry into the EC. And much of the right's lingering chauvinism opposes further European integration on purely nativist grounds, rather than because of the liberal principles of free trade and limited government.

So, whether it be High Tory nostalgia for 'the English way of life' or low British attachment to 'garden gnomes', indigenous reactionary sentiment will continue to resist the country's full integration into the Western commercial and financial system and continue to exalt national identity over popular prosperity. Such British reactionary sentiment has a coherence to it. The imperatives of the world economy do indeed increasingly threaten the traditional nation-state. National sovereignty implies, at the very least, that the lives of citizens within the sovereign boundary are determined more by decisions taken within, than outside, that sovereignty.

Yet we are now reaching a point where actions taken outside Britain affect the lives of its citizens more profoundly than any purely domestic decision: when men (usually men) meeting behind closed doors in Bonn, Paris, Brussels, Washington, Riyadh or Tokyo may collectively possess a greater purchase upon Britain's future than those meeting in Whitehall or Westminster. When the Chairman of the Federal Reserve Board in Washington DC increases the US prime interest rate, the consequence is higher unemployment in Liverpool or Birmingham or Manchester. When the US administration yielded to the OPEC cartel in the early 1970s, the result was an increase in inflation worldwide, including Britain. It was decisions taken in Bonn and Washington, as much as in London, which determined the outcome of the 1976 IMF loan, and the new economic course upon which Britain was set.

In fact, it could be argued that the single most important 'institution' affecting the lives of ordinary Britons in the late twentieth century is the G5 or G7 grouping of nations within the International Monetary Fund. It is within this framework, where Britain's economic destiny is co-ordinated with those of the other major Western nations, that its interest-rate policy, exchange-rate policy and, ultimately, taxation policy and unemployment levels, are all effectively determined. The fact is that politics (with its nation-states) still lags behind economics (with its interconnected world market-place). This discreprency tends to obscure from the view of citizens bounded by the nation-state what is, in effect, the new supranational reality under which they live.

For Britain, the cultural consequences of its full integration into the Western economic system are momentous. Further foreign penetration of British industry and markets will bring in its train patterns of work, and habits of mind, which can only reinforce the changes already induced by Thatcher's domestic bourgeois revolution. As the Europeans, Americans and Japanese establish themselves in the British market, their management techniques are unlikely to tolerate for long the 'officers and other ranks' mentality of the traditional English industrial culture. Nor will they accept the indigenous trade union restrictive practices. In response, British enterprises will modernize in order to compete.

More combustible still will be the cultural and social democracy which will flow freely to all members of the island race when Britain's airwaves are opened up to all manner of domestic and foreign competition. Public information (transmitted through a plethora of news and current affairs programming) will no longer be the preserve of domestic guardians; and public taste will no longer be dictated by the narrow culture of upper-crust English provincialism. A world bounded by 'garden gnomes' and 'castles and cottages' will dissolve amidst a cloud cover of receiving dishes from John O'Groats to Lands End.

This process of internationalization will ensure that British culture will become more cosmopolitan and egalitarian, more like those of its Western bourgeois allies. And there will, most probably, be no turning back.

Once the wind is behind a more mature and internationally integrated bourgeois society, its benefits will become increasingly apparent. Growing mass prosperity will bring its own rewards. The ugly features of contemporary life, such as violence, yobbery and philistinism (which the British had been told by their paternalists were the consequences of bourgeois materialism), will instead become associated with poverty, not prosperity. Also, greater contact with other Western countries will prove that materialism can be embraced whilst enhancing, rather than losing, civilized values.

In place of decline

Some years ago Peter Walker wrote an optimistic book called *The Ascent of Britain*. Published in the late 1970s, it struck a discordant note, for at that time all the best tunes were being composed around the theme of national failure and decline.

Postwar literary doomsterism had taken its first tentative steps in July 1963, when *Encounter* published its famous symposium, edited by Arthur Koestler, 'Suicide of a Nation'. Although *Encounter's* contributors were developing many of the themes later to become acceptable in the 1970s, they were then swimming against the high-tide of postwar complacency. However, when, in 1972, Correlli Barnett published his seminal work, *The Collapse of British Power*, his attempt to locate the seeds of national decline (in the character of upper-class English education in the nineteenth century) sparked a decade-long debate which accepted decline as a reality if not Barnett's explanation of its causes. The 1970s witnessed a spate of works – amongst which were Robert Moss's *The Collapse of Democracy*, James Bellini's *Doomsday*, Donald Horne's *God is an Englishman; So Why Is Britain in Such a Mess*, and my own work *The Death of British Democracy* – which attempted a contemporary analysis of the sour innards of the bitter fruit of decline. There was even a literature of violence and insurgency, in which Richard Clutterbuck's *Britain in Agony: The Growth of Political Violence* was the most widely publicized.

Writers from both left and right used decline as a peg upon which to hang some compelling arguments for radical, even revolutionary, change. Marxist analysts in particular had a field day, depicting, somewhat eagerly, a major crisis in the capitalist system. Andrew Gamble's *The Conservative Nation* and Ralph Miliband's up-dated *Parliamentary Socialism*, together with the serious-minded essayists of *The New Left Review*, produced a body of socialist argumentation which was increasingly formidable. From the right, there appeared an equally emphatic rejectionism of the postwar age, of which R. Emmett Tyrell's edited volume *The Future That Doesn't Work: Social Democracy's Failures in Britain* still stands the test of time. Even the normally careful world of academic contemporary political science and economics saw theories emerging about such startling issues as Britain's 'ungovernability', the system's 'over-load' and potential 'frag-mentation', and 'de-industrialization'.[27]

These books and essays were supplemented by doses of decline culture in the daily and weekly journals. During the mid and late 1970s hardly a week went by without a despairing commentary in the press. Britain was described by *Guardian* Columnist, Pe-ter Jenkins, as 'A Nation on the Skids', and by Paul Barker as 'Europe's Merseyside'. So profoundly ill-at-ease with the country were some of its leading commentators that the British people themselves came in for heavy criticism. Peregrine Worsthorne asked derisively 'Do The British Want To Lose Their Chains?', and Tom Forrester enquired into whether 'The British Sincerely Want To Be Rich?'. Decline also produced its black humourists. Auberon Waugh used national distress effectively to prod many an exposed nerve, as he appeared to help the country's literary class to 'giggle' (somewhat defensively) 'into the sea'.

Literary doomsterism was not, however, only the intellectuals' indulgence or fancy. The writers were simply replicating on the page what was the dominant concern of the politicians during the last phase of the paternalist era: how to manage – gracefully – what was seen as an inevitable and irreversible national decline, and in the process save the country from coups, communism or disintegration. Yet very few 'insiders' would spill these beans in public. *Cecil King's Diaries*, to this day the most complete (and undenied) inside account of an establishment in torment about the nation's governability, was an exception. The King *Diaries* were notable not only for their tales of crises, but also for the picture they painted of a governing class utterly at a loss about what to do.

There was, though, a self-defeating problem at the heart of the culture of decline. The alarms about national decline were normally raised by the well-meaning in order to help arrest the fall. Yet, at the same time, they ultimately served to create such a climate of despair that national decline became 'the solution, not the problem'. This defeatist mentality played into the hands of the paternalists.

Brian Walden has reported that, whilst he was an MP, 'I remem-ber being told by a very senior figure, the British are resigned to permanent decline and our task is to organize this decline in a civilised manner'.[28] In other words, only the paternalist habit

of mind – graced by sure-footed scepticism, custom and God –
could do this job of 'decline management' in a 'civilized' manner.
The seeming need for 'Decline Management' in the 1970s only reinforced the whole High Tory intellectual and cultural apparatus of
impossibility (dressed up as a 'judicious sense of limitation') – and
with it the position of the elites of collectivism who embodied this
Zeitgeist of despair. Those whose temperament was optimistic,
and whose politics were liberal, would only make things worse by
their reforming zeal.

There was present in the 1970s an unspoken analogy between
the 'civilized' way in which Britain's paternalist class believed they
had managed the End of Empire, and the way they looked at the
'civilized' solution to Britain's own national decline. Both were
inevitable, irreversible. This author remembers a lunch at the
Reform Club in 1975 when he was informed by a senior diplomat
that it had been his 'duty' in the 1960s to 'put to bed the British
Empire'; he then went on to offer the thought that 'one should
never swim against an irreversible tide . . . and at home now it
is running towards socialism'.

There was a sense in which the last, declining, phase of the
British Empire had dominated the thinking of all Britain's postwar
paternalist party leaders. After all, they were all literally children
of this Empire; all were fed upon the notion of British 'greatness'
being achieved through Empire; and, during their mature adult
lives the single most important global event for their country had
been the loss of this Empire.

Amongst the Tories, Winston Churchill was the only avowed
imperialist, although Anthony Eden acted like one during the Suez
crisis in 1956. Both Harold Macmillan and Alec Home possessed a
patrician manner of governorship which was 'to the Empire born'.
Even Edward Heath was dominated by 'the imperial problem', as
revealed by his inner drive to create 'Britain in Europe' as a substitute 'world role' for the country. Labour's leaders were no less
fixated upon securing a 'world role' for a country which could not
possibly sustain one. Clement Attlee was the political father of the
British nuclear bomb, then seen as the means, in the absence of
Empire, to keep Britain at the top table. Hugh Gaitskell evoked the
imperial memory of 'Vimy Ridge' during his famous 1962 speech
against British entry into the Common Market and retained a
deep personal commitment to the Commonwealth. Harold Wilson

declared whilst Prime Minister that Britain's 'frontier was on the Himalayas'. Jim Callaghan was almost the perfect embodiment of the instincts and values of the British imperial working class. And Michael Foot's socialist missionary zeal had an aspect about it of the 'White Man's Burden'.

The political psychology induced in this generation by the end of Empire – whether they were attempting to maintain it, extricate the country from it, or create a substitute for it – was careful, conservative and defensive. Political life existed in a world of shrinking horizons, and the key attribute of the trade of politics amounted to little more than 'the art of the possible', a term popularized by R. A. Butler, another son of late Empire, in his autobiography. Conserving what you had, rather than creating something new, was the governing political impulse. Scornful of 'solutions' and problem-solving, this mental framework of late Empire was deeply and decidedly un-radical.

In this sense both Margaret Thatcher and Neil Kinnock are Britain's first post-imperial party leaders. The last flickers of imperial imagery and sensibility would certainly have touched Kinnock's formative years. However, his Celtic origins have probably made the preservation of 'British greatness' (of its 'role in the world') one of the lesser forces working its will upon his personality and political beliefs. Margaret Thatcher's background and upbringing were (as with anyone in her generation) suffused with the belief that she belonged to the most powerful country in the world, a role secured by Empire. But her political style and opinions were not formed in the schools of Empire. Her womanhood, together with her Grantham public sector education, would not have taught her that she was 'born to rule' (either the globe or the country). Like many of her fellow Tory radicals, the paternalist impulses of 'the White Man's Burden' would have hardly touched, let alone influenced, her. What is more, Thatcher shares with the new generation of Conservatives a political background in which effort and achievement have counted, a legacy which has left them contemptuous of the lethargy and langour so characteristic of those many sons of late Empire whom they would have found everywhere around them on the Tory benches in the 1960s.

The modern nationalism of the Tory radicals has little to do with past imperial greatness. The differences between the High Tory Suez war of 1956 and the Low Tory Falklands war of 1982 tell the story. Whereas the Suez operation was the last fling of an imperial cast of mind, the Falklands war was a decidedly 'post-imperial' affair. The 1982 conflict in the South Atlantic (unlike Suez) was not even a traditional conflict between nations. In essence, the campaign against the Argentinians was a major NATO operation, conducted with the full logistical and intelligence help of the United States and the total diplomatic support of the European Community. On Britain's part, the conflict was conducted on the very un-imperial principle of 'self-determination'. It was also revealing that the Tory government's Falklands 'victory parade' was staged in the City of London, in the absence of the imperial totems of Crown and Church.

The patriotic emotions which this war unleashed at home were not those of Empire and conquest, but rather the more democratic sentiments of national resolve and success. The 'nationalism' which the more modern Conservatives both evoke and unleash at regular intervals is hardly that of the imperial notion of 'greatness' (with its connotations of geographic expansion and white rulership). Rather, it represents a morale-boosting exercise for a country so long attuned to failure; and it is also a ploy to use against Labour, which still seems incapable of associating itself with the more emotive aspects of public sentiment.

As Britain in the 1990s finally withdraws from under the lingering spell of Empire, political success will no longer be dependent upon the mysterious and the intangible (upon lineage, or the automatic tribal loyalties accruing to those associated with the running of an awe-inspiring Empire). Rather, politicians and political parties will be judged more rationally: by measurable criteria, primarily the country's economic performance. Just as the hold of paternalism depended on the success of Empire, so now Britain's bourgeois revolution will live and die according to the test it sets itself: whether it can continue to deliver the economic goods to a population with rapidly increasing expectations.

The economic recovery of the 1980s, however, may be only temporary; consequently, few opinion-formers are willing to commit themselves to a final verdict. By the late 1980s commentators hostile to Thatcherism were tending to hedge their bets about the lasting nature of the bourgeois revolution. Those sympathetic to Thatcherism were more willing to risk their arm. A pro-Thatcher Sunday newspaper could argue in 1988 that Britain's economic recovery 'is the story that most of the British Establishment has not wanted to tell, and has even tried to suppress'.[29]

By mid-summer 1988 Britain was in the seventh year of a powerful economic recovery. And nine years into the 'great experiment' government, Ministers were even beginning to suggest that Britain's economic performance was strong enough to insulate it somewhat from a world depression. These optimists (still faintly fashionable by the late 1980s) could point to some fundamental indicators for support. Inflation was stable at around 4 per cent; unemployment had fallen by over 550,000 since the middle of 1986; manufacturing productivity had averaged a growth rate of 6 per cent a year since 1980 compared with under 1 per cent between 1974 and 1979; and, incredibly, Britain's share of total world exports, after declining for three decades, stopped falling in 1983 and rose in 1987. Public finances were stronger than at any time for twenty years, and there was a huge government surplus.[30] Although some of the gilt had come off the gingerbread by 1989 – as inflation crept up, interest rates rose and the balance of payments slid into a considerable deficit – there still remained a sense that, outside of an international economic cataclysm, the British economy would not easily return to its erstwhile uncompetitive world position.

Should Britain's economic recovery continue well into the 1990s, then there will come a point of no return. For, even if the economy then falters, the contrast with the economic traumas and social dislocations of the 1970s will still be sharp enough to ensure that no party will be able to put the process into reverse. They will find themselves able only to tinker at the margins of the then prevailing economic structure. This will be the pivot for the fate of Britain's bourgeois revolution. Economic success, domestic social change and foreign capital penetration will, by then, have so modernized British culture and society that not even a Labour government (should it wish to do so) could restore the paternalist structures.

The forces in British life which have the greatest vested interest in a 'counter-revolution' are not normally to be found in the ranks of the political parties, even those of the left. Rather, they inhabit Britain's ancient 'establishment' of privilege, a High Tory caste (and a cast of mind) which attempts to transcend party. This High Tory establishment is as fearful of directly confronting Thatcher's bourgeois revolution as it was of confronting Labour's left wing in the 1970s. It might, in the process of such a confrontation, lose everything. Hence (as it did with the ascendant socialism of the 1970s) it seeks to moderate and limit social change.

Thatcher's bourgeois revolution places these 'High Tories' in a deadly quandary. They reluctantly supported the architects of the radical revolution (including Tory 'dries' like Thatcher, Tebbit, Howe and Lawson) because they saw them as saving the country from socialism. But 'High Tory' distaste for the socially egalitarian consequences of the radical revolution (a more open society, supported by merit and enterprise) leads them to resist its further progress.

4
The Paternalist Resistance

New battle lines

In Britain's demi-democracy – where the people are free, but not yet sovereign – it is only to be expected that England's traditional established order will not easily yield up power to insurgent arrivistes. Given half a chance it will fight back. And, three decades after Henry Fairlie coined the term 'Establishment', and one decade into the bourgeois turmoil of Thatcherism, it still has considerable resources at its disposal.

The present battle lines of the British polity are drawn rather differently from those normally sketched by media journalism, which still tends to see political conflict in terms of the battle between parties. In fact, the real lines of conflict do not run between the parties, but rather within them. For, just as paternalism transcends parties, so now does radicalism.

In the radical camp (or corner) we shall find not only the Tory 'dries' but also the growing band of supporters of the broad goals of the social-market economy who are embraced within the SDP, the SLD and Labour. In the paternalist camp (or corner) there is the High Tory faction within the Conservative party, the corporatist grouping in the SLD, and the socialist wing of the Labour party. It may seem bizarre to list Labour's socialists under the establishment banner. However, British politics is never as clear-cut as it seems; and, for the foreseeable future, High Tories and socialists may share a cause, and may become wary, but real, allies in a popular front against the new radicalism.

From the High Tory establishment's vantage point the strategy could look like this, should, that is, it ever be articulated in a frank, unvarnished, form:

> Thatcherism is fine: as long, that is, as it doesn't go too far along the road of change. Our fortunes are secure under Thatcherism, but the social stability and deference, which ensure that our remarkably lavish and, by modern standards, unproductive lifestyle goes both unnoticed and unchallenged, are being eroded as new money and new aspirations are unleashed. Let's face it, should a future general election bring Labour to power, the Labour government would be led by the mild kind of socialist chap. This would serve our interest in two ways. First, it would halt Britain's liberalization process by skewing the country back to a Keynesian profile. Secondly, the Conservative party in opposition would dump Thatcher, and respond to the new Labour government by reverting to a 'me-too' Toryism which would sing all our old tunes. The 1960s consensus would be re-established.

These unacknowledged alliances across the parties (often unrecognized even by the parties involved) are the stuff of which high politics is made. They are the real agencies for change or stagnation, the very forces which shape the future. Such was the case in late nineteenth-century Britain when seemingly disparate groups from across the formal political spectrum were essentially united by ideology, although divided by party. Then, the formal contest was between Liberals and Tories, although the real battle was between the individualists and the collectivists in both parties. In 1893 George Bernard Shaw summed up this real divide:

> The Old Whigs and the new Tories of the school of Cobden and Bright, the Philosophic Radicals, the economists of whom Bastiat is the type, Lord Wemyss and Lord Bramwell, Mr Herbert Spencer and Mr Auberon Herbert, Mr Gladstone, Mr Arthur Balfour, Mr John Morley, Mr Leonard Courtney: any of these is in England a more typical Anarchist than Bakunin. They distrust state action, and are jealous advocates of the prerogative of the individual, proposing to restrict the one and extend the other as far as is humanly possible, in opposition to the Social-Democrat, who proposes to democratize the state and throw upon it the whole

network of organizing the national industry, thereby making it the most vital organ in the social body.[1]

The defeat of this nineteenth-century alliance of 'Philosophic Radicals' by another disparate grouping which also cut across the formal political divide (that of Disraelian Tory Democracy, the New Liberalism of Simon, and the Fabians) helped determine the British future for a century.

The public sector resistance

By the late 1980s, the country has arrived at a similar turning point. This time, though, it seems that the radicals have the upper hand. For a start, they control the government, the formal seat and source of political power. Also, the threat to the enterprise revolution from one of Britain's most powerful conservative forces, the trade unions, has become a thing of the past.

Less directly threatening, but certainly as influential, was the bitter resistance to Thatcherism which emerged during the 1980s from 'middle-class' (non-manual) supporters of the public sector – from amongst civil servants, teachers, academics, artists heavily dependent upon public funding, and the journalists of the BBC. These groups possessed what amounted to an almost ideological commitment to the 'public interest', an interest which would be best served by a mixed economy and a universal welfare state. Yet, the notion that a 'public interest' – separate from the rhetoric to secure some private interest or aggregation of private interests – actually existed, was increasingly being challenged. (And the radical liberal suggestion that such was the case here, amongst the professional public sector middle classes, would often be treated with incredulity.)

These public sector talking, informing and managing classes, mainly domiciled in southern England, had found the dispensation of postwar Keynesianism a particularly beneficent mix. (And it became particularly benign at the top end of the public sector ladder.) Keynesian beneficence provided these public sector elites with everything which the vast majority of manual workers and their families either could not achieve or did not want: security for their incomes and property, status for their jobs, tax-breaks for their mortgage interest payments, many of the same welfare benefits

which went to the most disadvantaged, and a public subsidy (derived from general taxation or the BBC compulsory levy) for their
cultural life and leisure activities. All of this, and, at the same
time, a general 'progressive' social ethos which could appease
tender (if not exactly guilty) consciences. Herein lay the secret of
how those archetypal upper middle-class enclaves represented by
Hampstead, Islington and Richmond, together with many of their
lesser outposts in provincial England, felt so at home with 'leftish'
(if not left) politics and culture.

As the militantly bourgeois rhetoric of Thatcher burst upon the
scene in the latter half of the 1970s, and was then progressively
put into practice in the 1980s, this 'left of centre' public sector
intelligentsia became increasingly worried. It was obvious that,
should Thatcherism take hold, what had previously amounted to
a tame 'working-class' acquiescence in the 'middle-class' purchase
on the state would come to an end. As more and more manual
workers moved into tax-paying, or higher tax, brackets, they
would adopt a 'bourgeois ethic' which would translate itself into
an electoral force for lower taxes – and, consequently, a lower
public sector. Also, this more 'bourgeois' society would be bound
to assign to the public sector elites far less status and prestige than
they had enjoyed under either 'Butskellism' in the 1950s and 1960s
or the corporatism of the 1970s.

This public sector class voted overwhelmingly for Labour or the
SDP-Liberal Alliance in the 1983 and 1987 general elections, but
all to no avail. Hopelessness turned to impotence. This discontent
found its outlet not only in a generalized rage at Thatcherism,
but also in a striking animosity towards Thatcher personally – a
hostility which expressed itself somewhat piquantly when Oxford
University took the unusual step of refusing to bestow an honorary
degree upon a Conservative Prime Minister.[2] An image of the
alienation of Britain's unreconstructed Keynesian intelligentsia,
as it surveyed the 'wasteland of Thatcherism', was captured by
an editorial in a Thatcherite Sunday newspaper:

> . . . wandering aimlessly between Islington and the Grouch Club,
> stopping now and then at Channel 4 or Broadcasting House to let
> the world know how much it despises what is happening to the
> country, it has become increasingly divorced from the land it lives
> in . . . Rarely have the ideals of the country's intellectual elite been
> so out of kilter with the aspirations of plain folk.[3]

The High Tory resistance

By the late 1980s, when the public sector cultural challenge to Thatcherism had gone the same way as the trade union challenge, the remaining resistance to the new radicalism increasingly fell to its last organized redoubt: to England's High Tory 'established' or 'landed' institutions, their inhabitants, friends, supporters and aspirants.

High Tory opposition to the opening up of Britain is likely to be much more impressive than that mounted by the progressive intelligentsia – not least because the High Tory resistance has a serious hold on some of the real levers of power in Britain. High Tory power rests where it always has done, in that cluster of 'institutions' which have seemingly been untouched by modernity: the Royal Family, the Church of England, the House of Lords (which incorporates many of the older landed families and their servants and supporters), and the educational hierarchy (particularly amongst the governing bodies, Heads and Masters of the leading public schools and the Oxford and Cambridge colleges).

These 'institutions' remain not only sources of cultural power. They also express a deeper power reality: the possession of exceptional aggregations of wealth. In Britain, where a population of 55 million co-exists with a finite landmass of 43 million acres of usable land outside the urban areas, land indeed almost equals wealth. More land (and therefore more wealth) can, of course, be created by simply 'building up', but the High Tory resistance (led, in this case, by the Prince of Wales) has so far managed to temper any such additions to the 'landmass'. At the last, imperfect, count the Crown owned 404,000 acres, the Oxford and Cambridge colleges, 200,000 acres, the Church of England, 165,000 acres, and eight families, between them, 1,253,300 acres.[4]

Yet it is the influence, not the wealth, that is the real landed problem for modern Britain. For centuries, landed (High Tory) values have been skilfully transmitted downwards to a population in whose daily lives 'land' (and its values and lifestyle) meant very little. Thus, 'land' has tamed business, labour, even finance in a manner unknown in any other Western country. This ugly trick was played through the hold which 'land' maintained over the country's information (and education) systems.

James Bellini, writing in the first year of Thatcherism, argued that the grip of the 'landed interest' on the life of Britain would, in the future, tighten further still. He suggested that Britain was developing what he called a 'landfax aristocracy':

> The collapse of Britain's industrial economy is creating a new power structure – the landfax aristocracy. As industry fades away two areas of stability and profits remain: land and the technologies of information. As more and more wealth is pushed into these two areas, Britain's economy will take on a new shape. In outward appearance it will seem like the disparate mixture of old landed wealth and the prosperous world of banking, insurance and the City institutions. But the underlying pattern of ownership will be simpler. Old landed wealth is taking over the information world as well. The result is a new aristocracy with its feet planted firmly on both sides of Britain's declining industrial base. One foot will stay with the land, the other will grow with the explosion of the information technologies. This is the landfax aristocracy that will run Britain in the twenty-first century.[5]

Bellini was somewhat premature. These 'landed' families (and the anti-bourgeois High Tory culture for which they all, ultimately, stand) are certainly powers to be reckoned with in the modern media business. Many among them own a plethora of information outlets (such as television companies, publishing houses and newspapers). 'Land' did well in the information business during the century of paternalism, and particularly well out of its last quarter, as a tightly regulated TV mass media developed, thereby enabling 'prevailing values' to be transmitted to a wider and wider audience. Yet, in the 1980s, Britain's media and information business fell increasingly into 'non-established' (often foreign) hands, and this trend will become even more pronounced in the 1990s as the new broadcasting regime comes into being.

In the century of paternalism, however, land's High Tory value-system was primarily transmitted to the nation at large not by newspapers, journals or even television, but by an elite educational structure which (looking back on it) seems breath-taking in its anti-commercial bias. For most of the century the English public schoolboy or the Oxbridge graduate was brought up in a world in which the static values of landed life were imposed in an almost totalitarian manner. Barnett describes this imposition as dooming the variety, spontaneity and open-mindedness that had hitherto [before the mid-nineteenth century] been the saving graces of the British upper classes . . . In an era of tremendous change, it had accustomed him to a static society . . . In an epoch [nineteenth-century Britain] that required in men the itch to develop, create and exploit, school had fostered . . . cautious 'responsibility' rather than the taking of risk.[6]

Arcadian High Tory values and sensibilities were thus transmitted downwards – to any 'working-class' youths who made their way to Oxbridge – and then laterally to the seats of power and influence as these graduates entered, and determined, the world of business, finance and the professions.

The age of mass democracy, and the arrival of socialism, hardly affected the character and power of Britain's peculiarly un-modern elite educational system. All that happened was that the base of recruitment widened somewhat as the public schools took into their fold some few from the propertyless masses, and Oxbridge took under its wing larger numbers of grammar school and comprehensive graduates. The 'governing values' remained the same. The patrician state had served the landed interest.

It took some time, but by the end of the 1980s the freer market economy was ringing some changes even in this most protected and frozen area of British life. The 'guiding hand' over higher education of the 'top-down' patrician state was fatally weakened by the 1988 Education Reform Bill, which ushered in what is to become a demand-led (and, therefore, student-led) era. In Britain, to introduce popular demand into higher education is to upset the whole apple-cart of generations of imposed tradition. It is a dagger struck at the heart of the establishment's incubator, where landed England's mores and lifestyle have been passed on from generation to generation, replicating themselves only by imposition from above.

A 'bottom-up' market-place for higher education will not destroy elitism, but it will radically alter the character of Britain's future elites. Students will become consumers (rather than an officer corps moulded to serve); and they will insist upon an education more attuned to the modern competitive world. Should the public schools and the colleges of Oxford and Cambridge not be able to respond to this demand-led era we are now entering, they will be supplanted by other institutions which can.

Thus Thatcherism, whilst not harming the wealth of the High Tory landed interest (indeed, it has enhanced it) has nonetheless severely eroded its propaganda power bases in both the media and elite education. The British people can now look forward to a twenty-first century in which the volume of the ancient drumbeat of landed High Toryism is turned way down.

Turning the volume of the High Tory drumbeat down within the Conservative party, however, may be a very different matter. The High Tories handled the Conservative party with considerable skill during the paternalist century. They used it to bring the deferential working class into their fold in order to thwart nineteenth-century liberalism; it was used to tilt the country towards protectionism when free trade threatened too emphatic a liberalization of the economy; it has been used regularly to beat the xenophobic drum whenever domestic revolt threatened; it was even used (as the historian, Maurice Cowling, has pointed out) to nurture Labour as the main opposition party in the early decades of the twentieth century, and to extend, as necessary, the patrician state they controlled. 'In the long run', argued C. N. Parkinson, 'it was mainly the Conservatives who introduced socialism into Britain'.[7] This piece of historical hyperbole nonetheless contains more than a germ of truth; for the High Tories certainly pushed the Conservatives into the warm embrace of collectivism.

With such a record it is surprising that Mrs Thatcher ever came to lead, let alone dominate, such a party. She is, in fact, the first Conservative party leader ever seriously to espouse the nineteenth-century liberal verities. She is also the first Conservative leader since Neville Chamberlain properly to represent – both in social background and governing ideology – the ethic of provincial business. Her election as leader in 1975 represented no sea-change in Tory opinion, no fundamental shift away from High Toryism towards a neo-liberal world view (amongst either Conservative MPs or the party faithful).

Thatcher was elected leader by a combination of factions, the smallest and least influential being Tory radicals from backgrounds similar to her own. The rest – those who gave her her majority – were a combination of the disaffected: those MPs who had come to the conclusion that Heath's corporatism had failed, and those personally antipathetic to Heath because of personal wounds sustained by his arbitrary style of party and governmental management. As Chris Patten later observed, Thatcher's election to the top of the Tory tree was more a product of a 'peasants [backbench] revolt' against Edward Heath than a determination to radicalize the Conservative party.

Consequently, her first Tory Cabinet and government were packed with an array of High Tory paternalists, the kind of Tories who would have felt at home in the Home or Macmillan governments. Such High Tories 'To The Manor Born' as William Whitelaw, Francis Pym, Ian Gilmour, Peter Carrington and Norman St John Stevas all found themselves presented with leading roles in this first Thatcher government. These Tories would soon assume the role of a Cabinet praetorian guard – not, however, to protect the new Prime Minister, but rather to guard established interests from interference by her.

Under the pressure of radical success, however, the old landed 'establishment' began to crack at the seams. It divided between a faction (led by Ian Gilmour) which progressively left government for either the backbenches, the life of landowning, or the City and another faction (led by William Whitelaw) which remained within the Thatcherite camp – in order, as High Tory rhetoric would have it, 'to serve' (but also maybe, as more sceptical minds would later reflect, to salvage something for traditionalism out of the awesome ravages of the 'Great Experiment').

Each new general election, however, saw a new intake of un-landed MPs sliding onto the Tory backbenches, a radicalizing force which converged with a Tory party conference, which, with every passing year, was becoming more militantly middle class (almost 'poujadiste'). Yet, even during the 1983–7 Parliament, the majority in the Parliamentary Conservative Party was by no means in accord with the underlying assumptions of 'the revolution'. There was always something rather phoney about the clipped accents of privilege muttering approvingly about 'markets' and 'choice' and 'people's capitalism'. 'They all sound very dry', announced a Labour MP in the tea room of the House of Commons in late 1986 as he surveyed a group of middle-aged Tory MPs, 'but they all *look* very wet.'

High Tory 'wets' did bare their teeth during the 1983–7 Parliament, but only when Thatcher's radicalism collided head-on (and in a way which could not be obfuscated) with traditional Tory interests. During this second Thatcher administration, Keith Joseph, still Secretary of State for Education, made proposals to change the structure of financing for higher education. His idea was that the higher education science budget could be increased by forcing well-off parents (most of whom had already secured an advantage for their children by paying for their private secondary education) to pay more towards their costs of attending university or polytechnic. This unremarkable scheme nonetheless caused a classic modern Tory imbroglio, as Thatcherite theory clashed with Tory vested interest. On the one hand, Joseph's arguments were impeccable from a modern Conservative viewpoint. The ordinary taxpayer should not be asked to subsidize the sons and daughters of the relatively well-off. (Surely, only a socialist welfare culture would ask for such 'Dependency' to be induced in its upper class.) On the other hand, it would be mainly Tory parents who would be hurt. The 'wet' revolt succeeded, and Tory privilege prevailed over a radical attempt to take the well-off out of welfare.

During the same Parliament, Thatcher's radical zeal led her to give government support to proposals for liberalizing the archaic Sunday trading laws. The idea was that those millions of ordinary people who worked during the week could actually assume the role of consumers at the week-end. It was a modest liberalizing measure, although a classic example of an attempt to gain consumer over producer sovereignty. It was met by fierce resistance – this time from a trinity of Tory paternalism, Labour and the Church. Labour's angle lay in its support for the trade unions which opposed the measure. The Tory/Church imperative was altogether more elevated. In the name of 'preserving the English Sunday' (when, presumably, the happy English family gathers together in an idyll of rural peace and spiritual contemplation), the barbarity and vulgarity of commerce was to be held at bay by the guardians of civility. Here again, a commercial republic yearning to be free was to be put back in its place by a High Tory 'Nanny' – acting 'for the spiritual good of all of us', of course.

These minor, though significant, rebellions apart, the High Tories were neither able to oust Thatcher nor palpably to weaken the general direction of the government. Even so, the new radicalism (as during the 1980s it stepped forth into Toryland) had about it an air of the usurper – rather like John F. Kennedy and his first day in the White House, when he is reported as saying that he

expected the police to come in and eject him. The new radicalism, certainly in its early years, seemed such an unschlerotic and
purposeful insurgent (almost un-English in its constant need to do
battle, to win, to renew itself lest complacency play into the hands
of its enemies) that it could not possibly last. The *ancien regime*
was seemingly always lurking, always ready (like Kennedy's White
House police) to take back occupancy.

Nevertheless, the radical usurper was not, in turn, to be
usurped. As this reality became ever clearer, the High Tory
opposition decided upon a strategy of resistance by rearguard
action. In the autumn of 1987 they floated the notion that the
'gains' of Thatcherism needed to be consolidated, not extended.
In the name of this strategy of 'consolidation' they offered their
radical Tory colleagues 'much friendly advice to trim their radical
ambitions and settle for being the natural party of government'.[8]

However, this High Tory tactic backfired. More and more
Tory MPs were becoming convinced that radicalism was the
vote-getter, not 'consolidation'. It was becoming obvious that
continuing Tory victories at the polls could best be ensured by
larger and larger doses of radicalism. By pushing the market
economy further and further into traditional Labour territory,
Labour would be undercut amongst its traditional supporters.
By widening the bourgeois embrace to include more and more
people from social classes C1 and C2, the Tories could gain a
permanent hold on 'working-class England'. 'Consolidation', on
the other hand, although beguiling on the surface, might actually
lose votes to Labour. Labour could argue that the Tories had run
out of steam.

As always, Tories in Parliament would, of course, 'ride any
horse as long as it was jumping well'; and radicalism was jumping very well indeed! So the flirtation with 'consolidation' came
to an end, and Thatcher was able specifically, and roundly, to
reject it during her first conference speech following the victory
in 1987. High Tory England had suffered another set-back within
the Conservative party.

Following the 1987 victory Thatcher's ascendancy over her
party was such that hardly any Tory MPs could aspire to
government without at least pretending to support her radical
market strategy. In the post-1987 Parliament, only the most
unreconstructed High Tories would demur (and only then in

private) at the free market strategy. By 1987 the Prime Minister had seemingly won the battle for the economic 'soul' of her own party.

However, although the economic theories of neo-liberalism were widely accepted, the broader radical implications of these doctrines were not. Talk of a 'cultural revolution', or of the full development of an 'enterprise society', would still cause many a Conservative to raise an eyebrow. Even in the midst of Mrs Thatcher's third term, bitter resistance to modernity lurked in many a Tory breast; and it was still a matter of speculation as to how strongly the new radical writ actually ran within the Tory government. Although the Cabinet was virtually Thatcherized by 1989, some of the brighter young ministers – among them, William Waldegrave, John Patten, Chris Patten, Robert Jackson – came from a decidedly 'wet' political stable.

There has to remain a question-mark, however, over whether Britain's historic party of Crown and privilege will ever seriously seek to translate its new-found enthusiasm for a liberal economy into a commitment to an open, liberal society? *The Economist* suggested, wishing to push the radical revolution ever wider, that

> Unradical Tories are conservatives, and many of the features of modern Britain are not worth conserving . . . Near the top of society many groups remain largely immune from competition. In their different ways, farmers, doctors, dentists, teachers, lawyers, academics and civil servants have all retained either price-fixing powers or barriers against arriviste competitors.[9]

This was dangerous egalitarian talk, directly highlighting how the social implications inherent in Britain's liberal economic experiment could have set the country upon a course more radical than many of its adherents would have either contemplated or thought possible. Margaret Thatcher once told this author that she was not in business simply to 'bash' the trade unions but, rather, to reduce 'restrictive practices throughout the country, at whatever social level'. The theorists of the 'enterprise revolution' had long identified the restrictive practices of the upper middle-class professions as one of the major effects (and causes) of the social rigidities in modern Britain.

By 1989 the Tory government had begun a tentative process

of change. A new (Scottish) Lord Chancellor, Lord Mackay, advanced the heretical opinion that the courts existed for the benefit of the public, and initiated a discussion on how to unfreeze the rigidities in Britain's protected legal profession. An erosion of the restrictive practices which the paternalist state had constructed for broadcasters was also being proposed. These small steps were hardly revolutionary. The farming lobby, the doctors and dentists, and the civil servants seemed to have emerged from this first tranche of reforms unscathed. Yet a process of change was beginning; and a radical principle was clearly established – that market imperative (and consumer sovereignty) knew no social boundaries.

In its third term the Thatcher government was also proceeding with another 'social' phase of the radical revolution: its 'social agenda', involving education reform, health service reform, and, more generally, raising questions at least about the nature and character of the 'welfare state'. This was a difficult, tricky, area for radicals. The paternalist welfare state was obviously not working. The services it provided to both those in need (and its customers, more generally) were inadequate; the state sector of secondary education was not functioning as well as the private sector, and the health service was creaking. Many amongst the upper income groups (many of them socialists) had increasingly 'opted out' of the state sector by sending their children to public schools and taking out private health insurance schemes.

The solution, though, could no longer be found in increased public money, which could only be raised by unpopular taxes. And no one (Labour included) was even raising the (dubious) idea that the state sector could be improved by making private health and private education illegal.

So, by the late 1980s the Tory radicals were toying with the idea of adopting a revolutionary new model for the kind of welfare society appropriate for Britain in the third millennium. The principle at the core of the 'model' was the nostrum that the whole paternalist welfare structure would need to be slimmed-down, and a new balance struck between public and private provision of services. British incomes were going to rise by almost a half by the year 2000, and more and more people would be able to pay for better services than the paternalist state had been able to supply.

Some amongst the Tory radicals were arguing that a new

balance between public and private provision could be achieved without abandoning the fundamental national commitment to state provision for education and health. It became clear during 1988 and 1989 that the Conservative government agreed with them, and was not about to abandon such state provision. Instead, the theme behind the proposed reforms centred around the notion of extending 'choice' within the state sector by creating 'internal markets'. Those who could not afford private education or health would nonetheless be able to exercise some degree of choice (and therefore, it was argued, power) over these aspects of their life. It all amounted to 'embourgeoisement' within the culture of the state.

The Thatcher government, even in its third term, did not seek to abandon the state's role as a 'safety-net' for those who could not function in the market-place. Instead, it was argued that provision for those in need could be dramatically improved, but only if public resources were freed by weaning middle-income groups off their various dependencies on the state. After all, there was always something rather hypocritical about attacks on 'welfare scroungers' emanating from protected and comfortable 'middle-class' folk who themselves were taking full advantage of their rights under the same welfare state.

In the social security area it all came down to an argument in favour of abandoning the 'universality' of welfare benefits, and replacing 'universality' by 'targeting' benefits to those in need. Why, indeed, should a duchess get the same child benefit as a poor, single-parent mother? 'Targeting', though, was a pin that would prick, and might even draw blood from some Conservative-voting interest groups.

This model of transition to a bourgeois society (with its slimmed-down, though more efficient, bourgeois state) would meet more resistance from higher-income earners than from lower. Professionals would no longer be cosseted by restrictive practices; and, should higher-income earners wish to continue to use state provision, then they would have to pay more – for, amongst other things, their children's higher education and their prescription charges.

Of course, these higher-income earners would be doing well enough out of the bourgeois society because they would be paying less in taxes. This stark benefit would (no matter their loss of privilege in the state sector) keep the affluent in the radical column. Yet, average-income earners would also be paying less in taxes, and, in addition, would be beginning to enjoy the liberties, choices and individualism hitherto largely confined to the more affluent.

Michael Foot was fond of claiming on behalf of socialism majority support amongst the British. 'We Are The Many, They Are The Few' was the famous phrase he would use to taunt his opponents (and many a High Tory would secretly agree). Yet, by the late 1980s, 'the many' were beginning to be enlisted on the side of liberal change rather than socialist or corporatist stasis.

This epoch-making fact presented the most serious challenge yet to England's High Tory establishment as it surveyed the British scene ten years into Thatcherism. The High Tories (and their socialist allies) had lost the economic battle with liberalism, and it looked likely that they were going to lose the social battle too. All that was left to block Britain's path to modernity was reliance upon the elemental force of antiquity itself, upon its peoples' love affair with the past.

An anti-modern culture

That Britain in the 1980s is still almost tyrannized by its past (is cultivating it, and revelling in it, rather than using it to provide vision for the future) can be glimpsed from even the most cursory glance at TV screens, national newspapers or titles in bookshops.

The standard explanations for the grip of nostalgia vary from the country's unique evolutionary experience (a pattern of historical development unbroken by revolution or conquest) to the rather grim speculation that the British are settling for a role as an historical 'theme park' for tourists. Yet one 'theme' of Britain's history (from amongst the many) seems to possess a power out of all proportion to its role in the construction of the modern nation and the modern world. The country which pioneered the world's entry into the age of industry and capitalism seems to wish to forget this progressive heritage, preferring instead to remain under the spell of its medieval and feudal past.

'The Glamour of Backwardness' is the vivid term given by Scottish writer Tom Nairn to this British attraction for the feudal.

Nairn explains that 'glamour' is an old Scottish word for 'magical enchantment, the spell cast upon humans by fairies, or witches'; and that 'backwardness' was a term that 'was until around the middle of the [twentieth] century the condition attributed by Her Majesty's subjects to most of the rest of the world. It meant those incapable of industry and democracy, or still on the long uphill road of modernisation.'[10]

Britain's resistance to 'modernization' has taken numerous forms. By far the most conspicuous has been the continued evocation – still ringing in the ears of the modern British of the 1980s – of the superior value of rural life over that believed to have been the unsavoury product of the industrial and commercial centuries. How come? The American cultural historian Martin Weiner has suggested that:

> In the world's first industrial nation, industrialism did not seem quite at home. In the country that had started mankind on the 'great ascent' economic growth was frequently viewed with suspicion and disdain. Having pioneered urbanisation, the English ignored or disparaged cities. The more I explored these incongruities, the more important they seemed to become. Instead of peripheral curiosities, they turned out to lie near the heart of modern British history. Taken together, they bore witness to a cultural cordon sanitaire encircling the forces of economic development – technology, industry, commerce. One could begin to see this mental quarantine take shape in the social changes (and non-changes) of the Victorian era, watch it give from then on a particular softly rustic and nostalgic cast to middle and upper-class culture, and finally observe it intertwine with the modern fading of national economic dynamism.[11]

Past proponents of the arcadian vision (of the idyll of rural England) – they ranged from socialists like Morris, Blatchford and Ruskin, to radicals like Cobbett, to Liberals like Asquith, and through to Conservatives like Baldwin and Halifax – represented a formidable and powerful cross-section of opinion. In the 1980s, the current of rural sentimentality may be running as powerfully as ever, particularly amongst the well-off and the well-connected. In Thatcher's Britain, the money and wealth of southern commerce is still not reward enough: even now, it needs to be legitimized by some kind of rural sanction. The literary left are also in thrall to England's 'green and pleasant land'. Even Margaret Drabble,

the chronicler of Northern England, felt it necessary to round-off
a list of gritty, industrial Northern virtues with the triumphant
observation: 'and it [the North] has countryside' – as though
such a statement is the ultimate party stopper, the end point of
an emotional appeal.[12]

The 'village' is also being re-created in the city. Jonathan Raban
describes Highgate Hill:

> On the clear windy top of Highgate Hill there is a community of
> ardent villagers. They wear country clothes – riding macs and
> headscarves, tweeds and Wellington boots – and talk in gentry
> voices, braying bravely over the tops of taxis. They have their
> church, their tea-shop, their family grocer, their village green,
> three village pubs, and the Highgate Society with its coffee morn-
> ings, its knighted president and its evening lectures.[13]

What's more, today's 'rural longing' is no longer simply an
individual fancy, or just a talking-point for clubbable Old Codgers
as they 'grumble into their beer' about the rigours of modern life.
Support for rural values and 'the rural way of life' has now become
institutionalized, elevated to a special public status in the form of
the National Trust. This plays a more vital role in the life of Britain
than simply allowing families of aristocratic lineage to continue to
enjoy their homes and estates at the taxpayers' expense. As one
of the archetypal resting places for England's 'Good and Great',
the National Trust bestows a kind of official blessing on Britain
as a 'museum society' (one that lives in and worships the past). It
also presents a skewed vision of the country's history by giving a
selected sanction to those (usually rural) aspects of our past which
need to be kept 'in trust'. Historian Patrick Wright goes further,
suggesting that the National Trust is a profoundly reactionary
force, one that gives 'a distorted view of the past . . . promoting
what Arthur Bryant once defined as "the sweet and lovely breath
of conservatism"'.[14]

In the backward-looking modern mind the rural image often
merges into the image of 'community'. Rural life before the age
of commerce – so the mythic image often presents itself – was
not only enriching because of trees, clean air, soothing views and
'the sweet and lovely breath of conservatism', but also because
of the way these village folk lived. Their lives may have been
somewhat hierarchical and constricting, but the 'communities' of

rural existence were at least stable and certain – producing happy people who, if not always dancing round the maypole, were at least content and unfraught. By contrast the modern city-dwelling or suburban individual is atomized, lonely and rootless.

This positive image of a past, lost, sense of community emerges in the ideas and rhetoric of the politics of modern Britain. It can be seen in the left-wing nostalgia for the non-competitive world of 'Merrie England'; in modern socialism's evocation of the 'warmth' of the older 'working-class communities'; and in the High Tory communitarian ideal of 'England as a Garden'.[15] Thus (and inevitably) the virtues of 'community' become subtly enlisted in the crusade against Thatcherite individualism, which, it is claimed, has destroyed the past.

It remains fair to ask, however, how enriched by 'community' have the lives of Britons ever been? And what was the character of this 'community-based' life that was so rudely destroyed after 1979 by the free market? One only has to ask the questions to get the less than appealing answer.

Britain, like most of the advanced world in the modern age, has rarely known 'community' – at least not in the mythic sense portrayed by the rural romantics. The century of paternalism saw Britain develop not as a patchwork of village 'communities', but rather as a vast landmass of housing estates, sprawling suburbs and inner-city slums. Rural Britain was no 'community' idyll either. It may have been less anonymous than the city and suburb; but neither closeness (nor even familiarity) makes a 'community'. Village life was often constricted, segregated (between private and public housing), hierarchical, intrusive and poor. The life, for the majority of its inhabitants, was no fuller or richer (and often much less so) than in the suburbs. The British reality was then what it is now, and always has been: a very un-communal nation of individuals and families struggling to make ends meet.

Nevertheless, the myth of lost rural community continues, almost as a psychic need. And its hold on the imagination of Britain's elites remains as damaging as ever. This impress of mythic 'community' continues to weigh in the national balance against fully embracing the modern world, and hence fully benefitting from its pleasures and possibilities. Modern Britain consequently gets the worst of both worlds. Community spirit and sensibility hardly exist to be built upon as a way of life; yet they remain an 'ideal' whose overhanging and spectral presence prevents us from developing a rounded, individualistic, bourgeois society.

Reactionaries appeal to 'community' whenever change is upon them. Socialists appeal to it against capitalist consumerism. And, more generally, its almost religious power is used to keep people from fully expressing themselves and their personalities. It helps, in other words, to keep them in their place.

In the holy name of community, 'individualism' remains a dirty word. Individualism can be variously described in modern commentary as 'rampant' or 'excessive' or 'unbridled', adjectives which would never be appended to the word 'community'. 'Respectable folk' (taking a lead from their betters) still too often feel precluded from asserting themselves, their interests or their tastes, lest they be considered 'selfish' – an expression of 'individualism'.

Thus, our still cantankerously anti-modern culture allows no serious idea of the sovereignty of the consumer to take hold. Too many Britons still feel uneasy as 'consumers', still feel consumerism to be too pushy a business. That we are still treated (relatively) contemptuously by our bureaucracies, (relatively) badly in stores, given (absolutely) appalling conditions at the grounds of our 'national game' (not considered, incidentally, a concern to be put right by our 'national' Trust) is, ultimately, of course, our own fault. We consider complaints too assertive, and maybe even too vulgar. We have been taught not to measure the life around us by reference to our own needs, but rather to accept the power of tradition.

There is no surer measure of the resilience in Britain of anti-modern sentiment than the kind of brazen attacks upon 'bourgeois values' which have become a feature of life in Thatcher's era. On the eve of the 1987 general election Britons could read in a leader in the mass circulation newspaper, *The Sunday Telegraph*, a public declaration which would be inconceivable in any other Western country:

> Something rather ugly has happened in the last four years – the growth of bourgeois triumphalism – that decent people might want to check and chasten by denying Thatcherism the endorsement of a third term. Bourgeois triumphalism is a difficult phenomenon to pin down. But anyone who has heard yuppies at play and at table – and who can fail to have done so given the trumpet volume of their braying voices? – will know what is meant. Wealth creating

is a good thing. But in their case – and this is what is new – the possession of wealth seems to carry with it absolutely no sense of obligation or service whatsoever.[16]

'Yuppies' was a term originally coined in the United States in the early 1980s to depict (literally) 'Young, Upwardly Mobile Professionals' who earned enough money to lead a somewhat self-consciously 'stylish' life – exhibited by designer clothes, personal fastidiousness and a certain sexual androgyny. The British usage (introduced in the mid 1980s) means something quite different. Not surprisingly it has a class connotation, and a feudal one at that. The new bourgeois class (as seen by *The Sunday Telegraph* leader) were not just new people with new money. Rather, they were judged according to a feudal social sensibility which looks for 'leadership' or 'rulership' (and considers them unworthy because of their social manners and a perceived lack of social 'obligation').

In reality, of course, New Money was simply rubbing up against Old Money, and causing social grief. But the reaction of old money (and its supporters) seemed to lack an appreciation that Britain's so-called 'yuppies' were really little different from earlier new money generations. After all: who were these 'decent people' – who heard the 'braying voices' of the new bourgeoisie 'at play and at table' – other than those whose ancestors some generations before them had been as 'undecent' as to steal land. (By contrast, the 'Yuppies' were only earning very high incomes.) As for the rest of the British, they could probably not distinguish between new money 'braying' and the 'braying' which had assaulted their ears for centuries past.

This kind of anti-modern 'aristocratic' eruption against new wealth was a feature of the 1980s. But the older order of wealth which felt itself under threat from Thatcherism was caught in a bind. It could not reject Thatcherism because it had done rather well out of it. And it could hardly oppose, in principle, the creation of new wealth, or 'wealth generation'. So it appeared to argue that Britain needed new wealth, but not its social and cultural consequences; and that the new 'yuppie' bourgeois were alright, but only in their assigned place. The mental framework here was something out of the pre-war diaries of Chips Channon, themselves a story of the hypocrisies of 'aristocratic' life in which 'business and trade' were constant companions of 'nobility' and supposed financial disinterest.

Later, and after the actual 'bourgeois' electoral triumph of 1987, modern Britons were enjoined by the same *Sunday Telegraph* to join in a solemn lament:

> . . . with the exception of the martial values, none of the other old aristocratic values receive any public encouragement or endorsement. Quite the opposite, they have been consigned to the dustbin of history. Indeed the Thatcherite message to the rich seems to be almost identical to her message to the poor – get off your backsides and make even more money that you did before. [17]

Britain in the late 1980s had to be the only Western nation in which a nostalgia for aristocracy could be so openly propagated. This deeply felt feudal sensibility, which Thatcherism had unleashed into the open, obviously saw itself more seriously threatened by 'peoples' capitalism' than it had ever been by the postwar Labour governments.

Anti-modern sentiment not only exalted tradition against modernity but, at the same time, successfully constructed a partial (and therefore fake) view of Britain's historical images. Thus, 'British tradition' (the 'kind of thing we all stand for'!) is still seen in the popular mind of the 1980s as aristocratic rather than bourgeois, as regal rather than common, as ancient rather than modern.

During the century of paternalism 'British tradition' became increasingly associated with the soft 'civilizing' Tory attributes of Late Empire, rather than with the tougher, rawer, more liberal and individualistic values which had actually built that Empire. The 'traditional' British figure became the 'Gentleman' rather than the 'Player' ('The Gentleman in Trollope' was the subject of a learned work as late as the early 1980s[18]), Bertie Wooster rather than John Bull. The cultivated mandarin somehow became more 'traditionally English' than the entrepreneur. The core values of 'traditional England' were often portrayed as those of decency, moral sensibility and 'caring'. The values of an earlier England – where men were 'hard of mind and hard of will . . . aggressive and acquisitive . . . who saw foreign policy in terms of concrete interest: markets, natural resources, colonial real estate, naval bases, profits'[19] – were often considered 'foreign'.

Public ceremonials are no less skewed against the bourgeois forces of British history. The modern mass communications system brings to millions through television public ceremonials in which medieval, not modern, symbolism is evoked. The images presented to the watching public (and foreign tourists) are not those of industry, commerce or democracy, but rather those of anti-democratic ancient hierarchy. The most prominent national ceremony, Trooping the Colour, is full of pomp and circumstance, but, ultimately, signifies little. In reality it is devoid of historical continuity; for this ceremony is fake tradition, initiated in the late nineteenth century to bolster an unpopular Crown.

The winning side in Britain's great seventeenth-century contest between bourgeois modernity and regal tradition – Parliament – has no such national ceremony. A bejewelled and crowned figure certainly enters Parliament every year, but only to read 'The Queen's Speech' – and not to the House of Commons, but to the House of Lords. The Parliamentary heirs of Cromwell (one of which has actually written 'The Queen's Speech') stand bunched together off centre-stage, thereby diminished both ceremonially and symbolically.

So complete is the hold of antiquity upon the modern British perception of their own history, that no national ceremony of democracy for the 'common' man or woman has ever been contemplated. Even when Britain's war dead are honoured (in the annual ceremony at the Cenotaph in Whitehall) it is the symbol of medieval England that lays the first wreath, and the democratic leader of a free people who lays the fifth. Should this order ever be reversed then, in the words of the father of the English bourgeoisie, Oliver Cromwell, 'It may provoke some spirits to see such plain men made captains of horse'. Even so (and again in Cromwell's words), a dead 'plain russet-coated captain that knows what he fights for and loves what he knows' might prefer to be honoured by those who 'tend to be of the middling sort' rather than him 'you call a gentleman and is nothing else'.[20] Thus – by the imposed force of contemporary ceremony and symbolism – is the English liberal vision (of enlightened democratic progress) robbed even of its place at the centre of British 'history'. Modernization is 'positively un-English'.[21]

Instead of weakening during the early phase of Thatcherism, anti-modernism temporarily reasserted itself. There was a time-lag effect at work, as the anti-modernist reaction against the social instabilities of the 1970s took its toll, reaching something of a crescendo in the early 1980s. One young writer suggested that the early 1980s witnessed a 'romanticism about the English past that hadn't been seen since the war', a nostalgia which reflected itself, amongst other things, in 'the resurrection of *The Tatler* under the editorship of Tina Brown . . . [and] . . . the pageantry of the Royal Wedding'.[22]

Also, the continued growth of violence – both violent crime and football hooliganism (and what would, in the 1980s, come to be described as 'yobbery') – led to a discovery amongst opinion-formers of what some saw as a lost 'golden age' of English 'civilized behaviour'. Characteristically, liberal bourgeois modernity was often blamed for this growth in violence. One guru of antiquity even proclaimed that aspiring to 'civilized values' 'maddens because of their total impracticality in a secular, rationalistic, democratic and liberal society'.[23] For anti-modernists, the past, conveniently, became 'civilized', the present 'uncivilized'. Few thought to look abroad to the 'secular, rationalistic, democratic and liberal societies' of continental Europe and North America, to the countries in which proletarian hooliganism was unknown; instead the assumption developed that only an ordered and paternalist system could guarantee social tranquillity. During the mid 1980s, the new radicals (sceptical about the value of tradition, contemptuous of rural and landed values, and increasingly 'triumphant') must have appeared in the minds of 'establishment England' as 'positively un-English', the greatest threat to Britain's social stability since the Luftwaffe.

The children of paternalism

Perhaps the 'guiding hand' of a collectivist aristocracy is indeed more conducive to social stability than are the random consequences of liberal economics. Paternalist governance may, indeed, have ensured domestic tranquillity and the perpetuation of 'civilized social structures'. Yet there is, of course, no sure way of telling. These supposed virtues of paternalism are, ultimately, only unprovable assertions and conceits: simply historical speculations. They tend to stick only because they are still regularly promulgated.

What, however, can also be told (if not measured precisely) is the social toll which paternalism has wrought: a cost in national

attitudes unreplicated in any other major advanced nation. Ernest
Bevin once lamented, about the condition of people from whence
he came, that 'the working class has been crucified on the poverty of its own desires'. Britain's greatest trade union leader was
referring here, in characteristically blunt language, to the complex
of unassertive and unambitious personal attitudes which he saw
displayed by the working people of his time. Bevin had more than
a point, and it probably still remains, forty years after his death.
It can still hardly be said of modern Britons, as Robert Chesshyre
has said of the children of a century of bourgeois progress in North
America, that they 'are launched into life with enormously positive
[personal] impulses'.[24]

But to what can this low level of 'positive' personal impulses
be attributed? In a sense, it may merely be the product of the
hopelessness (for most of the British) of the general economic
climate in which they have found themselves. Amongst the
propertyless masses the ability to 'advance oneself in life' through
social or geographic mobility, or access to education, has always
been difficult and limited. Also with the end of Empire Britain possessed no 'frontier' (no 'West') which could fuel even
an imagination of opportunity. What individualism and personal
assertiveness existed, tended to be channelled into trade union
activity.

Paternalist cultural dominion cannot escape responsibility here
for low aspirations, for the 'poverty of desires'. Inevitably – and
probably deliberately – the 'top-down' paternalist structures and
mentality succeeded in infusing their subjects with a low level of
individual self-esteem. In such an environment, to seek personal
advancement, to improve one's position, was to go against the
grain. In a society whose national symbolisms placed such a heavy
emphasis upon the value and virtue of heredity, personal aspira-
tion amongst those who inherited little or nothing was bound to
be weak.

Nor were personal aspirations particularly encouraged in other
levels of society, where, no matter the prosperity or status into
which they were born, the British were essentially allotted an
assigned 'place' for life. What British parent could (or can) say
to their child: 'you may grow up to be President one day'? In this
sense, Britons (unlike Americans, French, Germans, Italians and
a host of others) simply could not, and cannot, aspire to 'anything'.

Thus, a culture of limited, rather than 'limitless', achievement was inculcated.

English nonconformity added to this regime of low expectations. Traditionally, nonconformist Protestantism in Britain (concerned only with 'saving souls', and lacking the corporate tradition of Catholicism) had been a force for the growth and development of the individual against authority. Religion was an individual's concern, and the social consequences of sin were not a particular concern of the pastor. Yet, during the century of paternalism 'the chapel' had emerged as the most powerful theological (and ideological) force amongst Britain's propertyless masses. By proselytizing about the virtues of 'self-sacrifice', the chapel became an instrument for social stagnation. It instilled in its adherents an ethic of personal moral rectitude which (unlike nonconformist Christianity abroad) translated itself into a sanctioned lack of personal ambition, a socially conservative 'acceptance of one's lot'.

Under the guidelines of this chapel-led selfless culture, a 'self-sacrificing' message was sent to Britain's manual workforce and their families. 'Rewards will be in heaven', it argued; seeking them on this earth thus became somewhat redundant. Losing became more virtuous than winning; indeed, 'winning' became somewhat vulgar and pushy. 'Fair play' was extolled (although a decent reticence and 'propriety' would preclude too many questions being asked when such 'fair play' was not forthcoming amongst 'one's betters').

This culture of 'self-sacrifice' made anything more than a minimalist personal ambition amongst the proletariat utterly prohibitive. In such an environment, even a *rhetoric* of individual possibility (let alone of 'limitless horizons') seemed not only embarrassing but ridiculous.

Victorian nonconformity (and its twentieth-century legacy) was thus not necessarily the great liberal force it has been cracked up to be. Aspects of its legacy have indeed fostered the notion of the primacy of the individual, of individual responsibility and individual character-building. That most Victorian of organizations, the Building Society (which insisted upon a 'down payment' for mortgages) stands testimony to Victorian nonconformity's encouragement of thrift as well as independence. Yet, ultimately, the Protestant chapel served to dampen down personal ambition and individual self-confidence among the masses (a purpose much

nearer to the heart of pessimistic conservatism within the High
Tory established church).

The pervasive cultural regime of self-sacrifice was later to
come in useful when the masses in their millions were enjoined
to sacrifice 'for King and country' during the First World War.
Later still, 'self-sacrifice' continued to be elevated to the status
of public collective virtue. We can hear its resonances all the
way from Churchill's ringing patriotic phrase during the blitz
that 'the Londoners can take it', through to the more dreary,
puritanical postwar exhortations of the 'joys' of 'rationing' and
'belt-tightening'.

By 1950, High Tory propaganda was projecting to the world
the image of Britain's masses as 'stout-hearted' folk, rugged John
Bull-type individuals struggling to be free of the dreary life of
postwar reconstruction. Bevin's rare insight into the underlying
reality of the lives of his own people is, however, more compelling.
A century of paternalist governance and nonconformist ideology,
together with the ravages of two world wars, had indeed induced a
'poverty of desire' (with the consequent low horizons and expectations) in a battered and tired working population.

However, although the flesh was weak, the spirit was, in reality,
more willing than in Bevin's dispirited depiction. Although blocked
from fully expressing itself individually through consumerism, the
human personality asserted itself (in economic terms) by becoming 'organized' – by developing through and within the trade union
movement. Suffocating paternalism had not destroyed human 'desire' (or dignity), it had only suppressed it. By the 1970s, an
assertive working class was expressing itself in the form of an
industrial scene of bitter working-class sensibility, and a street
scene of punks, yobs and football hooligans. Paternalism's proletarian children were acting up.

What though of other children born of the paternalist century?
What of those who, through luck or willpower, managed to advance through the layered social strata of collectivized Britain?'

The life of the upwardly mobile was, in one sense, even more
difficult than for those who remained behind: for the socially
mobile were breaking the rules. All the social pressures were
against them. The 'arriver' was an 'arriviste', a derogatory term.
The 1988 *Concise Oxford Dictionary* could still list 'arriviste' as
in current usage in the English of the day; and it was defined

as an 'ambitious or self-seeking person' (and 'self-seeking' was obviously somewhat unworthy).[25] These 'arrivistes' were often derided as 'social climbers', which, like 'self-seeking', was another disparaging term. The 'social climber' became a social type, whose deceits and affectations were vividly depicted by many a nineteenth-century novelist. Anthony Trollope (the reputed, and appropriate, favourite author of Harold Macmillan) perfected the art form in *The Way We Live Now*.

Of course, 'social climbing' is not a uniquely English 'vice'. It is simply the English class-system's variant of basic human opportunism (again, unfortunately, until recently at least, another faintly derogatory term). But opportunism and upward mobility became contorted in the century of paternalism. Those who acquired power through wealth (capitalists) or institutional position (politicians) somehow remained dissatisfied. Of course, wealth or institutional power was the only hold which the aspirant had on upward mobility, his only ticket to success. Yet neither money nor politics ultimately counted! The arrivistes wanted more. And 'more' always turned out to be that elusive 'social acceptance': a place in the scheme of a social realm redolent with the values and imagery of the past.

The upwardly mobile of the paternalist century were incapable of setting their own standards, their own fashions, their own realm. Richard Cobden, the spokesman for the bourgeois revolution of the early nineteenth century, finally gave up on the upwardly mobile of his time:

> We have the spirit of feudalism rife and rampant in the midst of the antagonistic development of the age of Watt, Arkwright and Stephenson! Nay, feudalism is every day more in the ascendant in political and social life. So great is its power and prestige that it draws to it the support and homage of even those who are the natural leaders of the newer and better civilisation. Manufacturers and merchants as a rule seem only to desire riches that they may be enabled to prostrate themselves at the feet of feudalism. How is this to end?[26]

This 'prostration' was not to end. It still has not. Generation after generation of the representatives of Cobden's 'newer and better civilisation' were to follow meekly in the footsteps of their forebears. Martin Weiner suggests that the feudal mentality of the post-Cobden newly rich became more pronounced, more entrenched over time. He reports Friedrich Engels as becoming as apoplectic on the subject as Richard Cobden:

> . . . in 1850 [Engels] announced the triumph of the bourgeoisie . . . [But he] observed in 1892, with a mixture of bewilderment and contempt, that 'the English bourgeoisie are, up to the present day, so deeply penetrated by a sense of their inferiority that they keep up at their expense and that of the nation, an ornamental caste of drones to represent the nation worthily at all state functions; and they consider themselves highly honoured, whenever one of them is found worthy of admission into this selected and privileged body, manufactured, after all, by themselves'.[27]

Engels's framework of analysis gave too much credit to the autonomy of Britain's nineteenth-century bourgeoisie. These manufacturers and merchants were hardly free-standing agents of change, able to create a world for themselves. Laurence Harris is nearer the mark when he argues that 'The entry of the industrialists to the national political scene was contained within the shell of the old ideas of deference and *noblesse oblige*'.[28] Engels's merchants were never free of the allegiant culture, and this servitude was what caused their 'sense of inferiority'. The 'ancient drones' were not 'kept' by the merchants; rather the merchants were domesticated by the 'drones'. And, as went the manufacturers, so went all others with ambition and talent.

Richard Cobden would have been no less furious had he lived in the twentieth century. He would have seen the almost daily 'prostration' of capitalism and commerce at the feet of feudal sensibility. In his own political world he would have seen a particularly marked aspect of it. Two twentieth-century Prime Ministers, Harold Macmillan and Stanley Baldwin, stand out as exemplars. Macmillan was born into a solidly bourgeois family if ever there was one, but (through both marriage and personal volition) he was to transform himself and act out his life as though he was a scion of the landed aristocracy. Baldwin was also a man of business, and (like his successor, Neville Chamberlain) his instincts led him to see politics, and particularly foreign policy, through mercantilist eyes. His life at the top was to convert the 'businessman in politics' into the Tory aristocrat. His assertion that 'the one eternal sight of England' was 'a plough team coming over the brow of a hill' was the stuff of pure High Tory romanticism. Yet, for all his efforts, Baldwin was to be dismissed as 'the ironmonger' – and by Brendan Bracken of all people. During the century of paternalism, such social tragi-comedy knew no bounds.

Even by 1988, Cobden might still have been somewhat disconcerted. In that year, Market and Opinion Research International carried out a poll in which 100 top company directors cast their votes for Britain's 'most impressive industrialist'. Of the top ten 'stars of the boardroom' who emerged from the poll, three were peers, eight were knights, and only Alan Sugar and Denys Henderson were still, as the term goes, 'plain Misters'.[29] Of course, ten years into Thatcher's era, personal achievement was becoming its own reward (and less in need of feudal sanctification). And peerages and knighthoods were often simply additional aids for both domestic and international business networking. Yet such a sanctification continued to send out all the wrong signals to a broader society still only emerging into the modern commercial world. The upwardly mobile could indeed jet upwards, but only straight back into the English past. Modern Britons had still not become their own men and women.

In 1983, Paul Theroux, the travel writer, could argue, following a visit to a village just outside Eastbourne:

> The English aristocracy has nearly always been recruited from the ranks of flatterers, cut-throats, boy friends, political pirates, and people of very conceited ambition. So it was not so strange that this blue valley on the coast of East Sussex was populated by wine-bibbing Lords who had formerly been Marxist union men named Jones and Brown.[30]

Many of these 'wine-bibbing' trade union lords, however, hardly 'prostrated' themselves in the usual manner. Whereas many of the men of commerce took peerages as part of a lifetime's process of social transformation, of denying their backgrounds, the trade unionists took peerages only for the money (the daily payment for attending the House of Lords). It amounted to a 'soulless liberal contract', not to a selling of the soul. Alan Bullock, in his biography of Ernest Bevin, tells of Bevin's incapability of wanting to be something other than he was. Bevin, declares Bullock, was 'his own man'; but, then, he was in his own words, 'a turn-up in a million'.[31]

By the 1980s, this feudal benediction of commerce and politics (and, thus, feudalism's psychological power within the nation) remained evidence of the fact that Britain had still not yet become a fully developed bourgeois society. It also highlighted a key, and uniquely British, class problem which lingered on, even though the century of paternalism was over.

A question of class

The Times, as late as 1 July 1988 (not 1888) could report that:

> This evening, 17 year old Zara Williams will attend her first ball of the season. Clad in her brand-new strapless gown, groomed and polished to perfection, she will follow in the dance steps of her mother, grandmother and great grandmother . . . of the 200 youngsters invited to her party, Candida will know most of the girls and about 40 per cent of the boys whose names her mother got from The List. This coveted document is compiled by The Tatler's social editor . . . Petra, studying for her A-levels says: 'There are 60 million people in Britain, and of them 172 girls are doing the season. It's not very important really. I think the whole thing is rather forced and a bit old-fashioned.'

The substantial differences of resources between individuals and groups to which Petra alludes are, of course, common to all modern societies, as are the more subtle characteristics of status (superiority and inferiority) based upon a whole host of factors – both including and excluding wealth and income. What *is* uniquely British is the extent to which feudal sensibilities are still present in class distinctions. Because of the social pathology about 'mobility' in Britain, stark wealth and income differences are often obscured (and thereby implicitly denied) by a camouflage of more gentle and noble imagery drawn from the imaginary civility of the past. Hence, instead of portraying Zara, Candida and Petra simply as lucky rich girls, *The Times* paints a social portrait involving 'The List' and *The Tatler,* thus evoking less raw imagery than 'mere' money.

This softening of the raw edges of wealth distinction is part of a discretion about wealth which, in Britain, has been awe-inspiring in its success. Whereas in the United States the only interesting thing about property tycoon, Donald Trump, and fictitious oil ty-coon, 'J. R. Ewing', is their money, the same is not true of the super-rich in Britain. What is (evidently) still important about the Duke of Westminster is not that he owns large tracts of central London and is extremely wealthy, but that he is a Duke. What is (evidently) still interesting about Britain's richest family is not their wealth (how it was acquired, and how it is spent) but the fact that they are 'royal'.

The 'entry post' to status in Britain certainly demands money. In this sense, Britain can count itself amongst the brasher nations where money can buy most anything! Peculiarly, though, financial resources are not the locus of status itself. Ivor Richard suggests that, for Britons, class has mystery, that it can be seen only in the eye of the beholder. He argues that our 'perception of class depends ultimately upon the belief in the mind of the beholder that the object of his deference is a person who has a greater claim to authority or superiority'.[32] He is, no doubt, right. Yet there is a subsidiary question: what kind of person is invested by the modern British as an 'object' of deference? The sad fact is that the century of paternalism has led us to invest as 'objects' of deference not those with money, but rather those with the largely intangible or unattainable characteristics (titles, manners and speech) associated with inherited authority.

'Attainable' attributes of status (like money or, in a free society, political power) are, of course, ultimately democratic. In a modern economy, almost everyone – apart, that is, from those groups discriminated against, and the physically and mentally disabled – can, over their life-time, at least *improve upon* the amount of money and power they hold. Liberal democratic capitalism is thus socially progressive. It wants to know only 'the colour of your money'. The 'colour of your skin', or, indeed, gender, reli-gion, race or background, are irrelevant criteria. In other words, within a regime of liberal capitalism, the public rhetoric (at least) is fundamentally egalitarian: 'Anyone' can make money. 'Everyman', in the words of the American populist, Huey P. Long, 'Can Be A King.'

In Britain, 'Everyman' is not only *not* a King; 'Everyman' is *not* even a citizen (possessed, as citizens are, of defined rights). Even a decade into Thatcher's era, Britain's great illiberal vice has remained the stubborn fact that it has continued to allot status to the 'unattainable' and 'intangible'. Thus, the country excludes its population not only from the status of citizenship, but also even from believing that, by the measurable yardsticks of work or achievement, they can improve their status. This, in turn, only reinforces the paternalist culture of low personal horizons and ambitions. As long as status is not linked, no matter how tenuously, to merit (that is, to some kind of work and creativity), then, inevitably, it will remain associated with its opposite – mediocrity, idleness and stupidity. And, in turn (in a downward spiral), the mediocre, idle and stupid will remain role models to be emulated.

The clever high Tory theorists of cultural pessimism oft-times consider most people to be, indeed, mediocre, idle or stupid. They argue therefore that a society which exalts work and achievement (rewarding these attributes with status) will only create a widespread sense of failure. This convenient formulation has underpinned paternalist ideology throughout the century of paternalism. It rules out a discriminating society: one in which workers, achievers and creators are encouraged and rewarded, and those who cannot work are cared for. Instead, it fosters an undiscriminating social ethos in which a paternalist elite exhibits an all-embracing 'compassion' for the totality of 'one nation'. In the model of the nation as an estate, 'Everyman' is not allowed citizenship, but 'Everyman' is allotted 'compassion'. This is the ideology which created the modern *universalist* welfare state, in which 'Everyman' can claim benefits irrespective of income or wealth. 'Everyman' is thus both a part of the state and also owned by it. Thus 'Everyman' is made dependent. And a sense of dependence, of course, induces a sense of inferiority (or a lack of worth).

A question of worth

Notions of worth (or, rather, unworthiness) are at the very core of the deeply insidious class system and sensibility which British paternalism has handed down to its children as their legacy.

Britain's peculiar system of social apartheid (in which people from different classes are cut off from each other both physically and culturally, and rarely mix) has always been unpleasing to a democratic temperament. By the 1970s – after two decades of relative economic decline and an increasing ability to compare Britain with more liberal and prosperous Western countries – its features had turned ugly. Britain was beginning to assume the proportions of a Latin American social profile (one in which some of the richest people in the Western world shared a small territory with some of the poorest).

During the century of paternalism the left-wing reaction against this ugliness led to a fixation with the class issue which focused solely upon inequalities of resources. Socialists argued that all would be well if only the productive process was socialized. Social democrats suggested that Britain's class system would be eroded if the economic rewards from the capitalist system were redistributed by the state. Yet, both these approaches – the governing passions of a generation of left-wing intellectuals – had little to say about the corrosive social and psychological inequalities (questions of unequal dignity and worth) which have marked out British social relations ('our class system') as unique.

Although the British left proclaimed a belief in an egalitarian society 'where all men were equal', they could simply not bring themselves to see that neither common ownership nor state-led redistribution would begin to solve Britain's fundamental problems of class; and certainly not whilst the more general structures of paternalism remained in place. Ultimately, it came down to a misreading on the part of the left about what an egalitarian culture or society, in fact, amounts to. Equality of resources, or economic 'levelling', does not make an egalitarian society. After all, economic equalities can be enforced under a benevolent despot who locks up his citizens, or secured by a paternalist state which denies citizenship.

The feudal notion – that some people were 'worth more' than others – was overthrown *not* by socialist revolution, but rather by democratic revolution. It was the democratic age which produced the egalitarian society; for, as political democracy replaced feudalism, there emerged a social (or public) recognition of the equality of human *worth*, of a fundamental moral equality inhering in all human beings within the society. This democratic notion of human equality was made specific both by the concept of citizenship and by the later emergence of 'one man, one vote'. Britain, having stood aside from the democratic revolutions of the eighteenth century, is still only (as argued in this book) a 'half-democracy'. The country's present-day subjects possess 'one man, one vote', but not citizenship.

This 'half-democracy' reflects itself in a quasi-feudal social sensibility, one still largely untouched by modern democratic sentiments of equality. The British people still exhibit, at all levels of society, alarmingly prevalent feelings of inferiority and superiority, deeply held personal convictions that one is more (or less) worthy than others.

What is democratic man to make of the mentality of a London hairdresser who, when asked whether Prince Charles should speak out on public issues, does not defend the right of all to free speech, but, rather, thinks it proper for 'better' people to air their views?[33] Alternatively, what is democratic man to make of a country in which the majority of the inhabitants can still be described as 'the common people'. (A nice vignette of this feudal social pathology of modern Britain appeared in the normally egalitarian *Independent* in January 1988. Under a head-line proclaiming 'Woodland "King" Fights To Save Ancient Rights', it reported: 'Deep in Gloucestershire's Forest of Dean a "King" is fighting for the common people's ancestral rights over an ancient woodland'. Hence, even as the third millennium approaches, a modern newspaper feels that it can best explain a battle over prop-erty rights only by reference to medieval sensibility and imagery: it is a 'king' who fights for 'rights'; there is a unity between 'crown' and 'common people'.)[34]

What, too, is to be made of the perpetual upper-class assump-tion that 'everybody' has the same lifestyle, standards and values as 'one' does. The notorious quote from prosecutor Griffiths Jones when addressing the *jury* during the *Lady Chatterley's Lover* obscenity trial was but a hilarious example of a more general attitude. 'Frankly,' he asked, 'is this a book you'd want your wife and servants to read?'[35]. Put another way, the assumption that 'everyone' has servants is really an assumption that those who don't do not in fact exist, not anyway as equals.

Simon Raven has neatly captured the sense of social superiority bred into Britain's army officers.

> I want to make clear how little the average officer regards himself as a professional man giving orders by virtue of his professional status, and how strongly such an officer is convinced, despite the

fact that his origins may be middle class or even lower in the social scale, that he has somehow been given the absolute and *personal* right to command, that this right is somehow rooted in him as a person as firmly as such a right was deemed to be rooted in a feudal overlord.[36]

This description of what Raven calls 'the feudal nature of the contemporary officer' could easily be applied more widely. Innate (or what Raven calls 'personal') sources of superior feelings have been inculcated into generations of British youth by that most impressive institution of paternalism, the English public school. The century of paternalism produced what amounted to a public school caste which one observer argues has been 'rooted in its own conception of superior, God-given status'.[37] Public schoolboys were made to feel, and felt, special. Status thus became *inherent*, rather than being dependent upon merit, talent and work. And those young men inculcated with 'superior, God-given status' were bound (notwithstanding their own excellences) to patronize those not so blessed: and, indeed, to patronize merit, talent and 'the work ethic' both in themselves and in others. In fact, an enquiry into why professional and technical expertise has been so undervalued in Britain need look no further than to the mental framework imposed upon these children of paternalism, and, through them, upon the rest of society.

Strangely, the considerable body of criticism aimed at these schools tends to concentrate on defects other than their function as a transmission-belt for the values and structures of paternalism. Modern socialist criticism of the public schools centres around the fee-paying aspect, the creation of an elite by parental income. An egalitarian criticism, however, would concern itself with the social consequences of the *type* of education which many of these schools still tend to perpetuate. The type of education deployed by public schools will continue to matter because they will, well into the next century, help to set the moral tone and social manners of a portion of Britain's educational elite. Thus, fee-paying or not, an unreconstructed paternalist ethos will still allow the social virus of inherent superiority to be passed into the nation's blood-stream.

Such deeply held sensibilities of superiority not only offend against democratic principles; they have also wrought a huge economic cost upon the wider nation.

A question of accent

Britain's soul-destructive inequalities of worth (the stubborn persistence of feelings of superiority and inferiority based upon class) are only compounded by the way in which the British can still 'assess' the 'class' of someone almost in an instant.

Not much has changed since George Orwell, in the aftermath of the Second World War, concluded that 'the great majority of the people can still be placed in an instant by their manners, clothes and general appearance'. Four decades later, Robert Chesshyre, after returning to Britain from America, found that:

> Looking around, I realised with a shock that, although I had been living in the United States for over three years, I could nonetheless make a shrewd guess at the circumstances of most of my fellow-travellers – their education, their income, their prejudices, their place in the pecking order, even perhaps where they took their holidays. It was not something I had been able to do in the States – neither, several friends told me later, could Americans – and I had grown accustomed to being around people less easy to read. [38]

Yet, even more than 'manners, clothes and general appearance', it is accent which identifies 'station and rank'. Shaw's dictum that 'it is impossible for an Englishman to open his mouth without making some other Englishman despise him' still holds. [39] That Britons are still 'branded on the tongue' (and that the tongue represents the most pronounced symbol of inequality of worth amongst them) is still probably the most insidious of all the cultural effects of the age of paternalism.

This question of accent and class so prods (as does little else) the deeply undemocratic exposed raw nerve of the culture of paternalism that it is often too delicate to discuss or handle. Britons themselves, once they have lived abroad, tend (no matter their own social background or political inclination) to agree about its corrosive social effects. Ivor Richard, after official diplomatic stints in New York and Brussels, could suggest that 'the moment a person opens his mouth, certain common attitudes come into play'. [40] Entrepreneur Miles Copeland appeared shocked to discover, on a trip back to Britain, that simply watching the television coverage of the 1986 Greenwich parliamentary by-election could, from the accent displayed by each candidate, tell him to which party each belonged. [41]

Yet, apart from the occasional mention, the subject of accent still remains taboo: a kind of guilty little secret which few wish to reveal. The one remarkable postwar exception occurred when Bernard Shaw's Professor Higgins (with his disdain for 'verbal class distinctions' in *My Fair Lady*) reached millions, but only through the glossy wrapping of a musical. Few of the great works of British social history or analysis consider the question at all. In E. P. Thompson's *History of the English Working Class* the subject is not mentioned. More recent social analysis – predominantly marxist in orientation – considers the issue frivolous and unimportant. Anthony Crosland alluded to it, but that was all. Even Richard Hoggart (whose works come closest to connecting language and accent with social stratification) tends to concentrate upon the horizontal accent distinctions across regional Britain, rather than the vertical distinctions.

The modern British literary scene also tends to leave the subject of accent and class alone. Of course, it is alluded to in a thousand detective stories, but the pungent, biting, social novel seems to be a thing of the past. In particular, no one seems prepared to take on what really is a sitting target for humour: what Ivor Richard calls 'that mode of speaking in which it is believed most powerful or superior people communicate with each other'.

The reasons for this reluctance are not difficult to fathom. Most social critics or literary figures are, of course, upper strata themselves or aspire to become so (and, unlike George Orwell, make no serious effort to immerse themselves in anything different). The 'proper accent' is still, alarmingly, a passport to success; and writers are amongst the most socially aspirant group in British society. By dwelling upon the subject, they might seem 'whining' or, worse, 'betray' their origins.

There is also very little that anyone, even social engineers, can *do* about accent. Attempts to become more socially egalitarian often seem forced and patronizing. The fact that the BBC has made a conscious attempt to 'import' regional accents into its national news broadcasting begs the question as to why such accents were not prominent, through normal democratic pressure, in the first place. [42]

Such lack of serious attention to the problem of accent has obscured the fact that, intriguingly, Britain's 'pukkah' accent of authority (like British paternalism's ceremonials) is of recent vintage. In the more liberal and socially fluid environment of pre-collectivist Victorian Britain many eminent figures retained their regional accents throughout their life-time. For instance,

> Sir Robert Peel (Harrow and Oxford, one of England's most famous Conservative Prime Ministers, never disguised his Midlands speech. Lord Stanley, later Eighteenth Earl of Derby (Rugby and Cambridge), spoke a 'sort of Lancashire patois'. His Liberal opponent William Gladstone, spent his childhood in Liverpool and his Lancashire 'burr' survived both Eton and Oxford, which suggests he was under virtually no social pressure to lose it. Even at Eton, the shrine of English private education, the Reverend J. L. Joynes, one of the poet Swinburne's tutors, is known to have pronounced 'died' as 'doyed', and to have attacked the 'oidle' in his sermons. All these idiosyncracies were noticed, but they were not stigmatised.[43]

Oddly enough, the kind of accent today's Britons would associate with the 'upper class' – the standard form of authoritative speech – was not only *imposed*, but this imposition coincided (almost precisely) with the strange death of liberal England, and the victory of paternalism over democracy. The need for a civil service for the Empire, and for 'outward and visible signs of belonging'[44] to a governing caste which would rule it, helped forward the need to standardize authoritative speech. The Education Act of 1870 was a key event, for it entrenched the English public schools into the educational infrastructure of imperial needs. And once these schools became the breeding ground for imperial governance, a new 'suitable' accent of imperialism appeared on the scene. The contrast between the English speech of the public school educated caste between the 1890s and 1870s was, reportedly, 'startling'.[45] The type of standard received speech which emerged – precise, un-generous, un-engaging, high-pitched, controlled, throwaway, non-confrontational, un-get-at-able, precious and slightly fey – simply reflected what was considered to be an appropriate governing ethos for the management of late Empire. Thus, paternalism had its language.

There was nothing particularly feudal in the tones adopted, save that the lightness and trippingness was more evocative of rural than industrial England, of birds rather than engines. What *was* feudal was the notion that speech patterns should accord with gradations of the social hierarchy: that a separate and identifying attribute of the lordly cultivated Englishman – 'one who can move his jaws and not swallow his words whole'[46] – should be established, and indeed, imposed.

By the 1890s, accent levelling amongst the imperial class was not only applied from above by the public school teachers. Peer pressure from among public schoolboys themselves became a powerful incentive for a new boy to acquire the approved tone of what later came to called Received Pronunciation (RP). This emerging RP became both more widespread and more entrenched because of imitation by the upwardly mobile of the day. Also, a distinction emerged between two types of RP: the mainstream version, 'unmarked RP', and the elite version, 'marked RP'. In the process of identifying the marked RP version, Professor Alan Ross coined his famous and controversial distinction between U and non-U, observing along the way that 'among European languages, English is, surely, the most suited to the study of linguistic class distinctions'.[47]

In 1920, the BBC (fully conscious of its monopoly power over information and manners in an emerging mass society) took a decisive step towards entrenching RP in the public mind as a 'right' and 'better' way to pronounce English words. Its Advisory Committee on Spoken English became a battleground over which the future of RP was fought out. It not only sanctioned standardization, but made standardized speech 'proper'. This single accent of authority was to last for at least for fifty years. From then on, the British – whether in Geordieland, Scouceland, Brummieland or Cockneyland – were asked to 'receive' the word. It amounted to an Orwellian attempt at social control, the single most 'totalitarian' exercise of the century of paternalism.

The received accent of British paternalism has carried on into the post-imperial period. In political life it has been 'received' by an array of politicians of all parties and backgrounds. Its 'reception' was still coming through strongly in the 1970s and 1980s amongst those politicians educated at the height of its influence. 'Edward Heath', declare McCrum and his colleagues, 'took elocution lessons to enhance his acceptability to the Conservative Party'.[48] Margaret Thatcher did the same and so did Roy Jenkins, who exhibited perhaps the most extreme form of the genre. The question remains: is there any other country in the world where thousands amongst the intelligent, talented and resourceful could (even sub-consciously) engage in such a terrifying self-abnegation as to change their accent? Also, can there be a more potent testimony to the continued, almost totalitarian, cultural power of upper-class manners than the fact that those from outside its breeding grounds can never (at least in public) be entirely themselves?[49]

The paternalist century has thus made actors of us all. Yet, the cost – for those who eschew the injunction 'to thine own self be true' – is much greater still. For, to alter (or change) the speech patterns of youth inevitably entails an alteration (or change) in personality, attitudes and values. Thus did paternalism reinforce itself. The century of paternalism has made us all paternalists.

A *ruling class*

'To Govern Is To Serve' proclaimed the feudal newspeak of the slogan perched high over the Conservative Party Conference platform as late as 1984. Such an aphorism is feudal in the sense that it attempts to unite opposites in an organic totality, binding 'together' rulers and ruled. It is 'newspeak' in the sense that, for modern democratic man, no such irrational formulas can seriously be expected to exist. 'To govern is to govern', and 'To serve is to serve'.

For High Tory England to survive, however, amidst what it must see as the holocaust of Thatcherite neo-liberalism, 'governorship' or 'rulership' must continue to inspire or, at least, be accepted. Traditionally, paternalists have attempted to 'justify' the need for a ruling class by extolling the positive virtues of inequality (so that the folks below could at least *understand* why they should remain permanently both less wealthy and less free.) Proselytizing in favour of inequality is now rare however – and, in modern times, it has almost assumed the proportions of a paternalist vice which can hardly speak its name. Instead, 'rulership' tends to be justified more neutrally, by assertions that a ruling class will always be needed. After all:

> The central thread – indeed the veritable backbone and spinal column – uniting all the various articulations of the Tory idea from

Tudor days into the twentieth century, through Bolingbroke, Burke, Disraeli and Randolph Churchill to Leopold Amery and R. A. Butler, is the commitment to authoritative leadership as a permanent social necessity. According to the Tory idea, whatever the economic or political order of the nation, a governing class is necessary – as much in the age of democracy, mass parties, and the welfare state as in the age of monarchy and aristocracy.[50]

High Tory journalist, the late David Watt, once enjoined the British (though not necessarily others) to live under 'some kind of elite'. He argued, as late as the mid-1980s, that, although

> Our class system is dying . . . only a very large, rich country can maintain stability and efficiency without some kind of elite, preferably as open as possible to talent, but still confident of its abilities and legitimacy. One of our problems is that our elite has lost that confidence, and many of those who have pulled and are pulling it down have neither the real self-confidence nor the instinctive 'feel' to take its place.[51]

Such a stark commentary gave the High Tory game away. For them, the highest priority of modern political statecraft is to ensure the 'legitimacy' not of the democratic state and society, but rather of the 'elite' – in the name, of course, of maintaining its own definition of 'stability' and 'efficiency'.

How revealing, too, to be told that England's world is divided between those who possess 'real self-confidence' or 'feel', and those who do not! Yet, one is lifted up here by Watt only in order to be let down. For the 'real' self-confidence, and the 'feel' which is referred to, are never explained or described. It is simply asserted. It *inheres*, old boy!

Of course, there was a sense in which Watt was, partly, right. The 1970s did witness the arrival on the scene of such an insurgent counter-elite in the form of a socialist vanguard movement; and, for a period, this insurgency managed to control the levers of power within the Labour movement and sought, through it, to guide the wider nation. High Tories were, rightly, terrified rigid. Yet Watt's fear was not that these insurgents were an elite, nor that they were 'socialists', but rather that they lacked 'self-confidence' and 'feel', an assertion which even a tangential relationship to the potential revolutionaries involved would have swiftly disproved.

Now that the Battle for Britain of the 1970s and 1980s is behind us, it can begin to reveal the story of how an old High Tory world crumbled: how, indeed, Watt's elite 'lost its confidence' as it fought a rearguard action with two new arriviste forces, both of which despised it. That the battle for the High Tory succession was won by the neo-liberal radicals rather than the marxists was in no small measure due to the fact that the High Tory paternalists threw their weight into the balance against the marxists.

They only did so, however, because they saw Thatcher's radicals as the lesser of two evils. It was the difference, for them, between the guillotine, or being put out to pasture. But, from the pasture, eerie calls for a return to a ruling class still echo across the valleys. Few give voice to as reactionary a sound as the editor of *The Sunday Telegraph* when in 1988 he argued, in a leader, that: 'there is nothing to stop the idea of a socially superior class once again resuming its old civilising role'.[52]

Ten years into Thatcherism, there is, on the contrary, *much* 'to stop the idea' of a return to a ruling class mentality. First, faith in 'rulership' seems increasingly incongruent with the new liberal age. A 'ruling class' is now associated in the public mind with an imperial Britain which is receding – not only from historical memory, but also from the imagination. More crucially, the traditional idea of rulership by a 'socially superior' class is now open to that most devastating of rejections: unfavourable comparison. Until the 1980s, the British had no reason to believe that any form of governance other than paternalism actually existed, let alone could work. But, now that a non-paternalist regime is a reality – and, under it, life carries on as normal (and, for some, much better) – the old magic of a class-run society loses its allure. Indeed, it can be tolerated as a kind of fabulous and enchanting national antique (worthy of framing and hanging in a High Tory museum of late Empire conceit, before, that is, the genre is forgotten).

The more sophisticated of Britain's paternalists have, however, rarely openly advocated the need for the country to be run by a 'socially superior' ruling class. Such naked propaganda on behalf of privilege has, indeed, been eschewed for some decades. Instead, the defence of rulership has been conducted in more acceptable rhetorical garb: by exhortations in favour of tradition, of the 'traditional way of doing things'. A holy trinity of 'tradition', 'habit', and the 'familiar way of doing things' is much more likely to tap popular feeling in Britain than is a direct appeal to class rule; and particularly so if the virtue of 'tradition' is counterpoised to liberal modernity's (and Thatcherism's) cold-hearted 'abstract theorizing'.

William Waldegrave, the 'impeccably aristocratic' younger son of a twelfth earl, educated at Eton, Oxford, and Harvard (and no mean 'theorist' himself), summed up the paternalist argument against Thatcherite liberal economic theory this way: the Conservative tradition had the force of relevance because it protected 'us' from 'the pathology of the forcible imposition of theory on people', and 'since no theory of organisation is complete, trust in this kind of theory should be abandoned . . . political advice, derived from Liberal economic theory . . . leaves governors and its own adherents always frustrated at the distance between their model of the world and reality'.[53] In consequence, 'we' should rely upon tradition instead of 'theory' – although the precise character of the tradition exalted, let alone a description of which of Britain's many traditions should inform us, was never fully spelt out.

Michael Oakeshott's metaphor of the state and society as a boat adrift in a 'boundless and bottomless sea' and needing to be guided safely to shore, was a popular image which underpinned a profoundly High Tory philosophical disposition. Society (Britain) as a 'boat' inferred an organic unified entity, encasing all of its inhabitants together with one single purpose; the vessel, particularly if it was to come safely to anchor, obviously needed a captain and 'other ranks'; the 'boundless and bottomless sea' was the unstructured anarchy of free market modernity. In order to reach safety, *practical* leadership, not crazed theoreticians, was needed. It amounted to a clever fusion of the ideas of traditional authority and more modern 'practical' technology, if not science.

Alongside this fashion of anti-theory, British paternalist 'theory' attempted to devalue the validity of human reason, and, by implication, reject the central postulates of the Enlightenment itself. Ian Gilmour's *Inside Right: A Study in Conservatism* called up from the deep such illustrious English thinkers as Burke, Bolingbroke and Disraeli in aid of the view that 'cold' reason could be dangerous, that passion and emotion were more humankind's guiding spirit, and thus needed to be tamed: all again by an unarticulated social 'tradition'.[54]

T. E. Utley, a friend of Gilmour's who, although a traditionalist, successfully straddled both the paternalist and Thatcherite wings of the Conservative party, virtually *campaigned* during the last years of his life for a moderation of neo-liberal rationalism. He argued that 'Human nature is violent and predatory and can be held in check only by three forces, the Grace of God, the fear of the gallows, and the pressure of a social tradition, subtly and unconsciously operating as a brake on human instinct'.[55] Again, the character of the 'social tradition' that was sought was unstated.

Utley was a major political and personal influence upon a school of young socially aspirant right-wing journalists who supported Thatcher but not the modernizing aspects of her revolution. He also, in the final months of his life, suggested that Roger Scruton be taken more seriously by the Conservative party as a coming Tory philosopher. Scruton viewed the whole modernization and liberalization aspects of Thatcherism with disdain. His journal, *The Salisbury Review* (together with some of the leading figures within the Tory Philosophy Group, particularly the philosopher-aesthete, John Casey) became the focal point for an attempted comeback by traditional paternalist Toryism. *The Salisbury Review* attempted to provide fresh ammunition to the older High Tory attack upon liberal reason and theory. 'We should', it urged, 'align our perception of the legitimacy of government with the unfathomable given-ness of human life, and so abolish that fruitless quest for abstract principles which inspires and embitters the constitutional theorists of liberalism.'[56]

'Given-ness', like 'tradition', was not explained or developed. 'Given-ness', as this tricky word implies, is simply *given*, and, being 'unfathomable', is conveniently beyond the reach of mere mortals. This rather obscurantist philosophy was the very stuff of High Toryism. In essence, it refused intellectual engagement. Its militant mysticism essentially told the 'embittered theorists' of liberalism (who had to include not only the great English liberal thinkers of the eighteenth and nineteenth century, the founders of the American republic, and anyone who wanted to think and question) that it would be best if they abandoned the estate of politics altogether. Politics, it tended to assume, was a preserve best left to those who could take part in the ancient ceremonies of magic, a ruling class that understood such things.

Beyond this, though, the whole High Tory attempt to set paternalism in a philosophic context put paternalists at a severe disadvantage. In attempting to enter into the modern game of theory, reason and argument, they were bound to lose. Their stated virtues (of tradition, 'given-ness', of a higher and nobler order of things not revealed or revealable to the rest of us) were best left unstated: as existing, rather than explicable, truths.

The 'power of tradition' either means something to people or it doesn't. It cannot be inculcated, except perhaps in totalitarian regimes, and then only for a while. A 'ruling class' either exists and is obeyed; or it dies. It cannot have proponents! The fact was that by the 1980s Britain's traditional 'ruling class' was indeed dying, incapable of resurrection, least of all by philosophers of magic.

'Culture' against the revolution

Of all the points of resistance to the new radicalism the fiercest is to be found amongst Britain's cultural elites. Although art, literature and music are politically neutral, they are created, interpreted, performed and consumed by *people*. And people, naturally, have political opinions. In Britain, as in other countries, the world of culture has its hierarchies, and its various *loci* of power and influence. The century of paternalism has seen to it that 'culture', like other areas of British life, is essentially a 'top-down' affair, with a relatively small number of people transmitting their tastes, opinions and predilections 'downwards' to the wider public.

There has always, of course, been an innate conflict between a bourgeois social order and 'culture'. Ever since the term 'culture' was invented by Immanuel Kant, culture (whatever it might be) has been thought of as high and profound, 'something before which we need to bow'[57]; and as something purer (both spiritually and aesthetically) than the 'selfish' and materialistic concerns of other aspects of human nature. Rousseau considered the bourgeoisie of his day particularly 'selfish', without even the pure simplicity of natural selfishness. 'Bourgeois man', he asserted, 'makes contracts hoping to get the better of those with whom he contracts, and thus he corrupts morality, the essence of which is to exist for its own sake.'[58] This tension between 'culture' and 'materialism' (between the character of the soul and the mind, on the one hand, and the more prosaic physical needs of the emerging masses in the democratic age, on the other) has even raised questions about whether high culture can co-exist with modern democratic society.

Democracy has not only introduced mass taste and popular culture, but is also egalitarian – denying (theoretically at least) that any aspect of life is superior to any other. The great historian of democracy, Alexis De Tocqueville, once declared that 'a permanent feature of democracy, always and everywhere, is a tendency to suppress the claims of *any* kind of superiority, conventional or natural, essentially by denying that there is superiority'.[59] Thus, in democracy, there is only diversity. Everything is as good as anything else, it is only a question of taste. It is hardly surprising that cultural enthusiasts must, often subconsciously, feel that the democratic age is their enemy.

In Britain, though, the clash between culture (on the one hand) and democratic mass society (on the other), as might be expected from the century of paternalism, has assumed a social twist. Culture and democracy do not compete as differing aspects of the human personality, with culture attempting to establish its ascendancy by virtue of its *inherent* superiority. Rather, the cultural enthusiast attempts to gain for himself (and for culture) a *social* superiority too.

This social superiority can be glimpsed in the way in which writers and artists have tended to see themselves somewhat self-consciously – as a group, or a class, decidedly separate from the rest of the populace. E. M. Forster exhibited this problem of self-consciousness (and, indeed, 'group consciousness) in his tract, *Two Cheers for Democracy*. He could write about artists and writers as being in some way decisively separate from the rest of the population, referring to them as 'cultivated people', and as 'us':

> What we have got is (roughly speaking) a little knowledge about books, pictures, tunes, runes, and a little skill in their interpretation. Seated beside our gasfires, and beneath our electric bulbs, we inherit a tradition which has lasted for more than three thousand years . . . judging by the noises through the floor our neighbour in the flat above doesn't want our books, pictures, tunes, runes, anyhow doesn't want the sorts we recommend. Ought we to bother him? When he is hurrying to lead his own life, ought we to get in his

way like a maiden aunt, our arms, as it were, full of parcels, and say to him 'I was given these specially to hand to you . . . Sophocles, Velasquez, Henry James . . . I'm afraid they're a little heavy, but you'll get to love them in time . . . they're really important, they're culture'. [60]

This picture of a cultural intelligentsia huddled around gas fires, and under naked light-bulbs in garrets, appears to the contemporary eye (which glimpses a more lavishly endowed cultural intelligentsia – in the universities, the BBC and the 'quality newspapers') as somewhat old-fashioned. It was also, on Forster's part, somewhat phoney (Forster lived in a grand flat in Kensington). Even so, Forster's picture of the artist as a humble seeker after truth and beauty, cannot disguise a more arrogant mental apparatus on his part – one which saw two utterly separated humans (one, indeed, maybe possessed of less humanity than the other), one with culture, the other without. It was little wonder that a 'Third Cheer For Democracy' was not forthcoming.

It is not a long jump from 'separate' to socially superior. This attempt to establish for the cerebral not only a distinctive character, but a higher social authority, has been described by Ernest Gellner. He suggests that England's cultural intellectuals often see themselves as: 'a sub-group consisting of people who belong to, or emulate, the upper class in manner; who differentiate themselves from the heartier rest of the upper class by a kind of heightened sensibility and preciousness, and, at the same time, from the non-U kind of intelligentsia by a lack of interest in ideas, argument, fundamentals or reform'. [61] (Here, 'heartier' is a term, deriving from the public school usage of the paternalist era, to denote a sporting character (normally a rugby player) who would tend to 'bully' less robust types. The term 'Non-U' merely means socially unacceptable.) Yet, democratic society inherently challenges this social status. The arrival of the masses (and mass culture) is seen as usurping the position of a revered class – not from its cultural domain but, rather, from the lofty social position which the domain of 'culture' tended to inhabit in pre-democratic epochs.

Artistic disaffection with democracy (and the bourgeoisie) is particularly pronounced in modern Britain. This is partly to do with the fact that during the century of paternalism the cultural intelligentsia (who, like all others, had their assigned and assured place) were virtually a protected class. During the Thatcher era, however, the emerging bourgeois society no longer assigns a place – let alone one that is socially superior – to the cultured class. All, now, tends to be more random.

Socially conscious artists and writers also tend to find a confident bourgeois society somewhat difficult to understand, and, consequently, to deal with. Thatcher herself typifies a new generation of the upwardly mobile who are less socially insecure than their forebears, and, consequently, do not need to be 'socially sanctified' by the world of art; nor do they accept what Marcus Cunliffe once described as the avant-garde notion that 'intellectuals know better than their society'.[62]

The Vice Chancellor of London University once suggested that Mrs Thatcher had upset the educational establishment not so much because she had allowed the higher education budget to be cut in real terms, but, because, as she displays no special interest in the political opinions of educators, 'she has trampled on their egos as well'. As a consequence, many of the cultural intelligentsia's criticisms of Thatcher have an element of unconcealed condescension and snobbery about them, the wounded riposte of the usurped to the usurper. The indictments tend to be moral, and laced with the undertone of a charge of 'philistinism'. The poet Peter Porter described Margaret Thatcher as 'arrogant, tasteless and vain'; playwright Jonathan Miller depicted her as 'loathesome, repulsive in almost every way'; author Jonathan Raban bemoans her lack of interest in novels and devalues her appearances at the opera as 'a social occasion not an intellectual pursuit'; former National Theatre Director, Peter Hall, sees Britain under her leadership as being taken over by 'American-owned companies spewing out plastic programmes . . . universities teaching nothing but science and technology'.

In the United States, the cultural-cum-intellectual condescension to Reaganism tended to approach its prey by attacks upon Reagan's 'simplicity' and 'lack of sophistication'. The Grade B movie actor was subtly counterpoised to the 'morally superior' government of opinion – which displays 'concern' instead of 'selfishness' and 'the public good' instead of private interest.

In Britain, the condescension also takes on a social form. Playwright Peter Nichols dislikes Thatcher because, he has argued, she speaks 'for a new class of rising working-class Tories . . . the taxi-drivers and wealthy butchers'. He further explained that 'he had met a lot of them [taxi-drivers and wealthy butchers] in London when looking for a suitable school for his son'. Lady Warnock, Mistress of Girton College, Cambridge, was also reported as commenting that 'there was something quite obscene' about Thatcher's presence in Marks and Spencer (Britain's main clothing store for ordinary people) 'picking out another blouse with a tie at the neck'.[63]

Thus, in Britain's developing bourgeois society, 'culture' (to the extent to which it is organized and speaks collectively) is inevitably a conservative social force. It tends to be hostile to social change (and new social groups) which it believes threaten its status; and hostile, too, to liberal economics which, inevitably, by rearranging the relationship between the private and public sectors (and by encouraging voluntarism in the financing of culture) erodes culture's public subsidy.

Britain's paternalistic epoch created a highly centralized public subsidy system for both higher education and the arts. British universities were funded directly by national government and, following the reforms of the 1970s, the polytechnics too were mainly financed by national taxation, although their funds were channelled through local government. The public subsidy for the arts was administered through the Arts Council set up in 1946. About a quarter of this national public subsidy was disbursed directly to national companies – primarily London-based – such as the Royal Opera House, the English National Opera, the National Theatre, the Royal Shakespeare Company, and the Royal Ballet. Local arts centres also received national government money. There was also an indirect public subsidy to the arts through the licence fee which funded the BBC.

As a result of this highly centralized and hierarchical disbursement apparatus, an educational and artistic bureaucracy (largely composed of a less than representative cross-section of civil servants, most of them indoctrinated during the high point of the paternalist era) was able to dominate the pattern of the nation's cultural development, and in a way which simply reinforced the dominant cultural ethos. Teachers, academics, writers, playwrights, actors and actresses, artists, painters, sculptors, all became enmeshed in a dependency culture which induced a general educated opposition to the more random and open funding mechanisms of a market system.

Consequently, the more commercially-minded society of the 1980s came to be seen as a direct threat to educational and artistic standards, rather than as an opportunity to create a more diverse cultural climate (one in which 'standards' would not be imposed by small cultural cadres but, rather, insisted upon by an informed citizenry). Yet, by the 1980s (at the fag end of the paternalist century) could it seriously be argued that Britain's educational and artistic 'standards' were, by international criteria, anything to boast about? The country did not possess a university of the first rank; nor was its contemporary artistic output any longer as globally impressive as its proponents often made out. British theatre still held centre stage. Yet, as one commentator remarked about contemporary British theatre (in an observation which could apply more widely throughout British cultural life):

> The skill and technical quality seem to disguise the fact that, as far as one can tell, little original creation is happening at the present time. It is almost as though this were an age that specialises in interpreting what past figures have said rather than saying anything itself. Is it perhaps an age which fears to speak out, which is afraid of commitment to any clear set of values?[64]

Contemporary English literature had also become less internationally impressive, certainly not 'the best in the world', certainly not a secure platform from which to launch political salvos against 'philistinism'. In fact, as Terry Eagleton argued,

> the paradox is . . . that with the exception of D. H. Lawrence the heights of modern English literature have been dominated by foreigners and émigrés: Conrad, James, Eliot, Pound, Yeats, Joyce . . . The unchallenged sway of non-English poets and novelists in contemporary English literature points to certain flaws and impoverishments in conventional English culture itself. That culture was unable, by its own impetus, to produce great literary art: the outstanding art which it achieved has been, on the whole, the product of the exile and the alien.[65]

By the 1980s, an examination of Britain's main cultural exports to the rest of the world would have revealed an unpleasant truth. The country's cultural output had largely descended to the interpretative and the presentational (dominated by a cultural industry which merely re-interpreted and re-presented to the world the great works of art from the British *past*).

A century of paternalist cultural governance – with its highly centralized control of the public purse strings, and its use of the force of social sanction to advance or hinder persons and forms – had taken its toll of contemporary British art. Not only had it restricted the very notion of what was 'good and 'bad', but it had also limited the public input. Consequently, we shall never know whether, had the whole ethos and structure been more democratic, a less interpretative and more creative contemporary 'culture' might have developed.

David Graham has argued that part of the problem with Britain's art establishment has been its fear of the popular:

> I have no fear of the tyranny of popular taste. But the discovery of popular taste is an exercise obscure to the intelligentsia, who are a conservative cultural force, educated in the thinking of a previous generation and determined to exploit their cultural capital. The intelligentsia would not have taken you or me to the Globe at Southwark: they would have taken us to a court mask. [66]

This fear of the popular is only part of the more general distaste on the part of the cultured class for democratic culture, and, indeed, for the artistic possibilities of democratic culture. Also, although 'we know that there is really no basis on whichh to tell other people what's good for them'[67] we feel that if we don't, artistic standards will slip, heralding a new dark age.

This anxiety about 'the popular' presents us with another paradox. Because of the fear of a new dark age, we tend to invest only in the past, remaining under its spell – beholden (according to taste) only to Shakespeare, Milton, Dickens and the Romantic poets. Consequently, as we feel there is nothing new to say, we say nothing that is new.

An insular disposition

The anti-democratic ethos which suffuses Britain's cultural establishment is only a reflection of the most damaging of all the social effects of class distinction in the century of paternalism, a seemingly endemic upper-class English attachment to exclusiveness. On one level, this is exhibited in the harmless fetish for clubs

– from the grand clubs of Pall Mall to the incestuous dining clubs of young aspirants at university. On another level, it has revealed itself somewhat more insidiously in those self-consciously intellectual interwar networks or coteries, ranging from the 'Bloombsury Nine' to the Cambridge Apostles.

The damage wrought to British cultural and intellectual life by this exclusiveness is rarely admitted. An anonymous writer, though, could argue that:

> The delight in excluding rather than including which is so characteristic of Britain's national culture has also deeply influenced the patterns of our intellectual life. In some instances this is blighted by an absurd kind of aristocratic privacy. Too many disciplines have clubbable standards which far exceed the standards of discrimination that can be justified by scientific or scholarly criteria. These powerful exclusionary instincts have to be modified if higher education is to reach out into our democracy to touch the whole people.[68]

But higher education is unlikely to 'reach out' into 'our democracy' whilst an exclusionary educational ethos still inhibits the country from either recognizing, or indeed creating, competing centres of excellence to Oxford and Cambridge.

A sense of the virtue of exclusiveness operates through another of the transmission belts of national culture, the BBC. On the one radio wavelength which the BBC has allocated to the public for serious music, Radio 3 purveys what one commentator described as: 'the famous knuckle sandwich: Mozart and Haydn with a filling of Schlumpnagel's Unstructured Opus For Computer and Strings'. This 'knuckle sandwich' is an appropriate example of a seemingly wilful BBC need to dilute the popular (in this case Mozart and Haydn) by eccentric obscurantism. Such a dilution helps to keep the audience figures down, and to encourage a sense of exclusiveness. And, when complaints are received about BBC music policy, the hapless complainants are often depicted as 'a bunch of philistines'[69], the favourite bugbear of the exclusive and cultivated.

Yet, as modern democratic man might ask, how was it that this upper-class cult of exclusiveness took hold? Part of the answer may lie in the inculcation in early life of a mental and social sensibility which has shunned directness, commitment and engagement. In the process, the upper-caste Englishman has developed an authoritative manner which (both to his compatriots and to foreigners alike) appears standoffish, overly self-contained, indeed almost 'withdrawn' from the world.

This 'withdrawn' personality is often exhorted as a virtue, as but an aspect of the 'Englishman's' noble reticence, shyness and sense of privacy. It has also been lauded as a social necessity – indeed a 'social good' – in a small and crowded island. Britain's upper classes may also have been tutored in repressing their emotions as part of the cult of 'rulership' inculcated at public school. 'Distance' and the 'withdrawn personality' may also have been induced (consciously or subconsciously) in order to cut off, and separate, rulers from ruled, as a supposed attribute of leadership. (In the end, of course, the authoritarianism of paternalist manners was self-defeating, creating a disposition amongst Britain's rulers which was not open to change, to new ideas, indeed to adaptation itself.)

This kind of assertive exclusivity was bred into young upper-class males by the paternalist public schools, which fostered in their pupils a notion of their exalted place in a separate educational structure, one which provided them with opportunities in life not available to others. Such a conscious education of separateness can only encourage an acceptance of exclusivity as a way of living. Malcolm Muggeridge, who attended Selwyn College Cambridge after Selhurst Grammar School, is reported as viewing his fellow students of this era with something approaching contempt – not because they had affairs with one another, but because of their separateness of being:

> Public schoolboys, whatever their particular school – from the most famous like Eton, to the most obscure – had a language of their own which I scarcely understood . . . The university, when I was there, was very much a projection of public school life and mores, and a similar atmosphere of homsexuality tended to prevail . . . I emerged unscathed. [70]

George Orwell also wrote eloquently on the subject in perhaps the most pointed essay ever written, from the inside, on public school life, 'Such, Such Were The Joys'. [71]

No serious discussion of the upper-class pathology of exclusiveness can be conducted without reference to the still largely closed world (and subject) of homosexuality. Homosexuality may, or may not be, 'le vice Anglais' (the joking accusation the Englishman tends to encounter at international conferences). Yet, there can be little doubt that Britain (during the century of paternalism) was unique in the stubborn insistence on the part of large numbers of its parents on consigning their sons to (mainly single-sex) boarding schools. This incarceration, as John Vaisey once put it, 'retarded heterosexuality' amongst Britain's narrowly drawn elite, even if it did not positively encourage homosexuality.[72] In any event, boarding schools produced an elite in which homosexuality was a pronounced aspect of life.

Homosexuals (whether from boarding school or not) tend to feel the need, because of continuing public antipathy, to hide their orientation; and a life time of furtiveness often ensues. This understandable culture of secrecy can also transform it-self into a cult of exclusivity. Secrecy, though, is usually self-defeating. Whilst homosexuality continues to hide from the world, the heterosexual population will continue to harbour suspicions of 'buggers' networks', indeed of conspiracies, and these tend to sur-face when people in leadership positions are thought of as having received special treatment because of their homosexuality. This particular conspiracy theory was recently given house room in a full-page article in *The Sunday Telegraph* entitled 'Is There A Homosexual Conspiracy?'[73]

The public school contribution to the withdrawn and detached personality may now be ending, but it will take years for the debilitating values it has fostered to work their way out of the system. A modern democrat does not have to agree with the prescription of the young Hugh Thomas, writing in 1959, to share his rage at the net effect of the older type of public schools upon Britain's national life. Thomas suggested that:

> We shall not be free of the Establishment frame of mind, permeating all aspects of life and society, and constantly re-appearing even when apparently up-rooted, until the public schools are completely swept away, at whatever cost to the temporary peace of the country.[74]

The cult of exclusiveness is not only the product of social arro-gance but also, paradoxically, of social insecurity (probably the obverse side of the same coin). England's traditionally privileged minorities could hardly have felt totally secure, or at home, in a country which was (during the century of paternalism) largely proletarian. This anxiety exhibited itself amongst the upper-class rich in their almost pathological abhorrence of overt displays of wealth or privilege. 'If you've got it, flaunt it' is certainly not an upper-crust English vice. The fear remains that, should wealth be 'flaunted', it will be expropriated by the majority who are not wealthy.

The cult of exclusiveness (of in-groups and out-groups, of 'U' and 'Non-U') can help explain how bourgeois society, and its associated liberal values of individualism and openness, is still suspect amongst large swathes of educated opinion. It certainly helps towards an explanation of how an earlier generation of upper-strata Englishmen in the interwar years (then the world's most privileged class) could have contained so many who were not only alienated from (but also actively loathed) the character and values of their own, wider, society. The historian, John Keegan, has argued that the Cambridge spies should be placed in this wider social context. They were, he suggested:

> . . . uniquely English, the products of a class-obsessed, over-secretive society. If they had been born in France they would have burnt out their radicalism in university politics . . . But, confronted as they were in this country by a culture of in-groups, each cherishing their own secrets, but conspiring automatically to defend the ethos of exclusivity, they opted for the one great contra-conspiracy that was in the market for recruits. The common thread . . . is the conspiratorial nature of communism. [75]

Keegan compared Britain with the United States:

> America is an open society in the largest sense. Its elites do not treat public life as an extension of the prefects' room or the club committee. And they do so because the nature of American democracy encourages a fullness of disclosure which still causes visible agony to their equivalents in Whitehall . . . Britain has never been a strong country in the way that America is today, and secrecy is one of its understandable defences.

The traitor, Anthony Blunt, was an almost perfect embodiment of this paternalist upper-class mix of collectivist sentiment, artistic sensibility, exclusiveness, snobbery and homosexuality. Blunt, though a communist, was also 'a snob about the Royal Family and he he hated the masses'. So reported George Zarnecki, a Polish colleague of Blunt's at the Courtauld Gallery, who was obviously somewhat bewildered by the British social scene. 'I remember' said Zarnecki, 'that he [Blunt] was thrilled when he was knighted.'[76]

As noted earlier, the upper-class paternalist culture of exclusivity was not particularly discriminating. It exhibited itself not only in an insular attitude towards 'the workers' or 'the middle classes', but also to *anything* beyond its narrowly drawn borders, including the world beyond Britain. How many purely British events are still depicted as 'moments in history' (as though what happens in Britain is of global consequence)? How often do we still refer (blithely, and without comparative information) to British institutions as 'the best in the world'? Alisdair Milne, whilst Director-General of the BBC, was once described in a serious national newspaper as possessing the 'most important job in the world'. This litany of excess and national self-centredness is long, but pride of place must still go to the mythic notion of Britain as 'the centre of the Commonwealth of nations':

> The conventional explanation of Britain's (or, better, England's) turning away from the world into narcissistic reverie, or exhibitionist violence, is still summed up most conveniently in Dean Acheson's aphorism: we have lost an empire but failed to find an alternative role. Not Europe, not a civilised and quietist insularity, not a rediscovery of nationhood in Britain's historical diversity. One escape route from this dilemma is to insist that we still have a kind of Empire – the Commonwealth of nations which continue to look up to us even if they are abominably rude much of the time.[77]

The insularity of the century of paternalism was often fostered unwittingly by the foreigners with whom Britons came into contact. Polite interest in things English is still often mistaken for awe. Foreign images of Britain – the cottage, the bowler hat, the nobility, the rustic beauty and the civil tranquillity – are deliberately cultivated by marketing firms for foreign audiences (as quaint amusements and diversions from the rigours of everyday life), but are often taken seriously, as accolades.

The insular disposition tends to become more pronounced the higher up the social ladder one proceeds. Ordinary people seem *interested* in foreign lifestyles, particularly if they are English-speaking and economically advanced. This explains the huge popular audiences for Australian and American soap operas, and the growing interest in foreign sport (particularly American football). Britain's social elites, however, remain militantly 'English': from the 'Britain is Best' cultural syndrome of the BBC, through to the pronounced xenophobia of the young Sloane Rangers.

At the very apex of English learning and scholarship, in the university environment of Oxford and Cambridge, where a measure of cultural breadth and cosmopolitanism might be expected, provincialism reigns. These ancient universities, although teeming with foreign students, tend (perhaps because of the foreign invasion) to be inward-looking places where traditional English customs and values are studiously protected. Stories abound of the insensitive and unwelcoming treatment meted out to foreigners. Witness one commentary by an American student about his time at Oxford, a viewpoint which, intriguingly enough, could easily have also been held by an average Briton:

> For most Americans [Oxford] is a social hell that either leaves you alone or traps you into being someone you are not in order to meet people. The most difficult thing for Americans in Oxford . . . is not how to complete two tutorials a week, but how to meet good, interesting English people and get the 'experience' they came for without compromising themselves.[78]

High Tory cultural ideology has tended not only to evoke, but also to encourage, a disposition towards the familiar. Lord Hugh Cecil could suggest that 'distrust of the unknown and the love of the familiar' should be nothing less than the guiding principle of the Conservative party. More recently, Michael Oakeshott has suggested, extravagantly, that 'change is a threat to identity, and every change is an emblem of extinction'.[79] This High Tory fear of the unknown hardly fits in with the image (certainly appropriate to Lord Hugh Cecil at the turn of the century, if not to Michael Oakeshott) of one of the world's most confident social groups, the English upper classes at the height of Empire. Yet, perhaps, there was something more at work here. For the fact is that the cultivation of 'the familiar' would serve towards instilling an acceptance of the social status quo in the population. Too strong an attachment on the part of average Britons to the unfamiliar – to other ways of thinking, living, and doing things – might lead them into asking too many awkward questions. At the height of Empire, few questions were, indeed, asked. Now that Empire is over (and unpleasant comparisons can be made between Britain and more prosperous and egalitarian countries) the questions are coming thick and fast.

The bloodless intellectual remnant

The cult of exclusiveness handed down from the century of paternalism has helped produce a quite remarkable 'other-world-liness' in Britain's intellectuals; a disengaged and disinterested sensibility which spread more widely to the broader upper middle class. Thus, the land known for rationality, hard-nosed practicality and an empirical turn of mind became, in fact, no such thing. Amongst the elite, the appearance of a 'withdrawn', refined and complex sensibility was what was called for.

Isaiah Berlin reports the literary critic Edmund Wilson as becoming increasingly irritated with 'the aestheticism, the prissiness, the superciliousness, the cliquishness, the thin, piping voices, the bloodlessness, the preoccupation with one's own emotions both in life and literature' which he discovered in the early postwar Oxbridge. Somehow, some way, the open and rumbustuous Edwardians of the turn of the century had degenerated into this bloodless remnant. Wilson thought, however, fancifully as it turned out, that the postwar Oxbridge he so derided could not possibly last, and that he was 'in at the kill'. Little did he know then that Attlee's generation would give the 'remnant' a lease of life well into the 1980s.[80]

The 'withdrawn personality' – detached, tentative, lacking in commitment – has not been without its defenders and promoters. W. B. Yeats' great line that 'the best lack all conviction, and the worst are full of passionate intensity' was a poetic aphorism which nicely captured the prevalent scepticism of the late Empire generations about false braggadocio and earnestness. Yet, since Yeats coined those famous words, the English upper middle class seems to have taken 'the tentative spirit' to new heights, indeed to have enthroned it almost as the unique mark of wisdom. This fainéant sensibility was still so pronounced in 1988 that Lindsay Anderson could declare:

> I have learnt to recognise qualities in myself which the English find 'tiresome': a dogmatic quality; a relish for argument; a preference for abrasion of principled judgement rather than the ease of non-committal toleration. Very un-English.[81]

The 'non-committal toleration' identified by Anderson had, in effect, become something far worse: a 'flinching from commitment' itself. In polite society, and in the world of polite letters, the English simply seemed incapable of making a stand. Upper-class dinner parties had become smooth, svelte occasions at which nothing incongruent should ever be uttered, no 'abrasive' points ever made, nothing jarring ever introduced. In such a repressed environment, points were often alluded to, rather than stated openly, so that no intellectual engagement could ensue. Everything was understated. 'Just a slight point' would often mean that an argument about to be offered was crucial; 'with due respect' was often a prelude to a remark containing no respect at all. Avowed feelings also became suspect, as exemplified by the constant repetition of such refinements as 'slightly', 'rather', and 'somewhat'. Anderson also suggested that under the pressure of this overlaid non-committal *politesse* of upper-class English life, reviewers of plays, art, creative writing, or indeed any activity at all, tended to find original work 'disturbing', 'unsettling' or 'alarming'.[82]

Fear of commitment produced in the cultural intelligentsia a strange form of cultivated and precious wit (which replaced the more basic and rounded humour of earlier times). Such 'wit' was less direct, less dangerous, less prejudiced, less open, less democratic. Its brand of humour was slippery, allowing its user to strike, but then to run and hide. 'We British at least possess our famed wit' was the sub-text of many a defensive argument to be heard amongst the talking classes during the era of acute decline in the 1970s. What is more, when aligned to half-serious self-deprecation, it became a powerful defensive shield.

As *The Economist* of 16 May 1987 put it:

Every travelling Briton knows the dispiriting sense of crossing the Channel or the Atlantic to find cleaner streets, fuller shops, snappier clothes and smarter hospitals than the ones at home. Although national decline had its moments of drama – the loss of Empire, Suez – its constant theme was that other countries were growing richer by the year. That fact spread into every corner of British life. It created a national cynicism which sneered at success, both foreign and (particularly) home-grown. The country's rulers – politicians, civil servants, industrialists – turned witty self-deprecation into an art form: it was less painful than the truth.

Dislike of commitment and engagement also led the postwar cultural intelligentsia into a love affair with self-proclaimed *style*. The shrewd 'bon mot', the witty 'throwaway line', the classical allusion, the foreign language aphorism (usually French), would too often suffice as the mark of intelligence. 'At least he has style' would become a defence in itself. In the musical, dramatic and literary arts (and echoed in academe and journalism) the British may indeed have become '. . . (to use the French terms) dazzlingly successful at *la forme*, but much less accomplished where *le fond* is concerned'.[83]

A consciousness of *style* and behaviour also affected the manners of personal relations. Honest human engagement with other people was replaced by a spurious civility. Flamboyance was decidedly out. 'You can tell an upper class twit before he opens his mouth', a visitor to London once proclaimed, 'he's the one who will give you a fish handshake, avert his eyes, and then shuffle away.' The obsession with *style* and behaviour may also help to explain the continued English educational bias during the century of paternalism in favour of the humanities. Correlli Barnett is at his most impressive on this subject:

> In 1887 an Oxford man informed prospective undergraduates and their parents that to the best young men 'Oxford will teach the graces which lend richness and interest to life, acquaintance with the great principles of literature and morality, respect for self and others, widened sympathies and admiration of human greatness'. For the average man Oxford would prove 'a means of employing pleasantly and not unprofitably, the years between boyhood and manhood, an opportunity of gaining a tone in the society of well-bred and cultivated men'. For Oxford's function was humanising the man rather than turning out the professional expert. Like the public schools the universities were monasteries, more lax in rule, more convivial, although scarcely less celibate. The universities lay remote from the clank and smoke and squalor on which the ease and assurance of British upper class life depended: they were serene, spiteful little worlds of college and university politics . . . Here for three years he was exposed to the silent propaganda of noble architecture deployed by the skill of centuries against trees and flowing water . . . Its debilitating charm has been portrayed in the memoirs of many, including men as diverse as Harold Macmillan, Hugh Dalton and John Betjeman. It is the Oxford of Pater and Max Beerbohm, the Cambridge of Rupert Brooke and E. M. Forster

> . . . Dr Benjamin Jowett, Master of Balliol . . . was a characteristic Victorian Englishman – characteristic in his concern for morals and ideals, his romantic love of the classical world and his distaste for the jarring note of realism struck by science or other modern studies. [84]

That a study of the humanities can sharpen instincts and encourage depth and maturity remains the primary argument for continuing to allocate a high national priority (though not a bias) to the discipline. However, teaching the humanities is not the same thing as 'teaching the graces'. In England, the humanities (as with much else) have tended to become not values in themselves but, instead, simply an aspect of 'behaviour', one which would often consciously set the recipient ('the educated') apart from the rest of society.

'Teaching the graces' was an indulgence of Empire; but as Empire faded towards the end of the century of paternalism and 'behaviour became all', 'the graces' became even more important. Such was a part of the way in which the imperial intelligentsia managed their successful offensive against science and technology.

Is the bias any less pronounced today? Modern Britain may, under the impact of economic necessity and social modernization, be wrenching the fulcrum back *somewhat* to a more balanced relationship between the humanities and science, and this new balance will eventually work its way through the system as the present generation of students enters the workforce. Even so, traditions (particularly in English academic circles) die hard. As Professor Norman Stone suggested in 1988,

> At times in the past universities have been almost comically out of joint with their age. In Spain in the middle of the eighteenth century, when the facts of modern science were already plain, there was in the once great university of Salamanca virtually only one question in only one examination in only one subject in only one faculty: 'which language do the angels talk?'. There are times when contemplating what we do, I wonder if we are not reproducing Salamanca. [85]

Discovering – on public money and in public time – which exact 'language angels talk' can hardly be the highest priority of an economy struggling to compete in the modern world.

E. M. Forster suggested during the Second World War, perhaps a little prematurely, that 'Today, people are coming to the top who are, in some ways, more clear sighted and honest than the ruling classes of the past, and they refuse to pay for what they don't want'.[86] But many of the country's established educators have carried with them through their lives the inner glow and the prejudices of an education gained during the decades when the humanities held sway. They can be expected to resist change. The most reactionary of all Britain's elites – its cultural intelligentsia – will still for some time believe that it can safely ignore the imperatives of national survival in the Low Tory, commercial, philistine world beyond its dreaming spires.

The constitution of the *ancien régime*

At the heart of paternalism's resistance to the emergence of a bourgeois society is the constitution of Britain itself, the formal political structures of the Western world's only remaining *ancien régime*.

Britain's constitution presents a paradox, and a contest. We live in a modern liberal economy and society – yet, at the same time, we inhabit a pre-modern, indeed, ancient, constitution. 'We the people' (to use Abraham Lincoln's great democratic phrase) have increasing economic power but 'we the people' do not own our own government. In fact, it is the other way round. Still, centuries after Magna Carta, the British people are owned by the state.

1688 is now generally accepted as the year in which the present constitutional framework (the template used to incorporate later political additions and adjustments) was constructed. William and Mary's so-called 'Glorious Bloodless Revolution' established the primary institutions of British politics, and set them in the context of an unwritten constitution. These institutions (a constitutional monarchy, a bi-cameral Parliament, an Established Church, and an independent, though politically unimportant, judiciary) are still with us today. There have, over the centuries, been adjustments. Power has been rearranged between the two houses of Parliament, and the composition of the lower house is now determined by universal franchise. But the basic pattern of political authority remains that which was programmed in 1688.

Yet, was even 1688 a revolution? In his 1975 Ford Lectures at

Oxford, the historian J. H. Plumb suggested that it was no such thing.[86]

> The seventeenth century had witnessed the beginnings and partial success of a bourgeois revolution that came near to changing the institutions of government. In this, however, it never succeeded. The Revolution of 1688 and all that followed were retrogressive from the point of view of the emergence of the middle class into political power. Socially and economically they continued to thrive, but not politically.[87]

Tom Nairn agrees that, although the political upheavals of 1640–88 did put 'a decisive end to the absolutist aims of the English Monarchy', the 'state form' (a marxist term for 'constitution') which emerged with William and Mary 'remained firmly tied to the epoch of the Rennaissance. As events were soon to demonstrate, it remained closer to Venice and the old mercantile city states than to post-1789 France; closer to the Dutch Stadholderate than to revolutionary America'.[88]

Conservative historian and Member of Parliament, Robert Jackson, also agrees that 1688 was a compromise, not a revolution. He suggests that Clarendon was the central, and successful figure, of the time; and that he 'sought to restore the historic institutions of the English Church and State. This was threatened on one side by sectarian fanaticism and ambition, and on the other by royalist aspirations to absolutism.'[89]

Should such diverse figures as Plumb, Nairn and Jackson be right, then 1688 was indeed something of a damp squib: a mere rearrangement of powers, certainly not a bourgeois 'revolution'. 1688 was liberal only in the negative sense of abandoning royal tyranny, not in the positive sense of ushering in a democratic constitution. Coming well before the cataclysmic events of 1776 in America and 1789 in France, the British thus missed the democratic boat. What emerged out of the 'Glorious Bloodless Revolution' was not popular sovereignty (in which 'we the people' set up and own government), but rather an aristocratic state constitution, an essentially High Tory political settlement.

The 1688 settlement certainly allowed room for change. Yet, as Plumb himself argued in the same Ford Lectures, 'no matter how frequently the constitution may have been reformed, the true anatomy of power, which goes deeper than institutions, remains'.[90] This 'true anatomy', the root of the matter, remains to this day, according to Plumb, 'a political and social authority devolved by inheritance . . . birth still remains a broad highway to power'.[91]

Of course, it can be argued that 'birth remains a broad highway to power' throughout the Western world, in countries which had had liberal revolutions as well as in Britain which did not. But *power* is not necessarily *authority*. What the true bourgeois revolutions of America and France managed to secure was a political settlement (lasting to the present day) which separated the constitutional from the economic spheres. In sum, 1776 and 1789 were republican revolutions. Thus, they (though not we) removed 'birth' and 'inheritance' from the constitution. 'You could have the money, but not the constitutional authority as well.'

Such a differentiation between 'inheritance' and political authority was the core of the matter. The French and the Americans made a systemic break from the monarchical past. In 1776 'We the people', not the inherited authority, became sovereign. In 1789, *égalité* ensured citizenship, not subjecthood. Britain's 'Glorious Bloodless Revolution', on the other hand, retained inherited privilege at the apex of its constitution. The aristocratic class (of Whigs and Tories) which engineered the 1688 revolution informed the British people that, although they would be allowed more power within the state, they could never own it. The monarch, not the people, was the sovereign.

Of course, the later bourgeois explosion during the Victorian epoch certainly posed a serious challenge to this aristocratic-inspired evolutionary and unwritten constitution. Had Weiner's famous 'wrong path' (of paternalism) not been taken, then the commercial and radical forces might have succeeded where they had failed in the seventeenth century, and established both popular sovereignty and citizenship as the base points of a liberal constitution. It was not to be, however. Britons, to this day, were to continue (unlike everyone else) to inhabit an evolutionary, irrational, magical, and unwritten polity.

Ann Hughes, though, strikes an optimistic note by suggesting that:

> Perhaps we are now in danger of becoming too cynical about 1688. It has been noted that there was radical and egalitarian potential in aspects of the 1688 revolution, in its combination of staunch

Protestantism and adherence to the rule of law and representative government. There was some care for the rights of individual 'Freeborn Englishmen' against the power of the Crown; and support for the jury system as a barrier against arbitrary interference in the law. Much of this was to be important in later movements of radical dissent. [92]

In sum: Britain may still be a half-democracy; but we have almost everything we need, and 1688 at least provides us with the potential for further democratization. Does living under the unwritten constitution of an *ancien régime* really matter?

Let us take first the question of 'rights' (or, rather the lack of them). The British – alone amongst the peoples of the free world – are 'subjects' rather than 'citizens'. As 'subjects', modern Britons, even as they approach the third millennium, can claim no inherent or entrenched rights. 'Rights' are no minor issue, for they form the cornerstone of the relationship between the state and individual.

The French in the 'Declaration of the Rights of Man and of the Citizen' resolved 'to set forth in a solemn declaration . . . natural, imprescribable, and inalienable rights'. The Americans, in their constitution, had earlier set forth 'inalienable' rights. By contrast, modern Britons' 'ancient freedoms' are both nowhere prescribed and nowhere able to be tested. Britain has no constitutionally entrenched Bill of Rights, and no Supreme (or High) Court which can enforce them. Britons live under benign provenance. The 'freedoms' which they possess were gained for them by aristocrats (in their fights against the Crown), and can be taken away from them, by Parliament; and, to this day, they are only ensured by the 'chaps in charge'. As far as the 'rights of Freeborn Englishmen' are concerned, paternalism's children still have to take pater's word for it.

The century of paternalism was noteworthy for its utter lack of interest in entrenching rights for the British. The rights of the freeborn were expected to be safeguarded by Parliament on the one hand, and by a caring judiciary on the other; and by and large they were. It was only towards the end of the century of paternalism – when Britain, in the 1970s, found itself confronted by an incipient socialist revolution – that the subject of 'entrenching' rights began to become a public issue.

A lead was taken by Lords Hailsham and Scarman, who began to discover that Britain's *ancien régime* (in particular, its unwritten

constitution and the undefined powers of the House of Commons)
could be quickly turned to the advantage of an incoming Labour
government. Hailsham and Scarman turned their guns in the direction of the House of Commons. Hailsham described Britain's only
popularly constructed institution as a potential 'elective dictatorship'. Scarman argued that

> The decline in the power of the King and the Lords has led to
> the House of Commons becoming the dominant partner in the
> constitution. And the House of Commons is almost all the time
> managed and controlled by ministers who exercise the executive
> power as well as, through their party's control of the Commons, the
> legislative power. We have achieved the total union of executive
> and legislative power which Blackstone foresaw would be produc-
> tive of tyranny. [93]

The only answer, they both argued, was to 'entrench rights'.

This welcome flirtation with 'entrenching rights' was to end
abruptly following the election of the Conservative government
in 1979. In any event, both Hailsham and Scarman were treading
on dangerous ground. 'Entrenched' rights can only be properly secured by a written constitution, a revolutionary step which would
threaten the whole edifice of the *ancien régime*.

Following the collapse of these initiatives, the British people
were back where they started from. Yet, during the late 1970s
and the 1980s, after Britain had entered the European Community, they were, arguably, in an even more undignified position.
The rights of the freeborn, which were not able to be upheld
domestically, could only be gained by an appeal beyond Britain's
shores, to the European Convention on Human Rights. It was
sad for the British, but it was a kind of vindication for Britain's
wayward liberal son, Tom Paine. His 'Rights of Man' had come
home at last.

The fact of the European Convention on Human Rights places
the British Establishment firmly on the spot. For the fact that
Britons can now go abroad to achieve rights can only mean
that questions will start being asked about why such rights
are not available at home. As the feel for citizenship emerges
amongst the British in bourgeois Britain, this question may
become more and more insistent. And the Establishment answer is bound to remain obscure. It can only run as follows:

As 'subjects' you owe allegiance to the Crown, the 'sovereign'. At the same time, you are technically governed by a formulation known as 'the Crown in Parliament'. One of the Houses of Parliament, the lower House, the House of Commons, represents you, and historically has protected your 'rights'. Yet, the House of Commons can also, by law (and by a majority of one), also take away your rights. It is to the House of Commons, therefore, that you should look for protection.

It is when the nascent citizen begins to look at the House of Commons that the *ancien régime* will begin to come into focus. For the anterior question will be: why is the House of Commons not sovereign? Why does it have to share sovereignty with other, unelected, institutions? Britain, alone amongst the totality of Western democracies, continues to allow two hereditary institutions – the Crown and the House of Lords – to be involved (no matter how minimally) in the law-making function.

The *ancien régime* also allows a peculiar relationship between church and state, a fusion which the French call 'intégrisme'. None of Britain's great constitutional reforms have been able to put asunder what was forged in 1534, when Henry VIII became head of the Church of England. Consequently, unelected bishops of an established church join unelected peers in possessing legislative powers over a free people. Although the old radical objective of 'disestablishment', of separating church and estate, is now creeping upwards onto the margins of the national agenda, the issue is still treated with considerable care. Witness the weasel words of even the most progressive of Britain's journals of opinion:

No longer would the Archbishop of Canterbury or his brother bishops have to watch their step before they spoke their minds. No longer would Downing Street have to ponder which prelate to advance up the ecclesiastical ladder. English Anglicans would be free at last, just as the Anglican communion is in the rest of the world, to elect their own bishops, make their own rules and make their own way, freed of the constitutional lumber of another age. The Church of Wales has managed extremely well since Lloyd George disestablished it. The Church of England should not be denied its chance to go it alone. [94]

Thus, even this most blatant of the excesses of the *ancien régime* is not posed in terms of the fundamental democratic postulate (which obtains everywhere else) of a separation of church and state, but, rather, in terms of 'helping out' the church! The sheer tentativeness exhibited by otherwise robust democratic souls as they address the questions of the House of Lords or the Established Church can be explained only by the sad fact that criticism of these undemocratic aspects of British governance inevitably leads the critic to having to get to grips with the linch-pin of the *ancien régime*: the seemingly intractable problem of the monarchy.

The taboo of monarchy

One of the great advantages of living in a republic is that a democratic citizen will know where sovereignty lies. He or she can read their constitution. In modern Britain, our enquiring nascent citizen, emerging slowly out of the chrysalis of 'subjecthood', can only read the works of constitutional sages. And unhappily (for such is the nature of the constitution of the *ancien régime*) the answers can only be unauthoritative, opinionated, ambiguous and numerous. The poignant fact is that no Briton can actually know what his or her constitution amounts to. Neither Bagehot, nor Dicey, nor Jennings, nor Mackintosh nor Rose can agree; and all we are left with is mystery.

Some sages even declare that the sovereignty of the *ancien régime* is located in the Mace. 'In a political system that lacks both a sense of the state and a constitution', argues Richard Rose, 'the Mace is the appropriate symbol of political authority.'[95]

Tom Nairn, whose recent book, *The Enchanted Glass: Britain and Its Monarchy*, is the first serious work since Bagehot to deal with the British monarchy, seems to be as bewildered as anyone else about where sovereignty is located. Along the attempted voyage of discovery, he quotes C. H. Sissons as arguing that 'it would be perfectly possible to govern England without Parliament or elections although it would certainly not be possible to govern it in this way for long with any efficiency', and Samuel Finer as declaring that Britain's constitution is one where democracy has been 'poured into an antique medieval mould . . . still stuffed with officials, terminology and procedures that originated in the middle ages'. Nairn himself concludes that British democracy 'is in a real and not token sense the servant of the Crown; the converse is not true'.[96]

The standard textbook answer to the enquiring subject would be that sovereignty lies in a conception known as 'The Crown in Parliament'. This particular interpretation seems fairly near the mark, because, in reality, a Bill, in order to become an Act, needs the monarch's signature. Although Britons are assured that a monarchical veto would never be used, the enquiring amongst Her Majesty's subjects (attempting to discover the very system of government under which they live, and which they may still have to fight and die for) have only the sages' word for it.

Certainly, Britain's constitution is redolent with the symbolism of monarchical sovereignty. The executive is 'Her Majesty's Government', and the Opposition is 'Her Majesty's Opposition'. Although Parliament forms these institutions, they are not Parliament's (or 'the people's) own. The monarch may be politically powerless, but she 'reigns' nonetheless. 'A Sovereign is a Sovereign for all that.'

The fact is that Britain's *ancien régime* has personified its state and, through the state, its loyalties. For instance, oaths (including military oaths) are taken to the Queen and not to Parliament or the constitution (although this may be yet another aspect of trivial flummery that democrats should not worry their heads over).

Because the constitutional and political role of the monarchy is shrouded in mystery, the growing debate about Britain and its monarchy centres not upon the institution itself, but upon tangential questions of its form and manners. Appeals are made to 'Modernize the Monarchy'. *The Sunday Times*, in something of a break with the then traditional media silence on the question, argued, in 1988, that 'Where the oddities of monarchy offend the susceptibilities of an increasing number of people – as the restrictions based upon gender and religion surely will – then it is in the interests of the monarchy to move to reflect contemporary mores'.[97] Suggestions are also offered that the Prince of Wales may not be properly employed;[98] and criticisms are made of the conduct of the Queen by popular newspapers. One in the *Daily Mail* of 27 January 1989 read:

> But one must ask whether the Queen is displaying not a royal tradition of political and cultural leadership, or a noble tradition of service and obligation, but the aristocratic tradition of holding

on to, and increasing, landed and inherited wealth at all costs . . .
The Queen, acting like an aristocrat rather than a royal, could
certainly not legitimately complain, although Charles would be fully
entitled to do so, were republicanism to start rearing its head in
Britain once again.

Although there is a growing body of radical Tory sentiment
which believes that there is an innate conflict between the royal
role as head of the Commonwealth and the royal role at home,
this domestic role is hardly discussed.

Part of the explanation for the strange silence of modern democrats in the face of this most irrational, mystical and reactionary
institution, may have little to do with a lingering paternalism in
the political culture. It may simply reflect a popular desire to
avoid embarrassing a popular monarch (certainly more popular
than many members of her family). After all, members of the
Royal Family did not seek their positions: they are, quite literally,
paternalism's eldest brothers and sisters. Should the institution of
monarchy be dispensed with, then even the most fervent democrat, the most modern bourgeois, would still have to ask the
awkward and sensitive questions: What would they do? Where
would they go?

Of course, another fear is that open discussion of monarchy
could, *ipso facto,* destroy the institution altogether, and together
with its demise could go: 'who knows what'? 'Above all', said the
arch-paternalist theorist, Walter Bagehot, 'our royalty is to be
reverenced, and if you begin to poke about it you cannot rever-
ence it . . . Its mystery is its life. We must not let in daylight upon
magic.'[99] Another explanation of the taboo over the role of the
monarchy is that, because the monarchy, more than any other of
the institutions of the *ancien régime,* has successfully appropriated
to itself the symbolic representation of nationhood, criticism of the
institution – even on the part of people whose families have lived
in the island home longer, and who have served in wars to defend
it – implies disloyalty, even, possibly, treason.

Perhaps, though, the most important of all the constraints upon
public discussion of the monarchy's role (and of the republican
alternative) is the question of loyalty. Monarchy in Britain is
sustained by all kinds of residual oaths and vows of loyalty (or
'fealty') taken, over generations, by virtually every major public
servant – from members of the armed services, through to the

judges, and even to Members of Parliament. There is hardly a senior official who has not sworn allegiance to the Crown, and thus made a pact, in honour, to uphold it (even though the oath to the Crown does, normally, include the caveat: 'under law'). And as well as the official vows, there is an unofficial vow – one of silence – that has seemingly become a convention of modern Parliamentarians.[100]

Although the House of Commons is the 'forum of the nation', it hardly raises a voice on matters royal. The bewigged Speaker, the guardian of Parliament's prerogatives against the Crown, often serves only to preclude democratic discussion about the monarchy. On every occasion in recent times when MPs have attempted to raise any matter relating to the Royal Family, Parliament (through 'Mr Speaker') assumes a self-denying ordinance. When a motion, criticizing Neil Kinnock's alleged 'long-standing hostility' towards the monarchy, was tabled by Conservative MPs on the eve of the 1987 general election, it was ruled out of order by the Speaker. When Conservative MP, Anthony Marlow, raised a question about the nature of the royal succession (he asked: 'Isn't it a bit strange that in a modern society the succession to the Throne is by the eldest male heir rather than the most suitable heir?'), this, too, was ruled out of order. The Speaker's rationale was a mandarin's delight: 'I don't think that question is appropriate'.[101] When Labour front bench spokesman, Frank Dobson, sought to give his opinions about remarks on defence questions made in West Germany by Prince Charles, that, too, was ruled out of order.

Britain's *ancien régime* seems to have produced the worst of all possible worlds. A polity, unrooted in popular sovereignty, has nonetheless produced, in its one democratic institution (the House of Commons), a monster which, by a majority of one, can erode even the most basic of freedoms. And it also sustains a overwhelmingly intrusive and expensive monarchy, whilst (rightly) not being able to look to this institution as a counterweight.

Yet, it is the weakness of the House of Commons which is the problem, not its strength. The Commons is, after all, the only democratic institution upon which Britain's nascent citizenry can build. It will have to be the locus of power around which Britain constructs its post-*ancien régime* constitution. At the moment, the Commons is hobbled. It is constricted on one level by strong, oligopolistic political parties. On another, it is virtually neutered by a modern British executive whose reach (vis-à-vis its own polity) far exceeds that of any other executive in the Western world.

This infirmity of the House of Commons, of course, suits Prime Ministers who, although ultimately accountable to the majority party, will tend to place themselves in the balance against any serious reforms which weaken the strength of the executive. Also, the weakness of the legislative branch suits the needs of the less accountable administrative apparatus of Whitehall, the mandarin class of first division civil servants.

It is somewhat ironic that, in its first decade of power, the anti-collectivist and anti-bureaucratic Thatcherite regime has, nonetheless, presided over a highly centralized Whitehall machine. 'The paradox of Mrs Thatcher's radicalism', argues David Owen, 'is that while intervening to introduce market forces she also intervenes to centralize power in Whitehall.' He suggests, instead, that Whitehall needs 'a far greater two-way traffic of civil servants into commerce and industry and of young managers into the Civil Service [which] would be mutually beneficial. We have allowed the Civil Service to become too insulated from the market-place in which Britain has to earn its living.'[102]

The seemingly endemic secrecy of Britain's government can, to a large extent, be laid at Whitehall's door – at the refusal of Whitehall to divulge or share what it considers to be its most precious asset: information. Yet, the kind of consumerist and individualistic society being created by Thatcher's era tends also to become voracious for information. And it will, ultimately, insist upon getting it.

It is here that the needs of an open society can come into conflict with the needs of national security. Britain's problem during the century of paternalism has been that its 'national security', and the reputation of those who administer it, have been seen as synonymous. Few British governments have been able to make a distinction between safeguarding national security, on the one hand, and protecting those who run the security services on the other. Hence, too often, the impression is created (and not wholly unreasonably) that Britain's cult of secrecy primarily exists to protect the vices and peccadilloes of an established class. Getting this balance right (protecting secrets, but not people) is perhaps the most difficult aspect of running a security policy in a democratic society.

Symbols and images of yore

The institutions of the *ancien regime* constitution may be able to *evolve* into what will amount to the constitution of a modern, liberal polity. We shall see. But *ancien regime* symbolism and imagery also count. And Britain's symbols and images are all wrong, out of joint with both the times and the free world.

For instance, 'One Nation' Tories, so often seemingly in search of social divisions, might ponder the 'divisiveness' of a public and political language which classifies its people according to social types deriving from medievalism. As has been argued, a 'monarch' inevitably entails 'subjects' (when free peoples should be citizens); 'Lords' inherently suggest their counterpart – 'serfs' (and indeed the 'commoners' in the lower house are only a terminology away from being so depicted). The roll call of medieval imagery – Kings, Queens, Princes, Princesses, Lords, Ladies and Knights – is not something out of a medieval theme park set harmlessly aside for tourists to poke at and ponder. The theme park is the present island home.

As of 1982, there were the Royal Family, 3 peers of royal blood (or the Blood Royal), 25 dukes, 30 marquesses, 160 earls and countesses, 105 viscounts and 792 barons and baronesses. The culture of medieval kingship bears down upon the British in the very daily routine. Letters are delivered by the 'Royal Mail', 'tax demands come in envelopes marked 'On Her Majesty's Service'[103], you go to hear music at the *Royal* Albert Hall, drama at the *Royal* Shakespeare Company, opera at the *Royal* Opera, ballet at the *Royal* Ballet; you pass by the *Royal* Academy (an experience which once turned the mind of the young Hugh (now Lord) Thomas into wondering about whether an 'establishment' existed), you walk in *Royal* parks, to enjoy *Crown* land, to study at *Royal* institutes and *Royal* colleges, to serve in the *Royal* Air Force and the *Royal* Navy; you can eat, drink, and use, goods made by *Royal* 'appointment'; you can live in (or visit people in, or write to people in) *Royal* Boroughs in streets like *Queen's* Terrace or *King's* Row; and you can go to, or watch, the pleasures of *Royal* Ascot.

You can't become Royal yourself, but you can be bestowed with an honour redolent of ancient chivalric or imperial symbolism. There is the Order of the Garter, the Order of the Thistle, the Order of the Bath, the Order of St Michael and St George, the Royal Victorian Order, and the Order of the British Empire (still awarded even though the Empire no longer exists). These awards produce 'Knights' and 'Dames', 'Companions' and 'Commanders'. It is all very complicated, yet deadly serious.

Thus, by linking social recognition and acceptance to the symbolism and imagery of yore, the 'glamour of backwardness' is skilfully ensured, whilst, by comparison, democracy and modernity are made to appear soulless and unglittering. And the imagery percolates well down the social scale, as the pointed designation 'subject' appears on the average Briton's passport as a kind of servant's international calling card to alert the world that – at home on the estate at least – all men are not born equal.

The paternalist reflex, when challenged, is still to argue that none of this matters: that these symbols and imagery are (like the monarchy itself) essentially harmless, ultimately devoid of serious meaning, and therefore not in need of reform. But our medieval honours system certainly has meaning to those who, whilst proclaiming progressive values, fall over themselves to be draped in ermine, and engage in all the little corruptions and compromises of life not just to advance themselves materially – as any good bourgeois should – but to achieve an ancient honour. Whilst so many still find the trappings of antiquity so personally alluring, the argument that Britain's ancient and imperial trappings 'do not count' will remain hollow.

5

The Emerging Democratic Polity

An end to paternalism

The forces of paternalism are more politically hesitant today than they have been for a century. What remains of the paternalist class faces a similar dilemma to that which confronted the oligarchy of the Venetian Republic in its last half-century. As C. P. Snow suggested:

> They knew, just as clearly as we know, that the current of history had begun to flow against them. Many of them gave their minds to working out ways to keep going. It would mean breaking the pattern into which they had crystallised. They were fond of the pattern, just as we were fond of ours. They never found the will to break it.[1]

Perhaps the person who has, more than any other, given his mind to 'working out ways' of keeping paternalism going in the late twentieth century, is that scion of Eton and Balliol, the 'tall spare former Guards officer; grandson of the Duke of Buccleuch and Queensberry', Sir Ian Gilmour.[2] At various meetings with this author, Sir Ian seemed to be in a constant state of slightly wistful agony, both politically (about what to do) and intellectually (about what to think). An avid reader, a strange pursuit for a man

of his background, Gilmour represents the very best of his class –
socially secure, ironic, supple of mind, generous, and effortlessly
charming. During the 1980s, he was to become the intellectual and
political personification of the passing of a world (and a class) which
knew it was on the run.

Gilmour's own writings reflected an uncertainty as to whether
his brand of Tory paternalism could be effectively advocated, let
alone covertly pursued, in the democratic age. The failure of his
fall-back position – he championed the concept of social democracy
and, with his friend Roy Jenkins, helped forward the birth of the
Social Democratic Party and its Alliance with the Liberals – could
only have reinforced his sense of inevitable loss. Gilmour, in many
respects both the political and intellectual chief of the forces of
High Toryism in the 1970s and 1980s, lost the battle before he
contested it; and primarily because he, perhaps more than many
of his troops, understands its limitations and weaknesses as it
confronts its liberal bourgeois foe.

Paternalist political authority rests, in part, upon public appreciation of its supposed singular attribute of disinterested rulership and
political leadership. The end of Empire dealt a potentially fatal blow
to this myth, as did the political traumas of the 1970s. For, when
the going got tough in the 1970s its exemplars abandoned the field
to a Low Tory liberal visionary. This, of course, was not surprising. High Tory political leadership has no want of, and no theory
of, change – frowning as it does upon zest (which it dismisses as
zeal), and especially upon political vision.

Britain's old establishment could provide no alternative vision to
the allure of marxism, and its opposition to the marxist challenge of
the 1970s was feeble because it had no map to follow. It can only,
by definition, retreat into the past.

Paternalist support for the new radicalism has been grudging
and curmudgeonly. T. E. Utley once confessed:

> I do not like her [Thatcher's] habit of describing herself as 'a
> radical'. To an old-fashioned high Tory like me, the word 'radical'
> is not pleasing. It conjures up the spectacle of a man (or worse
> still a woman) who is determined to go around setting everything
> to rights according to some abstract principle and without regard
> either to practicality or the sentiments of the people.[3]

Yet, Britain's paternalists supported her nonetheless. As one
Tory paternalist after another fell in behind Thatcher, whilst at the

same time criticizing her radicalism, sceptical observers came to see Britain's old establishment in a new light. 'Traditional Toryism' wrote Brian Walden in 1987, 'lost its grip, not because it was the possessor of all the noble qualities upon which it congratulated itself, but because its inherent selfishness eventually became apparent. It was protecting itself from the wolves by throwing its retainers off the sledge. So deference died, and then came Thatcher.'[4]

There is no more perfect exemplar of the death of the old English establishment than the strange and distempered career of Enoch Powell. Something of a Low Tory by background – a Midlands Conservative, an admirer of Macleod and a populist – Powell was, nonetheless, a High Tory paternalist by *conviction*, and thereby one of its most effective NCOs.

Although entranced by the High Tory magic of the British constitution and the mysteries of imperial rule, Powell nonetheless allowed his Low Tory impulses free rein in economics. During the 1960s, he led an intellectual crusade for the free market, which was to become a populist stable door through which many a Low Tory rushed, not least Margaret Thatcher, who had sat at Powell's feet throughout the 1960s and 1970s. During the 1970s, however, she was to turn Powell's dry and technical approach to the free market into a real Low Tory zeal for Free Enterprise, and, later, was to go even further and advocate, and then implement, that most dangerous (to High Tories) of all modern conceptions – the 'Enterprise Culture'.

Thus, during the 1970s the two most impressive postwar populist Conservatives had both, separately and differently, resolved the contradiction at the heart of modern Conservatism. Powell resolved it in favour of the mystical High Toryism to which he had been attracted ever since his formative experiences in the Raj. He was to declaim that in any conflict between the free market, on the one hand, and national sovereignty, on the other, he would be on the side of national sovereignty. (It was thus deemed to be 'better' for the British people – indeed in their interest – to inhabit and enjoy the heritage and tradition of a sovereign slum than to suffer the psychic damage of inhabiting a marginally modern and relatively wealthy part of an international community.) Thatcher, on the other hand, resolved the postwar Tory contradiction in favour of neo-liberalism and democratization.

Yet, although the modern Conservative party may – by the 1980s – have resolved its own historic inner contest between antiquity and modernity, the same cannot be said of those formal structures of the nation (our *ancien régime*) within which all political parties, and the British people, still work and live. Of course, *ancien régime* Britain faces no such inner conflict, as it represents and embodies only the past. All it can do is to attempt to survive; and this it will seek to achieve by attempting the only thing it knows when pushed into a corner – compromise and appease in order to live another day. We therefore witness the spectacle of some of Britain's most ancient institutions, forged centuries before the democratic age, attempting to appropriate to themselves the attributes of modernity.

Yet, modernity is not to be appeased. Such compacts with the modern age appear patently phoney, and further undermine the credibility of the ancients. For instance, Prince Charles's attempt to use the power of traditional authority in the name of modernization can backfire in ridicule. As John Lloyd declared in the *Financial Times*:

> He [Prince Charles] is a man pointing the way to modernisation while preparing himself to receive the most gorgeous hereditary crown in the world. He is a man commending efficiency while his palaces are stuffed with flunkeys and his family drains the public purse of some £25 million a year. He is a man conjuring up a more equitable society while being heir to one of the biggest fortunes in the world. He is a man who will soon stand at the apex of a social pyramid whose snobbery, jobbery and frippery is the envy of the idle rich of this world, whose philistinism has been legendary and whose late conversion to good works is transparently self-serving.[5]

Mass democracy, which holds in its hands the power to destroy antiquity, can nonetheless also *demand* it. At the moment it has a taste for it, and in ever heavier doses. Ancient Britain – kings, lords, judges in fancy dress – is in popular demand. The 'infotainment' sector of the mass communications industry (primarily the domestic print media and worldwide TV) seems to possess an insatiable appetite for Britain's *ancien régime*. It is the island home's contribution to the democratic world's need for fantasy; and, because these folks are 'real' and 'live', they have an edge even on the actors and actresses of Hollywood.

Yet the dangers here – for antiquity – are obvious. Pop star popularity is ephemeral. It demands a consistency of glamour and sparkle which is unattainable. Here is the real problem which democracy poses to the institution at the apex of the *ancien régime* pyramid. 'As the Royal Family joins hands with showbiz', suggests Craig Brown in the *Sunday Times*, 'it should be aware that its own meagre talents place it on roughly the same pegging as the type of resoundingly average family so often chosen by Esther Rantzen to appear on 'That's Life', a family of no greater consequence than its possession of a cat which whistles or an auntie who pulls funny faces.'[6]

And fantasyland, no matter how magical the fantasy, can also call forth competitors in the art. Moreover, such fantasy popularity, as any faded actress can testify, is no guarantee of survival. It is an interesting point that most deposed kings of the Continent were, on the very eve of their dethronements, 'very popular with the people and many were loved and, indeed, almost considered divine'.[7]

Popularity in a democratic age imposes democratic demands upon the popular. A beguiled democratic people are not slaves to the fantasy of antiquated authority; rather, they are increasingly instrumental in their public fantasies, wanting of them what *they* want, not necessarily what is on offer. It has been suggested that:

> The British people want their royals to pretend to be middle class and have those values. The Prince of Wales is not doing that. He's openly smarter, more engaged, more educated, more sensitive. In the long run this will work against him. He won't make it because the people don't want him to be this way. They'll ultimately insist he give up his ideas and drift into the concerned idleness they demand from their royals.[8]

So:

> The royal family is caught between two social forces. On the one hand, there is the pressure to move with the times . . . At the same time, another section of society wants the royal family to cleave itself to more traditional values. It is a difficult balance to maintain: many fear that if the distance between the general public and the royal family narrows too much, royalty will start to lose its magic.[9]

The *ancien régime*, therefore, needs more than the ephemera of popularity. Its continuing hold over its subjects is dependent upon its having a continuing *political* (or *constitutional*) role within the democratic polity, a dimension which guarantees a longevity beyond the stars and starlets. This constitutional aspect however, leads the ancients into murky political waters. For instance, the *ancien régime* is now supranational, having demanded for itself a Commonwealth role as a consolation prize for the loss of Empire. Thus the monarch, the House of Lords, the Privy Council and the judiciary, all of which still possess varying degrees of jurisdiction outside the domestic realm, can hardly escape the conflicting pressures of real-world political change which may eventually cause Britain and many of the Third World Commonwealth nations to part company. For instance,

> Should the Commonwealth leaders decide to jettison the Queen, she would have few important duties to perform abroad and would thus become no more important than the Queen of Holland or the Queen of Denmark. At this point the future of the Monarchy would indeed be in question because if political and ceremonial functions are removed it is unlikely that the people would support a King or a Queen and a republic would almost certainly follow.[10]

So, the Western world's only remaining *ancien régime* (with its mix of paternalist political culture, High Tory ideology and pre-modern constitutionalism) will fight for its existence against the democratic pressures bearing down upon it. And, now that its domestic political base is exhibiting decided signs of modernity, it seems that it will have to fight on without the strong underpinnings of a national political class dedicated, almost as a governing principle of political existence, to its survival.

The new polity

As Britain emerges from under the wing of paternalism, its replacement by an un-servile state and society will not need an act of creation. Rather, all that will be necessary is an act of description, for its forms are already present.

Britain is no longer a sovereign nation in the old-fashioned sense. The term *sovereign* is far too singular a nostrum to describe the present plural power realities under which the British live. For instance, in the economic realm, the City of London already has stronger real links with the worldwide financial system than it does with the domestic economy. The economy of the South–East of England is already tied into the Western trading system to a greater degree than it is linked with the North of Britain.

Britain, of course, will retain its nationhood. Prophets of dismemberment can still be heard in the land, but it would seem that, apart from Northern Ireland, the rest of the nation has settled for some form or other of unitary state.

But, although united, Britain will have to exist within the context of the sharp restructuring of the Western system which is now under way. That the US budget and trade deficits will ultimately work their way through to a smaller troop commitment to Western Europe almost goes without saying. The only questions left are ones of degree and about the character of the political management of the NATO alliance. In any event, Britain's relationship with Western Europe will become stronger, not weaker – whether in terms of new defence arrangements (even including nuclear defence) or because of the natural, though still incremental, integrative effects of the single market of 1992.

Britain's polity at the turn of the century, therefore, cannot be seen outside the context of Western Europe, its evolution and development. Although Western Europe is unlikely to take on the characteristics of modern nationhood (a centralized executive, legislature and armed forces), the coming generation of Britons can probably still look forward to the privilege, unknown to any of their forebears in the island home, of inhabiting a continent-wide civilization.

Britons, particularly the newly affluent and mobile, will become ever more cosmopolitan. As they get Empire out of their system, increased contacts and relations with foreigners will be established on an equal footing! Mass travel, transferability of professional qualifications, ever closer (though competitive) commercial and financial relations, even intra-national marriages, all these, and more, will give the new generation of Britons a new and liberating sense of space, of frontier, of opportunity.

The sense of belonging, not to a cramped and constricted nation-state, but rather to a continent-wide civilization, will affect the character of British political culture as much as any of the domestic changes brought about by the new radicalism. Paternalism thrived upon the fact that its subjects were confined within the island home. Now, the barriers to that confinement are being removed one by one – whether by the forest of television dishes about to appear across the sky-line of Britain, or by the increase in transnational mobility, or merely by continued membership of the European Community.

The politics of that Community will inevitably evolve rather hesitantly and slowly. Nationhoods will be protected, as they are now, by the strength of the various nation-state governments. Yet, the growing plurality of political authorities which the Briton of the 1990s will confront (Westminster, Whitehall, local government, the EC Commission, the European Court, the European Parliament) can only make for more individual manoeuvrability and, consequently, more freedom. Above all, Britons will, at least in principle, finally take possession, through the European Convention on Human Rights, of those 'inalienable rights' which have for so long eluded them.

Domestic British politics will continue to be the largest single factor determining their lives, and here the political effects of the radical bourgeois revolution have still to run their course. As paternalism winds down, Britain's socialist tradition, no longer able to grow in the rich soil of a culture of deference and authority, will similarly wither on the vine. The end of the socialist era is also foreshadowed by hard political and electoral realities. Politically, Britain's trade unions no longer pose a threat to the democratic system, nor can they perform their half-century-long role of tilting the balance of power within the polity towards collectivism.

In the absence of an international economic cataclysm – and, maybe, not even then, as the ensuing social instability will call forth a reactionary High Tory response – the Labour party is unlikely to be able to form a government until well into the late 1990s. Britain's electoral system, its two-and-a-half party political structure, and Labour's electoral *laager* in North Britain which only reinforces the larger Conservatives' electoral *laager* in the south, all conspire to ensure that Labour as currently constituted cannot possibly secure during normal political times a Parliamentary majority.[11] Consequently, all the pressures over the next decade will be upon Labour (which will easily remain the main opposition party) to abandon its socialist ideology, either dramatically and cleanly (as Hugh Gaitskell attempted in 1959 or as the West

German Social Democrats succeeded in the same year at Bad Godesberg) or by stages.

In the meantime there is now enough evidence to suggest that some form of 'Thatcherism' will succeed Margaret Thatcher within the Conservative party. Also, that, whatever may happen to the centre parties – whether they remain separate from each other or not, or separate from the main parties or not – they too, like Labour and the Conservatives, will increasingly accommodate themselves to a new, non-socialist and non-collectivist political consensus. That neither socialism nor collectivism will be on Britain's agenda in the 1990s is the measure of the success of Thatcherism.

Living without socialism will take some getting used to. British politics will no longer be constrained by having to react to organized labour, no longer be governed by the Cowlingesque statecraft of appeasing labour, and no longer exist uneasily under the shadow of an imminent national descent into socialism.

Also, political debate between left and right will no longer be informed by a paternalist culture which distorts the real debate. The left's impulse towards equality, towards a stronger state to redistribute resources, will be able to make its appeal directly to the democratic society rather than to paternalist authority. The right's emphasis upon economic freedom, upon a limited state, will no longer be viewed as a conspiracy of authority, but rather as an alternative political position. The state itself, decoupled from paternalist authority, will increasingly be viewed as the neutral mechanism of an elected government (to be used or not according to political taste), not as the tool of social control.

Ultimately left and right within the coming liberal polity will no longer divide between public and private ownership, between socialism and capitalism. The left will place a greater emphasis on equality than on freedom, on the state than on the individual (and the right, vice versa).

Politics will also become less ideological (in the old-fashioned 'socialist' versus 'capitalist' sense) and more populist, reverting to the question of which set of leaders, and which party, is seen to be more in tune with 'the people' and less 'elitist'. Also, with the decline of old-fashioned ideology, electoral campaigns will increasingly centre upon which set of leaders, or which party, is more competent to run the country and its foreign policy. The

future political debate (no longer turning on 'socialism versus
capitalism') will be more technical and less emotive: revolv-
ing around subtle and complex issues, such as the appropriate
relationship between environmental concern and development,
the nature of the evolution of Britain in NATO and Europe, the
proper response of Britain towards the Third World.

Parties will tend to retain 'natural constituencies' of region,
'class' and income (Labour retaining the underlying sympathies
of the 'North', manual workers and their families, and ethnic
minorities in the inner cities; the Conservatives retaining the
'South', and rural and suburban England). But, depending upon
how the fluctuating leaderships of each party contest the campaigns, these constituencies will not be unerodable. Should Labour
be able to take its place in the new liberal consensus, and should
the Conservatives back away from their radical populism, then
Labour could easily become the majority party within the new
consensus, just as the Democratic party remains the natural party
of government in the US Congress.

It would be strange indeed if the Britain of the 1990s, as it
sloughs off paternalism, does not, at some point, arrange a
new constitutional settlement. The obstacles to the creation of
a new, written constitution (including a Bill of Rights) will remain
formidable, seemingly impossible to overcome. Who will write the
constitution? Who (or what) will ratify it? Will there be enough of
an agreement across the parties about even its central provisions?
Simply to ask these questions is to reveal the intractability of the
problem.

Yet, although the way forward to a written constitution may
be blocked, the removal of the *ancien régime* aspect of the
constitution presents no such difficulty. Its key characteristic –
the formal, constitutional, linkage between inherited privilege and
the legislative process – can simply be 'legislated away', whilst
retaining the present unwritten and evolutionary system. There is
no reason why – within our present unwritten system – we cannot
simply remove inherited authority from any role whatsoever in the
legislative process. All that is needed is to build upon Britain's one
democratic institution, and locate formal constitutional sovereignty
in the House of Commons. The unaccountable (and undemocratic)
elements in our constitution – the monarchy, the hereditary element in the upper house, and the bishops of the established

church – would no longer have any say, no matter how minimal or formal, over legislation governing a free people. There would be no Royal Assent needed for Acts of Parliament, no audiences between Queen and Prime Minister, no Privy Council, no royal appointment (by the 'kissing of hands') of the chief executive, and no hereditary or ecclesiastical element in the upper house. All oaths and declarations of loyalty would be made to Parliament, not to a Head of State. There would be no need to abolish the monarchy, which could be established under an Act of Parliament purely for ceremonial purposes.

Of course, in any new constitutional settlement arranged by the initiative of the House of Commons, it is unlikely that the Commons would allow a competing democratic assembly (an *elected* upper chamber) to be brought into being, at least not initially. Britain, for a while, would have to live with an upper chamber which was nominated by the elected lower house; over time, however, an elected second chamber (perhaps based upon federal principles and elected by proportional representation) might emerge.

Such a new constitutional settlement could be instituted by a single Act of Parliament, and ratified by the simple mechanism of submitting a rearranged constitutional settlement to a referendum.

As Britain enters the twenty-first century, it may, finally, come to terms with itself. It will, certainly, have 'lost an Empire', but it will, by then, have found 'a new role'. Images of Empire (and the accompanying illusions of a 'world role') will have receded, indeed have become meaningless for most of its people. And a new democratic domestic polity (one shorn of the *ancien régime*) will have consigned paternalism (like Empire) to the past. In such a new environment Walter Bagehot's stricture delivered in 1860 at the dawning of the century of paternalism that 'there has ever been a structure in English society and every man has not walked by the light of his own eyes . . . the many have subordinated their judgement to that of the few . . .'[12] will have finally become redundant. In the new century Britain could become, once again, a confident nation, existing at ease within an increasingly confident continent – a country no longer defensively trumpeting its virtues, no longer resentful of foreigners and things different, but a nation enjoying the life of the mature Western civilization to which Britons, before the age of paternalism, did so much to give birth.

Notes

Preface

1　See: Neal Ascherson, *Games With Shadows* (London: Radius, 1988).
2　See: Tom Nairn, *The Enchanted Glass* (London: Century Hutchinson, 1988);
　　Correlli Barnett, *The Collapse of British Power* (London: Eyre Methuen,
　　1972); and Martin Weiner, *English Culture And The Decline Of The Industrial
　　Spirit 1850–1980* (New York: Viking Penguin, 1987).

Chapter 1　A nation in transition

1　*The Sunday Times*, 31 May 1987.
2　*The Thomas Paine Reader* (New York: Penguin, 1987). Editor's Introduction,
　　p. 22.
3　Geoffrey Wheatcroft, *The Spectator*, 24–31 December 1988.
4　W. H. Greenleaf, *The British Political Tradition, Volume Two: The Ideological
　　Heritage* (London: Methuen, 1983), p. 51.
5　*The Spectator*, 31 January 1981.
6　*The New Statesman*, 3 June 1988.
7　John Dunn, *Times Literary Supplement*, 1 July 1988. Also see Nairn, *The
　　Enchanted Glass*, who argues that 'Her [Margaret Thatcher's] contempt for
　　its [Britain's *ancien régime* government structure] archaism has been effaced
　　by the enjoyment of its powers', p. 385.
8　Paul Webb, *The Spectator*, 24–31 December, 1988, p. 49.
9　Philip Norton, *The British Polity* (New York, Lougman 1984), p. 27.
10　Greenleaf, *The British Political Tradition* p. 197.
11　J. E. Gorst, quoted in ibid., p. 217.
12　Quote is from Greenleaf *The British Political Tradition* (p. 363) as part of
　　the author's description of the cameralist school of political thought which he
　　cites Michael Oakeshott as arguing possessed views very similar to those of
　　the 'improving socialists'.
13　*Political Anecdotes*, edited by Paul Johnson (New York, Oxford University
　　Press, 1986), p. 226.

14 James Callaghan, *Time and Chance* (London, Collins, 1987), p. 441.
15 Reported in Hugo Young, 'The Callaghan Offensive', *The Sunday Times*, 21 May 1978.
16 Callaghan, *Time and Chance*, p. 429.
17 See both Greenleaf *The British Political Tradition* and Samuel H. Beer, *Britain Against Itself: The Political Contradictions of Collectivism* (New York: Norton, 1982).
18 Johnson, *Political Anecdotes*, p. 225
19 Greenleaf, *The British Political Tradition*, p. 257.

Chapter 2   The revolt against paternalism

1 See: C. A. A. Crosland, *The Future of Socialism* (London: Jonathan Cape, 1956) and J. Strachey, *Contemporary Capitalism* (London, 1956).
2 *The Establishment*, edited by Hugh Thomas (London: Anthony Blond Ltd., 1959), p. 20.
3 Michael Young, *The Rise Of The Meritocracy* (London: Penguin, 1958) pp. 26–7.
4 There has been no serious academic study on the general question of 'working-class' deference, although T. McKenzie *Angels in Marble* (University of Chicago Press, 1968) deals with the subject of deferential 'working-class' Toryism.
5 Quoted in Weiner, *English Culture*, p. 92.
6 *The Sunday Telegraph*, 30 September 1973.
7 Drawn from the unpublished memoirs of the Rt Hon. Sir Reg Prentice.
8 Ibid.
9 Callaghan, *Time and Chance*, pp. 420–21.
10 Ibid., pp. 425–6.
11 See Bernard Donoughue, *Prime Minister* (London: Cape, 1987), p. 168.
12 ITN-Harris Exit Poll, 11 June 1987. Published in *The Independent*, 13 June 1987.
13 *The New York Times*, 13 June 1987.
14 Quoted from *The Sunday Times*, 31 May 1987.
15 Matthew Oakeshott, a former political adviser to Roy Jenkins, produced for the Radical Centre for Democratic Studies, and for the nascent SDP leadership, a detailed analysis of projected Alliance seats based upon varying popular vote assumptions. This survey, together with other polling evidence, persuaded Jenkins of the impossibility of the Alliance ever being able seriously to dent Labour's hold upon its 'heartland' seats – except in by-elections. In a discussion with this author on the eve of his decision to contest the safe Labour seat of Warrington in a by-election in 1982, Jenkins was certain in his mind that the best he could do would be to dent Labour's majority.
16 See *The Times*, 11 June 1987.
17 Both quotations are from Labour Party Annual Conference reports, the first from LPACR, 1955, p. 175, the second from LPACR, 1959, p. 111.
18 Roy Jenkins, review of Hugh Gaitskell's Diaries, *The Observer*, 11 September 1983.
19 Prentice memoirs.
20 ibid.
21 *The Times*, 1 September 1987 (report of *David Owen Speaking Personally to Kenneth Harris*, (London: Weidenfeld and Nicolson, 1987).
22 *The Sunday Times*, 23 August, 1987, (review of *Family Quarter* by John Catlin).

Chapter 3   The radical challenge

1   *The Times*, 5 March 1988.
2   *The Sunday Times*, 9 July 1987.
3   *The Observer*, 20 March 1988.
4   *The New Statesman*, 11 March 1988.
5   David Marquand, *The New Statesman*, 11 March 1988.
6   *The Times*, 14 September 1987.
7   *The Independent*, 9 January 1988.
8   *The Times*, 11 June 1987: report by political correspondent.
9   T. E. Utley, *The Times*, 8 June 1987.
10 Beer, *Britain against Itself*, p. 179.
11 *The Sunday Telegraph*, 27 December 1987.
12 Speech to Cambridge University Conservative Association, 25 January 1987.
13 Speech to Conservative Central Council, Buxton, March 1988.
14 Norman Tebbit, Inaugural Lecture to The Radical Society, London, 25 April 1988.
15 *The Independent*, 16 February 1988.
16 Reported in *The Times*, 27 April 1988.
17 *The Economist*, 16 May 1987.
18 From: George Orwell, *The Lion and the Unicorn: Socialism and the English Genius* (London: Secker and Warburg, 1941).
19 See Crosland, *The Future Of Socialism*, p. 152.
20 *The Times*, 3 February 1988.
21 Joel Krieger, *Reagan, Thatcher And The Politics Of Decline* (Oxford: Polity Press, 1986) p. 74.
22 Quotes are from 'Britain's onwardly mobile society', *The Times*, 11 September 1987. Statistics are from the 1987 Population Census. Maclennan is Director of the Centre of Housing Research at the University of Glasgow.
23 Quoted from: Stephen Haseler, 'The Spectacle of Tory Radicals Hoist By Their Own Petard', *The Independent*, 16 June 1988.
24 *The Times*, 3 February 1988.
25 Nairn, *The Enchanted Glass*, p. 242.
26 ibid.
27 See, amongst other works: Anthony King, *Political Consequences of the Welfare State* (University of Essex, 1984); Richard Clutterbuck, *Britain In Agony: The Growth Of Political Violence* (London: Faber, 1978); Stephen Haseler, *The Death Of British Democracy* (London: Elek Books, 1976).
28 Brian Walden, *The Sunday Times*, 27 December 1987.
29 *The Sunday Times*, 1 May 1988.
30 Figures from *The Sunday Times*, 27 December 1987.

Chapter 4   The paternalist resistance

1   Greenleaf, *The British Political Tradition*, p. 280.
2   The congregation of Oxford University refused to award the incumbent Prime Minister an honorary degree in 1985 by a margin of 2 to 1 because of government 'cuts' and 'underfunding' of higher education.
3   *The Sunday Times*, editorial, 20 September 1987.
4   James Bellini, *Rule Britannia* (London: Jonathan Cape, 1981), p. 115. (Statistics taken from: Northfield Report, Cmnd 7599, HMSO, 1979).
5   Bellini, *Rule Britannia*, p. 11.
6   Barnett, *The Collapse of British Power*, pp. 36–7.

7   C. N. Parkinson, *Left Luggage* (Boston, Houghton Mifflin, 1967) p. 70.
8   *The Economist*, 13 June 1987.
9   Ibid.
10 Nairn, *The Enchanted Glass*, p. 214.
11 Weiner, *English Culture*, preface.
12 'The North Beyond The Grit', *New York Times*, 26 July 1987.
13 Jonathan Raban, *Soft City* (London: Hamish Hamilton, 1974), p. 59.
14 *The Guardian*, 8 June 1988.
15 See Weiner, *English Culture*, Chap. 4.
16 *The Sunday Telegraph* (leader), 7 June 1987.
17 *The Sunday Telegraph* (leader), 20 September 1987.
18 Shirley Robin Letwin, *Gentlemen in Trollope: Individuality and Moral Conduct* (London: Macmillan, 1982).
19 Barnett, *The Collapse of British Power*, p. 20.
20 Christopher Hill, *God's Englishman* (London: Weidenfeld and Nicolson, 1970), pp. 66–7.
21 Weiner, *English Culture*, p. 16.
22 *The Oxford Myth*, edited by Rachel Johnson (London: Weidenfeld and Nicolson, 1988).
23 See *The Sunday Telegraph*, 7 June 1987.
24 Robert Chesshyre, *The Return of A Native Reporter* (London: Penguin, 1987), p. 13.
25 *The Concise Oxford English Dictionary* (Oxford; Clarendon Press, 1988) p. 48.
26 John Morley, *Life of Richard Cobden vol. II* (1981) pp. 481–482.
27 Weiner, *English Culture*, p. 174.
28 Quoted in Nairn, *The Enchanted Glass*, p. 378.
29 Reported in *The Sunday Times* (Section C), 18 December 1988.
30 Paul Theroux, *The Kingdom By The Sea* (Boston, Houghton Mifflin 1983), p. 51.
31 See Alan Bullock, *Ernest Bevin, Foreign Secretary* (London: Heinemann, 1983), p. 856.
32 Ivor Richard, *We, The British* (New York: Doubleday, 1983), pp. 106–7.
33 In a conversation between the author and a hairdresser in London, in the autumn of 1988.
34 'Woodland King Fights to Save Ancient Rights', *The Independent*, 12 January 1988.
35 Quoted in *The Sunday Times*, 17 May 1987. Extract from Philip Knightley and Caroline Kennedy, *Trial Of The Century* (London: Jonathan Cape, 1987).
36 Simon Raven, 'Perish By The Sword' in *The Establishment* (London: Anthony Blond, 1959), p. 70.
37 Ibid., p. 79.
38 Chesshyre, *The Return of a Native Reporter*, p. 10.
39 Robert McCrum, William Can and Robert McNeil, *The Story Of English* (New York: Viking, 1986), p. 21.
40 Richard, *We, The British*, p. 107.
41 UK LATE, Channel Four, 11 September 1987.
42 This, indeed, is the word, rightly used, in Richard, *We, The British*, p. 108.
43 McCrum et al., *The Story of English*, p. 24.
44 Ibid., p. 21. The exact argument here proceeds thus: 'The emergence of Received Pronunciation – the outward and visible sign of belonging to the

professional middle class – went hand in hand with the rise of an imperial Civil service and its educational infrastructure.'

45 Ibid., p. 24.
46 From: Emily Post, *Etiquette* (New York, 1937) p. 93.
47 See: 'The English Aristocracy' by Nancy Mitford, *Encounter*, September 1955, which popularised a paper by Alan Ross.
48 McCrum et al., *The Story of English*, p. 29.
49 One of the saddest stories of the contortions which England's continuing sense of class has wrought upon its people was recounted by an American to a gathering in Washington in the mid 1980s. The American, an impression-able young woman from the Mid-West, had come to London some years previously, and had befriended an older woman from the 'county set'. The American grew fond of the older woman, and was taught by her (Professor Higgins-like) to be 'a lady'. The American was present at the death-bed of the old woman, who, just before she died, threw off her lifetime's RP patois and croaked out her final farewells in raw, uninhibited cockney.
50 Beer, *Britain Against Itself*, p. 175.
51 David Watt, Posthumous commentary, *The Times*, 3 April 1987.
52 *The Sunday Telegraph*, 19 June 1988.
53 Beer, *Britain Against Itself*, p. 173.
54 See: Ian Gilmour, *Inside Right: A Study Of Conservatism* (London: Hutchinson, 1977).
55 Greenleaf, *The British Political Tradition*, p. 198.
56 *The Salisbury Review*, No. 3. Spring, 1983.
57 Alan Bloom, *The Closing of the American Mind* (New York: Simon and Schuster, 1987), p. 185.
58 Ibid.
59 See also ibid., pp. 246–56 for further discussion on the subject of a 'democratic intellectual life'.
60 E. M. Forster, *Two Cheers For Democracy* (London: Penguin, 1951) p. 12.
61 Ernest Gellner, *Words And Things* (rev. edition) (London, Penguin 1979), pp. 263–4.
62 Quoted in Seymour Martin Lipset, 'American Intellectuals', *Daedalus*, (Summer, 1959) p. 475.
63 Quotation from Graham Turner, 'Why Britain's Eggheads Look Down On Mrs Thatcher', *The Sunday Telegraph*, 10 January 1988.
64 Richard, *We, The British*, p. 269.
65 Quoted in Nairn, *The Enchanted Glass*, p. 276.
66 *The New Statesman*, 2 October 1987.
67 Ibid.
68 *The Times Higher Educational Supplement*, 8 April 1988.
69 Both quotes from Simon Jenkins, *The Sunday Times*, 24 January 1988.
70 Malcolm Muggeridge, *The Infernal Grove*, (London: Collins, 1973).
71 George Orwell, 'Such, Such Were The Joys', *The Collected Essays, Journal-ism and Letters of George Orwell* (New York, Harcourt Brace, 1968), pp. 330 ff.
72 *The Establishment*, p. 370.
73 See: 'Is There A Homosexual Conspiracy?', *The Sunday Telegraph*, 26 April 1987.
74 *The Establishment*, p. 20.
75 From: Barry Penrose *Conspiracy Of Silence: The Secret Life Of Anthony Blunt* (New York, Vintage Books, 1988, pp. 595–6).
76 Ibid., p. 33.

77   *The Times Higher Education Supplement*, editorial, 24 June 1988.
78   Johnson, *The Oxford Myth*, p. 148.
79   Gilmour, *Inside Right*, pp. 87 and 92.
80   *New York Times* Book Review, 12 April 1987.
81   *The Sunday Times Magazine*, 26 June 1988.
82   In the Film 'Plenty', the actress Meryl Streep played the part of an English-woman who had been a courier behind enemy lines in the Second World War. She returned to the postwar England of 'plenty' to find it bland and uninteresting. She continued to seek commitment, engagement, 'life' in her native country, but found, instead, only form and a cultivated sense of manners. In a scene at the end of the film, this English problem was explained to her by a diplomat in the Foreign Office. He summed it up by suggesting that, for the postwar English elite, as they had lost an Empire, and no longer counted for much, then 'behaviour, not commitment, becomes everything'.
83   Richard, *We The British*, p. 269.
84   Barnett, *The Collapse of British Power*, pp. 38–9.
85   *The Sunday Times*, 24 January 1988.
86   Forster, *Two Cheers for Democracy*, p. 112.
87   J. H. Plumb, *The Growth of Political Stability in England, 1675–1725* (London, Macmillan, 1967), p. 187.
88   Nairn, *The Enchanted Glass*, pp. 151–2.
89   *The Times* (Letters Page), 11 April 1988.
90   Plumb, *Growth of Political Stability*, p. 18.
91   Ibid., p. 187.
92   Ann Hughes, *The Guardian*, 27 June 1988.
93   *The Guardian*, 27 June 1988. Excerpt from Radcliffe Lecture delivered by Lord Scarman at Warwick University.
94   *The Sunday Times*, 31 January 1988.
95   Quoted in Nairn, *The Enchanted Glass*, p. 374.
96   Ibid., pp. 70 and 369.
97   *The Sunday Times*, editorial: 'Modernise The Monarchy', 17 January 1988.
98   From Transcript of 'Panorama', BBC TV, 11 April 1988.
99   Quoted in *The Economist*, 12 December 1987.
100   *Today*, 30 October 1987.
101   Ibid.
102   *The Listener*, 2 June 1988.
103   Richard, *We, The British*, p. 152.

Chapter Five   The emerging democracy polity

1   Cited in Haseler, 'Can The Social Democrats Devise Policies For Political Power'? *Encounter*, January 1982, p. 17.
2   Professor Beer's own depiction in: Beer. *Britain Against Itself*, p. 171.
3   *The Times*, 8 June 1987.
4   *The Sunday Times*, 11 October 1987.
5   John Lloyd, *Financial Times*, 14 April 1988.
6   Craig Brown, *The Sunday Times* 14 February 1988.
7   Harold Brooks–Baker, *Majesty*, June 1988.
8   Harold Brooks–Baker, *Esquire*, April 1988.
9   *The Economist*, 12 December 1987.
10   *Esquire*, April 1988.
11   It would take a swing unprecedented in the postwar period for Labour to gain enough seats for an *over-all majority* in the House of Commons at the next

general election. For Labour there is the additional complication that in seats held by the Conservatives in the election of 1987 the Alliance came second in more seats than Labour.

12   Walter Bagehot, 'The History of the Unreformed Parliament and its Lessons', *National Review*, January 1860.

Index